Kaplan Publishing are constantly finding new ways to support students looking for exam success and our online resources really do add an extra dimension to your studies.

This book comes with free MyKaplan online resources so that you can study anytime, anywhere. **This free online resource is not sold separately and is included in the price of the book.**

Having purchased this book, you have access to the following online study materials:

CONTENT	AAT	
	Text	Kit
Electronic version of the book	✓	✓
Knowledge Check tests with instant answers	✓	
Mock assessments online	✓	✓
Material updates	✓	✓

How to access your online resources

Received this book as part of your Kaplan course?
If you have a MyKaplan account, your full online resources will be added automatically, in line with the information in your course confirmation email. If you've not used MyKaplan before, you'll be sent an activation email once your resources are ready.

Bought your book from Kaplan?
We'll automatically add your online resources to your MyKaplan account. If you've not used MyKaplan before, you'll be sent an activation email.

Bought your book from elsewhere?
Go to **www.mykaplan.co.uk/add-online-resources**
Enter the ISBN number found on the title page and back cover of this book.
Add the unique pass key number contained in the scratch panel below.
You may be required to enter additional information during this process to set up or confirm your account details.

This code can only be used once for the registration of this book online. This registration and your online content will expire when the examinations covered by this book have taken place. Please allow one hour from the time you submit your book details for us to process your request.

Please scratch the film to access your unique code.

Please be aware that this code is case-sensitive and you will need to include the dashes within the passcode, but not when entering the ISBN.

BUSINESS AWARENESS

STUDY TEXT

Qualifications and Credit Framework

Q2022

This Study Text supports study for the following AAT qualifications:
AAT Level 3 Diploma in Accounting
AAT Level 3 Certificate in Bookkeeping
AAT Diploma in Accounting at SCQF Level 7

BUSINESS AWARENESS

KAPLAN PUBLISHING'S STATEMENT OF PRINCIPLES

LINGUISTIC DIVERSITY, EQUALITY AND INCLUSION

We are committed to diversity, equality and inclusion and strive to deliver content that all users can relate to.

We are here to make a difference to the success of every learner.

Clarity, accessibility and ease of use for our learners are key to our approach.

We will use contemporary examples that are rich, engaging and representative of a diverse workplace.

We will include a representative mix of race and gender at the various levels of seniority within the businesses in our examples to support all our learners in aspiring to achieve their potential within their chosen careers.

Roles played by characters in our examples will demonstrate richness and diversity by the use of different names, backgrounds, ethnicity and gender, with a mix of sexuality, relationships and beliefs where these are relevant to the syllabus.

It must always be obvious who is being referred to in each stage of any example so that we do not detract from clarity and ease of use for each of our learners.

We will actively seek feedback from our learners on our approach and keep our policy under continuous review. If you would like to provide any feedback on our linguistic approach, please use this form (you will need to enter the link below into your browser).

https://forms.gle/U8oR3abiPpGRDY158

We will seek to devise simple measures that can be used by independent assessors to randomly check our success in the implementation of our Linguistic Equality, Diversity and Inclusion Policy.

British Library Cataloguing-in-Publication Data

A catalogue record for this book is available from the British Library.

Published by
Kaplan Publishing UK
Unit 2, The Business Centre
Molly Millars Lane
Wokingham
Berkshire
RG41 2QZ

ISBN 978-1-83996-873-0

The text in this material and any others made available by any Kaplan Group company does not amount to advice on a particular matter and should not be taken as such. No reliance should be placed on the content as the basis for any investment or other decision or in connection with any advice given to third parties. Please consult your appropriate professional adviser as necessary. Kaplan Publishing Limited and all other Kaplan group companies expressly disclaim all liability to any person in respect of any losses or other claims, whether direct, indirect, incidental, consequential or otherwise arising in relation to the use of such materials.

© Kaplan Financial Limited, 2024

Printed and bound in Great Britain.

All rights reserved. No part of this publication may be reproduced, stored in a retrieval system, or transmitted, in any form or by any means, electronic, mechanical, photocopying, recording or otherwise, without the prior written permission of Kaplan Publishing.

BUSINESS AWARENESS

CONTENTS

	Page number
Introduction	P.7
Progression	P.9
Unit guide	P.11
The assessment	P.30
Study skills	P.32

STUDY TEXT

Chapter

1	The business organisation	1
2	The legal framework for companies and partnerships	19
3	Business stakeholders' interactions and needs	41
4	Organisational structure and governance	61
5	The role of the finance function	87
6	Risk and risk management	109
7	External Analysis – the PESTLE model	131
8	The microeconomic environment	155
9	Sustainability	177
10	Professional ethics in accounting and business	197
11	Money laundering	223
12	Technology affecting business and finance	243
13	Data protection, information security and cybersecurity	269

BUSINESS AWARENESS

14	Information and Big Data	281
15	Visualising information	299
Mock Assessment Questions		331
Mock Assessment Answers		355
Index		I.1

BUSINESS AWARENESS

INTRODUCTION

HOW TO USE THESE MATERIALS

These Kaplan Publishing learning materials have been carefully designed to make your learning experience as easy as possible and to give you the best chance of success in your AAT assessments.

They contain a number of features to help you in the study process.

The sections on the Unit Guide, the Assessment and Study Skills should be read before you commence your studies.

They are designed to familiarise you with the nature and content of the assessment and to give you tips on how best to approach your studies.

STUDY TEXT

This study text has been specially prepared for the revised AAT qualification introduced in 2022.

It is written in a practical and interactive style:

- key terms and concepts are clearly defined
- all topics are illustrated with practical examples with clearly worked solutions based on sample tasks provided by the AAT in the new examining style
- frequent activities throughout the chapters ensure that what you have learnt is regularly reinforced
- 'examination tips' help you avoid commonly made mistakes and to focus on what is required to perform well in your examination
- 'Test your understanding' activities are included within each chapter to apply your learning and develop your understanding.

BUSINESS AWARENESS

ICONS

The study chapters include the following icons throughout.

They are designed to assist you in your studies by identifying key definitions and the points at which you can test yourself on the knowledge gained.

 Definition

These sections explain important areas of knowledge which must be understood and reproduced in an assessment.

 Example

The illustrative examples can be used to help develop an understanding of topics before attempting the activity exercises.

 Test your understanding

These are exercises which give the opportunity to assess your understanding of all the assessment areas.

 Foundation activities

These are questions to help ground your knowledge and consolidate your understanding on areas you're finding tricky.

 Extension activities

These questions are for if you're feeling confident or wish to develop your higher level skills.

Quality and accuracy are of the utmost importance to us so if you spot an error in any of our products, please send an email to mykaplanreporting@kaplan.com with full details, or follow the link to the feedback form in MyKaplan.

Our Quality Co-ordinator will work with our technical team to verify the error and take action to ensure it is corrected in future editions.

BUSINESS AWARENESS

Progression

There are two elements of progression that we can measure: first how quickly students move through individual topics within a subject; and second how quickly they move from one course to the next. We know that there is an optimum for both, but it can vary from subject to subject and from student to student. However, using data and our experience of student performance over many years, we can make some generalisations.

A fixed period of study set out at the start of a course with key milestones is important. This can be within a subject, for example 'I will finish this topic by 30 June', or for overall achievement, such as 'I want to be qualified by the end of next year'.

Your qualification is cumulative, as earlier papers provide a foundation for your subsequent studies, so do not allow leave too big a gap between one subject and another.

We know that exams encourage techniques that aid short term retention, however you will simply forget much of what you have already learned unless it is refreshed (look up Ebbinghaus Forgetting Curve for more details on this). This makes progression more difficult as you move from one subject to another: not only will you have to learn the new subject, you will also have to relearn all the underpinning knowledge. This is very inefficient and slows down your progression which makes it more likely you may not succeed at all.

In addition, delaying your studies slows your path to qualification which can have negative impacts on your career, postponing the opportunity to apply for higher level positions and therefore higher pay.

You can use the following diagram which shows the whole structure of your qualification, to help you keep track of your progress.

BUSINESS AWARENESS

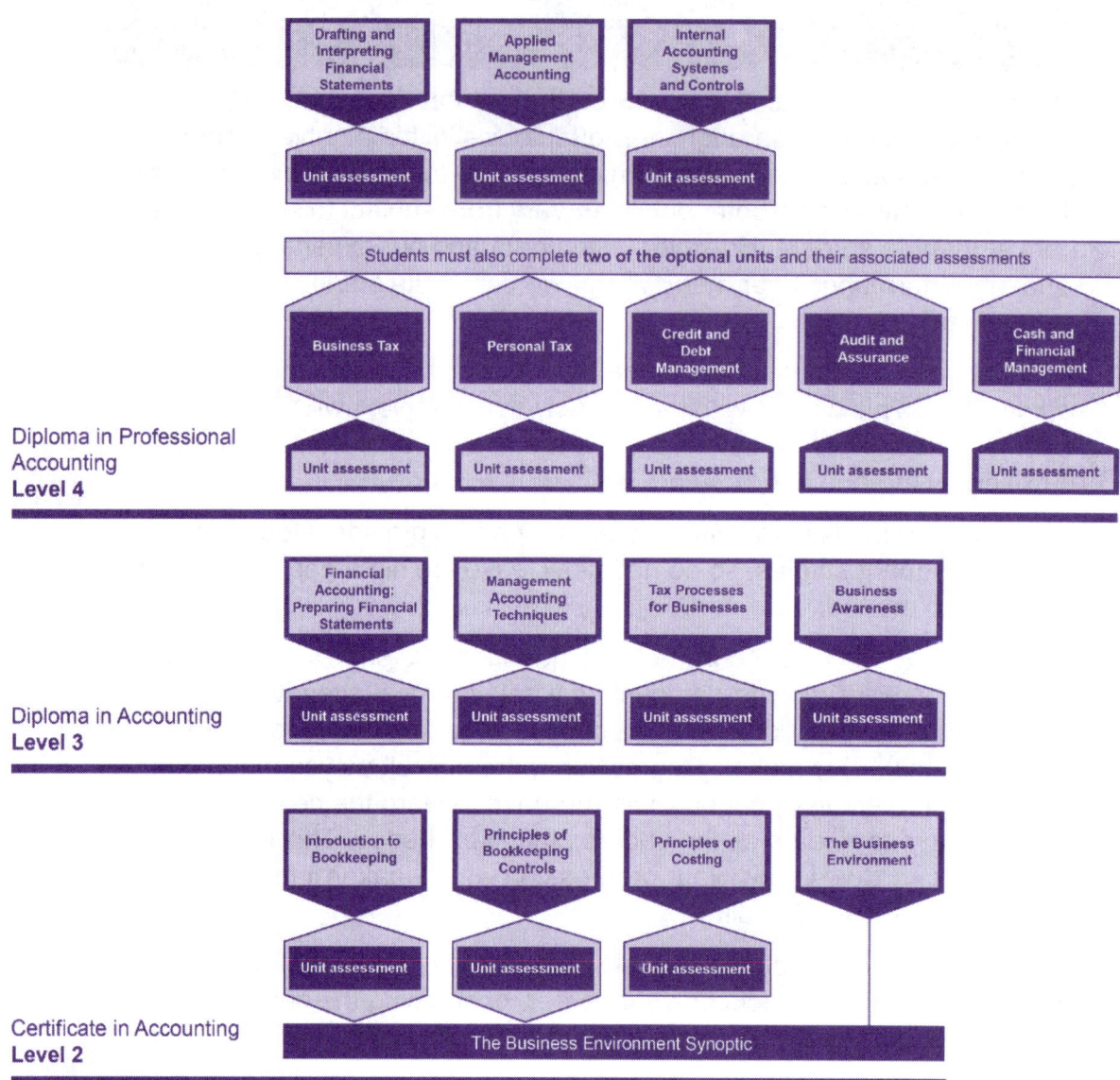

BUSINESS AWARENESS

UNIT GUIDE

Introduction

This unit provides students with an understanding of the business, its environment and the influence that this has on an organisation's structure, the role of its accounting function and its performance. Students will examine the purposes and types of businesses that exist, and the rights and responsibilities of key stakeholders. Students will learn what the micro- and macro-economic environments are and the impact and influence that changes in these environments can have on performance and decisions. This will include an understanding of the basic business law relating to the preparation of financial statements for different types of entities. Students will learn about the concepts of risk, types of risk and risk management for a business.

Students will understand the importance of professional ethics and ethical management, and how the finance function interacts with other key business functions to enhance operational efficiency. Students will learn the core aspects of the ethical code for accountants and will apply these principles to analyse and judge ethical situations which could arise in the workplace. They will also understand how acting ethically stems from core personal and organisational values, as well as the legal and regulatory framework for anti-money laundering.

The role of the accountant is changing. This change is particularly driven by emerging technologies, so students will learn about types of technological changes that affect the accounting profession and the impact of these on performance, data analysis and accounting processes. An important skill for accountants is being able to analyse, understand and interpret information gathered and communicated in different formats. Students will understand the use of and impact of big data, the key features of blockchain, artificial intelligence (AI) and cloud accounting. Students will gain the skills required to visualise and interpret data to support understanding and decision making for businesses.

BUSINESS AWARENESS

Learning outcomes

- Understand business types, structures and governance, and the legal framework in which they operate.
- Understand the impact of the external and internal environment on businesses, their performance and decisions.
- Understand how businesses and accountants comply with principles of professional ethics.
- Understand the impact of new technologies in accounting and the risks associated with data security.
- Communicate information to stakeholders.

BUSINESS AWARENESS

Scope of content

To perform this unit effectively you will need to know and understand the following:

Chapter

1 **Understand business types, structures and governance, and the legal framework in which they operate**

1.1 **The types of businesses**

   1.1.1 The standard organisation types and their key characteristics: 1

   - sole traders
   - partnerships (unlimited liability)
   - limited liability partnerships and limited partnerships
   - private limited companies
   - public limited companies
   - not-for-profit organisations including public sector

   1.1.2 The impact of business type on the organisation's governance: 1

   - degree of separation of ownership
   - control/management

   1.1.3 Types of funding used by businesses: 1

   - new capital introduced
   - profits retained
   - lending
   - working capital

BUSINESS AWARENESS

	Chapter

1.1.4 Common features of business organisations: — Chapter 1

- a structure determined by groups of interrelated individuals
- achievement of common objectives, i.e. goal congruence
- co-operative relationships
- defined responsibility, authority, relationship individuals working together as teams division of work

1.1.5 the differences between manufacturing and service businesses: — Chapter 1

- availability of internal information
- the processes and activities
- reporting requirements

1.2 The legal framework for companies and partnerships

1.2.1 The key elements of companies legislation: — Chapter 2

- the rights and roles of shareholders
- the role and duties of directors
- regulates company formation and reporting

1.2.2 The key elements of unlimited liability partnerships: — Chapter 2

- what a partnership agreement typically contains
- that formal partnership agreements may not exist for all partnerships
- the definition of goodwill and its relevance to the partnership
- the impact of a change in partner on the partnership

BUSINESS AWARENESS

	Chapter
1.3 Business stakeholders' interactions and needs	
1.3.1 Different business stakeholders:	3

- customers
- suppliers
- finance providers
- owners
- government
- employees
- regulatory/professional bodies
- the general public

1.3.2 Stakeholders' objectives and requirements from the business — 3

1.3.3 Stakeholders' contributions to and impact on the business — 3

1.3.4 The relative significance of stakeholders to the business (including attitudes to risk) — 3

1.4 Organisational structure and governance

1.4.1 Organisational structure — 4

- different organisational structures: functional, divisional, matrix
- the impact that the span of control has on the organisation structure, i.e. tall or flat

1.4.2 the importance of governance in different organisation types: — 4

- what is meant by the term 'governance' in a business context
- the impact of organisational structure and size on governance
- the difference between centralised and decentralised control

1.4.3 The role of operational, managerial and corporate/strategic levels within an organisation — 4

BUSINESS AWARENESS

	Chapter
1.4.4 The role of the finance function in contributing towards the operation of the other business functions and the organisation's plans and decision making	5

- operations/production
- sales and marketing
- human resources
- information technology
- distribution and logistics

1.4.5 The concept of risk and risk management — 6

- difference between risk and uncertainty
- types of risk:
  - business risk
  - financial risk
  - strategic risk
  - operational risk (cyber risk and reputational risk)
- risk management:
  - transfer
  - accept
  - reduce
  - avoid

BUSINESS AWARENESS

		Chapter
2	**Understand the impact of the external and internal environment on businesses, their performance and decisions**	
2.1	**The use of PESTLE model for analysing the external environment**	7
	2.1.1 The use of PESTLE to analyse the impact of the business's macro environment	7
	2.1.2 Political factors affecting a business	7
	• government policy	
	• taxation	
	• imports and exports	
	• public spending	
	2.1.3 Economic factors affecting a business	7
	• interest rates	
	• exchange rates	
	• changes in disposable income	
	• business cycles	
	• demand-pull and cost-push inflation	
	2.1.4 Social factors affecting a business	7
	• demographic changes	
	• trends	
	• unemployment	
	2.1.5 Technological factors affecting a business	7
	• changes in technology	
	• impact on structure	
	2.1.6 Legal factors affecting a business	7
	• trade regulations	
	• changes in law and regulations	
	2.1.7 Environmental factors affecting a business	7
	• environmental changes	
	• sustainability	

BUSINESS AWARENESS

		Chapter
2.2	**The micro-economic environment**	
	2.2.1 The concept of supply and demand	8
	2.2.2 How prices are determined by the price mechanism (supply = demand, i.e. shifts along the supply/demand curves) and market forces (shifts of the supply/demand curves) and the impact of the type of goods (normal, necessity, substitute and complementary)	8
	2.2.3 The impact of price changes on volumes, revenues, costs and profitability	8
	2.2.4 How the levels of competition in the micro-economic environment are influenced	8

- product features
- number of sellers and buyers
- barriers to entry, i.e. licences and regulatory controls, cost to set up, expertise
- location
- availability of information

2.3	**The importance of sustainability**	
	2.3.1 The meaning of sustainability	9
	2.3.2 The three aspects of sustainable performance:	9

- social
- ecological/environmental
- economic/financial

2.3.3 The importance of: — Chapter 9

- taking a long-term view and allowing the needs of present generations to be met without compromising the ability of future generations to meet their own needs
- considering the needs of the organisation's wider stakeholders
- long-term responsible management and use of resources
- operating sustainably in relation to products and services, customers, employees, the workplace, the supply chain and business functions and processes
- the accountant's public interest duty to protect society as a whole and the organisation's sustainability

3 Understand how businesses and accountants comply with principles of professional ethics

3.1 The relevance of the ethical code for professional accountants

3.1.1 The principle of integrity — Chapter 10

- the effect of accountants being associated with misleading information
- the key ethical values of honesty, transparency and fairness when liaising with clients, suppliers and colleagues
- how integrity is threatened by self interest and familiarity threats

BUSINESS AWARENESS

	Chapter
3.1.2 The principle of objectivity	10

- what is meant by a conflict of interest, including self-interest

- threats arising from financial interests, and compensation and incentives linked to financial reporting and decision making

- the importance of appearing to be objective as well as actually being objective

- the importance of professional scepticism when exercising professional judgement in relation to financial accounting and the link between compromised objectivity and possible accusations of bribery or fraud

3.1.3 The principle of professional behaviour 10

- how compliance with relevant laws and regulations in relation to financial accounting is a minimum requirement but an act that is permitted by the law or regulations is not necessarily ethical

- the link between bringing disrepute on the profession and disciplinary action brought by a professional accountancy body

3.1.4 The principle of professional competence and acting with due care 10

- how professional qualifications and continuing professional development (CPD) support professional competence

3.1.5 The principle of confidentiality 10

- how financial accounting information confidentiality may be affected by compliance with data protection laws

BUSINESS AWARENESS

	Chapter
3.1.6 Professional scepticism	10

- The meaning of professional scepticism: assessing information critically, with a questioning mind, and being alert to possible misstatements due to error or fraud

- The importance of professional scepticism when exercising professional judgement in relation to transactions recording and financial reporting be used as safeguards to prevent threats and ethical conflict from arising

	Chapter
3.1.7 The difference between a principles based approach and a rules-based approach	10
3.1.8 How documented organisational policies on relevant issues can be used as safeguards to prevent threats and ethical conflict from arising	10
3.1.9 The types of safeguards that may be applied	10
3.1.10 What an accountant should do when a threat cannot be eliminated or reduced to an acceptable level	10
3.1.11 Recognise threats to integrity in financial accounting: intimidation/self-interest threats to present misleading information to users of financial statements	10
3.1.12 Recognise threats to objectivity: intimidation, self-review, advocacy, self-interest, familiarity threats resulting in bias	10
3.1.13 Recognise professional competence and due care threats; keeping knowledge up to date, pressure in working role, self-interest, self-review, familiarity threats	10
3.1.14 Recognise areas in which up to date technical knowledge can be critical and the consequences of not maintaining CPD	10
3.1.15 Recognise when confidential information can or must be disclosed when it must not be disclosed, and when situations pose a threat to confidentiality	10

		Chapter
	3.1.16 Recognise situations when professional scepticism should be applied and the action to be taken	10
	3.1.17 Recognise which safeguards may be appropriate	10
3.2	**Ethical conflicts and reporting unethical behaviour**	
	3.2.1 How ethical conflicts arise	10
	3.2.2 How to determine whether behaviour is ethical or unethical	10
	3.2.3 Key organisational values and compliance with regulations	10

- Being transparent with customers and suppliers
- Reporting financial and regulatory information clearly and on time
- Whether to accept and give gifts and hospitality
- Paying suppliers a fair price and on time
- Providing fair treatment, decent wages and good working conditions to employees
- Use of social media

3.2.4 The stages in the process for ethical conflict resolution when a situation presents a conflict in application of the fundamental principles

3.2.5 What happens when a course of action is unethical

- When disciplinary action by the relevant professional accountancy body may be brought against the accountant for misconduct, and the possible penalties that can arise
- When internal disciplinary procedures may be brought against the accountant by the employer for unethical or illegal behaviour

BUSINESS AWARENESS

3.2.6 The link between lack of professional competence and due care and claims for breach of contract and professional negligence

3.2.7 The requirement for professional indemnity insurance

3.2.8 When and how to report unethical behaviour to responsible persons at work, including:

- When it is appropriate to report that a breach of the unethical code has taken place

- Report in line with formal internal whistle-blowing or 'speak-out' procedures that may be available for reporting unethical behaviour

- Seek advice confidentially from relevant managers or helplines as appropriate

- Circumstances when there may be public interest disclosure protection available under statute for blowing the whistle externally in the public interest in relation to certain illegal or unethical acts by the employer

- Seeking third-party advice before blowing the whistle externally

3.3 Money laundering

3.3.1 Money laundering law and regulations   11

- The consequences for an accountant of failing to act appropriately in response to money laundering, including the potential for the offences of 'tipping off' and 'failure to disclose'

- The consequences for any person of 'prejudicing an investigation'

- The nature of the protection given to accountants by protected disclosures ad authorised disclosures under money laundering law and regulations

- All accountants will be regulated by their professional body or by HMRC

BUSINESS AWARENESS

	Chapter
3.3.2 The importance of reporting suspected money laundering in accordance with regulations	11

- Select the information that should be reported by an accountant making a required disclosure in either an internal report or a suspicious activity report regarding suspicions about money laundering
- Timescales for disclosure of suspected money laundering

4 Understand the impact of new technologies in accounting and the risks associated with data security

4.1 Technology

4.1.1 The impact of emerging and developing technologies on accounting systems — 12

- automation of processes
- AI and machine learning
- blockchain
- electronic filing of documents
- electronic signing of documents
- data analytics

4.1.2 How technological developments have increased outsourcing and offshoring, which has impacted business development — 12

- cost structure
- markets
- locations

4.1.3 The effect of automation and AI in accounting systems on the role of the accountant and the finance function — 12

	Chapter
4.1.4 The key features of cloud accounting:	12

- access to data and information from anywhere
- remote data storage so no backup by the business is required
- automation capabilities
- availability of apps/plug-ins/add-ins
- interactions with stakeholders
- real-time data

4.1.5 Benefits and limitations of cloud accounting for an organisation	12

4.2 Data protection, information-security and cybersecurity

4.2.1 The principles of data protection:	13

- lawfulness, fairness and transparency
- purpose limitation
- data minimisation
- accuracy
- storage limitation
- integrity and confidentiality (security)
- accountability

4.2.2 The impact of data protection breaches on the individual and business	13
4.2.3 The importance of maintaining information security:	13

- accounting systems access levels
- security controls, i.e. firewalls
- integrity controls (input, processing and output controls)

4.2.4 The importance of cybersecurity to address cyber risks	13
4.2.5 The risks to data and operations posed by cyberattacks	13

BUSINESS AWARENESS

		Chapter
5	**Communicate information to stakeholders**	
5.1	**Information requirements in a business organisation**	
	5.1.1 The attributes of good quality information	14
	5.1.2 The type, purpose and characteristics of information at operational, managerial and corporate/strategic levels within an organisation	14
	5.1.3 The characteristics of big data:	14
	• value	
	• variety	
	• velocity	
	• veracity	
	• volume	
	5.1.4 The benefits and limitations of the use of big data	14
	5.1.5 The sources of internal and external big data	14
	5.1.6 The need to apply professional scepticism in relation to big data	14
	5.1.7 The use of data analytics from external sources	14
5.2	**Visualising information**	
	5.2.1 The importance of being able to visualise information in different formats	15
	• images	
	• charts	
	• diagrams	
	• tables	
	• matrices	
	• graphs	

BUSINESS AWARENESS

	5.2.2 Patterns or significant anomalies within data	15
	5.2.3 The importance of choosing the most appropriate forms of visualised data for communication purposes	15
	5.2.4 That accounting software packages use dashboards to communicate to non-technical stakeholders	15
	5.2.5 Interpret visual information to indicate relationships and trends	15
5.3	**Communicating information**	
	5.3.1 The principles used to determine the appropriate method of communication to use both internally and externally by the business	16
	5.3.2 The characteristics of professional communication:	16
	• meeting different stakeholder requirements	
	• use of appropriate communication medium for desired outcome	
	• importance of communicating valid information	
	• importance of confidentiality	

BUSINESS AWARENESS

Delivering this unit

When delivering this unit, tutors could refer to a range of organisations of differing types and sizes. This will enhance students' understanding of how the finance function supports the other functions and inputs into the short-, medium- and long-term decision making at all levels in an organisation. The structure of the business will have an impact on how it is controlled and how the processes and reporting in a business will interact. Through use of different examples, students will gain an awareness of the differences between tall and flat organisations and the impact that this has on the span of control.

Students need to know the different business types and the differences in regulatory and legal requirements of these business types. Service industries have increased, and students should appreciate the characteristics and challenges of these businesses and how the processes and activities differ from manufacturing businesses. They should also understand the regulatory requirements for the different business types, including partnerships.

Students should be able to identify who the stakeholders are and, through case studies, or real business examples, students can identify stakeholders. Students will also identify stakeholder needs and their expectations and consider their power over and influence on the business.

Throughout the delivery of topic areas associated with external and internal business environments, students could apply PESTLE analysis to known organisations, either as part of a project or as group work. Students could explore how the analysis can be used by businesses to gain an understanding of threats and opportunities that exist in the macro-economic environment, as well as understanding what political, economic, social, technological and environmental factors are and how changes may impact on performance and decisions.

When learning about the micro-economic environment, students should understand the relationship between supply and demand and the effect of changes in price, including what is meant by price elasticity of demand and how the level of competition in the environment is influenced.

Ethics are fundamental to everyone working in accounting and finance, and it is key to have a thorough understanding of ethical principles and how to apply them to practical situations. Throughout the delivery of associated topic areas, tutors can help to prepare students by providing practical examples and opportunities to apply professional ethics to a number of situations, so that students can identify ethical issues and the courses of action to be taken. They should appreciate the importance of

BUSINESS AWARENESS

personal and organisational values, culture, policies and the code of ethics in acting ethically. They will need a sound understanding of the legal and regulatory frameworks that provide safeguards to the ethical principles, and when and how they should report unethical behaviours.

There have been changes in the industry as new technologies have been developed, which have changed the nature of accounting and the role of the accountant. It is therefore important for students to understand what technologies are used, the processes or activities for which they are used and the impact they have on the work undertaken by the accountant/ finance function. Students should understand key features of blockchain, machine learning and AI, and the impact that these have on the processing of transactions, the available data, and the speed and complexity of reporting. Cloud accounting and electronic filing are increasing used by the industry, and students should know what these are as well as their key features, how they work in real time (such as bank feeds), the benefits they offer and the opportunities for add-ons/apps/plug-ins to undertake specific processes, activities or reports. As well as digitalisation, it is important to appreciate the risks posed to data; students should have a basic understanding of the risks of cyber attack and how data can be protected. Showing examples of these or providing the opportunity to use cloud software would aid students' understanding.

Students need to understand how to provide information in different formats and are encouraged to practise interpreting and communicating financial information by visualising data, for example in graphs, images and diagrams. Students should be prepared to communicate information as well as understand the most appropriate method for specific audiences. Students need to know what big data is, where it can come from and the benefits that it can provide to organisations. Students should also be aware of the number of risks that are associated with big data and the need to use big data with caution in some cases.

Links with other units

This unit links with:

- Level 2 The Business Environment
- Level 3 Financial Accounting: Preparing Financial Statements
- Level 3 Management Accounting Techniques
- Level 3 Tax Processes for Businesses
- Level 4 Applied Management Accounting

BUSINESS AWARENESS

THE ASSESSMENT

Test specifications for this unit assessment

Assessment type
Computer based assessment

Marking type
Partially computer/ partially human marked

Duration of exam
2 hours 30 minutes

Learning outcomes		Weighting
1	Understand business types, structures and governance, and the legal framework in which they operate	25%
2	Understand the impact of the external and internal environment on businesses, their performance and decisions	20%
3	Understand how businesses and accountants comply with principles of professional ethics	20%
4	Understand the impact of new technologies in accounting and the risks associated with data security	15%
5	Communicate information to stakeholders	20%
Total		100%

BUSINESS AWARENESS

APPRENTICESHIP LEARNERS ONLY

UNIT LINK TO THE END POINT ASSESSMENT (EPA)

To achieve the Assistant Accountant apprenticeship leaners must pass all of the assessments in the Diploma in Accounting, complete a portfolio and reflective discussion and complete a synoptic/knowledge assessment.

The synoptic/knowledge assessment is attempted following completion of the individual AAT units and it draws upon knowledge and understanding from those units. It will be appropriate for learners to retain their study materials for individual units until they have successfully completed the synoptic assessment for that apprenticeship level.

With specific reference to this unit, the following learning objectives are also relevant to the knowledge assessment:

LO1 Understand business types, structures and governance, and the legal framework in which they operate.

LO2 Understand the impact of the external and internal environment on businesses, their performance and decisions.

LO3 Understand how businesses and accountants comply with principles of professional ethics.

LO4 Understand the impact of new technologies in accounting and the risks associated with data security.

LO5 Communicate information to stakeholders.

STUDY SKILLS

Preparing to study

Devise a study plan

Determine which times of the week you will study.

Split these times into sessions of at least one hour for study of new material. Any shorter periods could be used for revision or practice.

Put the times you plan to study onto a study plan for the weeks from now until the assessment and set yourself targets for each period of study – in your sessions make sure you cover the whole course, activities and the associated questions in the workbook at the back of the manual.

If you are studying more than one unit at a time, try to vary your subjects as this can help to keep you interested and see subjects as part of wider knowledge.

When working through your course, compare your progress with your plan and, if necessary, re-plan your work (perhaps including extra sessions) or, if you are ahead, do some extra revision/practice questions.

Effective studying

Active reading

You are not expected to learn the text by rote, rather, you must understand what you are reading and be able to use it to pass the assessment and develop good practice.

A good technique is to use SQ3Rs – Survey, Question, Read, Recall, Review:

1. **Survey the chapter**

    Look at the headings and read the introduction, knowledge, skills and content, so as to get an overview of what the chapter deals with.

2. **Question**

    Whilst undertaking the survey ask yourself the questions you hope the chapter will answer for you.

BUSINESS AWARENESS

3 **Read**

Read through the chapter thoroughly working through the activities and, at the end, making sure that you can meet the learning objectives highlighted on the first page.

4 **Recall**

At the end of each section and at the end of the chapter, try to recall the main ideas of the section/chapter without referring to the text. This is best done after a short break of a couple of minutes after the reading stage.

5 **Review**

Check that your recall notes are correct.

You may also find it helpful to re-read the chapter to try and see the topic(s) it deals with as a whole.

Note taking

Taking notes is a useful way of learning, but do not simply copy out the text.

The notes must:

- be in your own words
- be concise
- cover the key points
- be well organised
- be modified as you study further chapters in this text or in related ones.

Trying to summarise a chapter without referring to the text can be a useful way of determining which areas you know and which you don't.

Three ways of taking notes

1 **Summarise the key points of a chapter**

2 **Make linear notes**

A list of headings, subdivided with sub-headings listing the key points.

If you use linear notes, you can use different colours to highlight key points and keep topic areas together.

Use plenty of space to make your notes easy to use.

BUSINESS AWARENESS

3 Try a diagrammatic form

The most common of which is a mind map.

To make a mind map, put the main heading in the centre of the paper and put a circle around it.

Draw lines radiating from this to the main sub-headings which again have circles around them.

Continue the process from the sub-headings to sub-sub-headings.

Highlighting and underlining

You may find it useful to underline or highlight key points in your study text – but do be selective.

You may also wish to make notes in the margins.

Revision phase

Kaplan has produced material specifically designed for your final examination preparation for this unit.

This includes pocket revision notes and a bank of revision questions specifically in the style of the current syllabus.

Further guidance on how to approach the final stage of your studies is given in this material.

Further reading

In addition to this text, you should also read the 'Accounting Technician' magazine every month to keep abreast of any guidance from the examiners.

BUSINESS AWARENESS

The business organisation

Introduction

In this chapter we will define 'business organisations' and explain why they are formed. We will also describe common features of business organisations, outline how business organisations differ, list the industrial and commercial sectors in which business organisations operate, and identify the different types of business organisation: commercial, not-for-profit, public sector, non-governmental organisations.

ASSESSMENT CRITERIA
The types of businesses (1.1)

CONTENTS	
1	Business organisations and the reason they are formed
2	Different types of organisations
3	Separation of ownership and control
4	Types of funding used by businesses

1. Business organisations and the reason they are formed

1.1 What is a business organisation?

Defining an organisation is challenging. There are many types of organisations, which are set up to meet a variety of needs, such as clubs, schools, companies, charities and hospitals.

What they all have in common is summarised in the following definition:

Definition

Organisations are social arrangements for the controlled performance of collective goals.

Considering the three aspects of this definition in more detail:

(a) 'Social arrangements' – someone working alone cannot be classed as an organisation. Organisations are structured to allow interrelated individuals to work together towards a common goal. This may include the creation of divisions to organise teams as part of an organisational hierarchy. Usually, the larger the organisation, the more formal its structures.

(b) 'Controlled performance' – an organisation will have systems and procedures in place to ensure that group goals are achieved. Managers and individuals will be given specific roles and responsibilities, and held accountable for their performance. For a company this could involve setting sales targets, or periodically assessing the performance of staff members.

(c) 'Collective goals' – organisations are defined by their goals, so we need 'goal congruence' i.e. everyone working towards the same goals. For example, the main goal of a school is to educate pupils. It will therefore be organised differently to a company that aims to make profits.

It is worth noting that a major similarity between most organisations is that they are mainly concerned with taking inputs and transforming them into outputs.

For example, a manufacturing company, this could involve taking raw materials and transforming them into a finished product that can be sold onto its customers.

An accountancy training firm will also take inputs (students and syllabuses) and transform them into outputs (qualified accountants).

BUSINESS AWARENESS

Example

A football team can be described as an organisation because:

- It has a number of players who have come together to play a game.
- The team has an objective (to score more goals than its opponent).
- To do their job properly, the members have to maintain an internal system of control to get the team to work together. In training, they work out tactics so that in play they can rely on the ball being passed to those who can score goals.
- Each member of the team is part of the organisational structure and is skilled in a different task: the goalkeeper has more experience in stopping goals being scored than those in the forward line of the team.
- In addition, there must be team spirit, so that everyone works together. Players are encouraged to do their best, both on and off the field.

Test your understanding 1

Which of the following would be considered to be an organisation, according to the definition presented earlier?

(i) A company owned and managed by one person, with no employees.
(ii) A tennis club
(iii) A hospital

A   (i), (ii) and (iii)
B   (i) and (ii) only
C   (ii) and (iii) only
D   (i) and (iii) only

1.2 Why do we need organisations?

Organisations enable people to:

- **Share skills and knowledge** – this allows people to perform tasks that they would be unable to achieve on their own. Knowledge can be shared between all the people within the organisation.
- **Specialise** – individual workers can concentrate on a limited set of tasks. This allows them to build up a greater level of skill and knowledge than they would have if they attempted to master everything.
- **Pool resources** – whether money or time.

This results in **synergy** where organisations can achieve more than the individuals could on their own.

> **Test your understanding 2**
>
> Jared is organising a social event.
>
> **Which of the following would be benefits of him forming a committee to manage the planning process and the event itself?**
>
> (i) It would help to overcome his limitations, by bringing on board other people with different skills to him.
>
> (ii) It would save time through the joint efforts of everyone on the committee.
>
> (iii) It would help to satisfy Jared's social needs.
>
> (iv) All members of the committee would have to be skilled in all aspects of managing the social event.
>
> A (i), (ii) and (iii) only
> B (i), (iii) and (iv) only
> C All of the above
> D None of the above

1.3 Common features of business organisations

Different business organisations are defined around their structure, their processes, as well as the relationships, authority and responsibility of the individuals that make them up.

BUSINESS AWARENESS

Business organisations have the following features in common:

- They are made up of a group of people who work together for the achievement of set goals – different people do different things or specialise in one
- They define business strategies to achieve goals/objectives
- They have a vision and a mission
- They have a culture which is formed by organisational values
- They have structures (such as department, teams and divisions) as well as systems and procedures
- They have inputs which are processed and provide an output
- They have customers, as well as other stakeholders.

2 Different types of organisations

Different organisations have different goals. We can therefore classify them into several categories:

2.1 Commercial versus non-profit

Commercial organisations

Commercial (or profit-seeking) organisations see their main objective as maximising the wealth of their owners.

There are three common forms that a commercial company can take:

- **Sole traders** – the organisation is owned and run by one person. In this type of organisation, the owner is not legally separate from the business itself. If a sole trader's business is sued by a customer, the customer is actually suing the owner themselves.

- **Partnerships** – the organisation is owned and run by two or more individuals. Traditionally, partnerships (like sole traders) do not have a separate legal identity from their owners. However in recent years many countries have created alternative partnership structures (such as Limited Liability Partnerships (LLPs) in the UK) which mean that the business exists as a separate legal entity and the owners' liability is limited to the amount they have invested into the partnership.

- **Limited liability companies** – a company has a separate legal identity to its owners (who are known as shareholders). The owner's liability is limited to the amount they have invested into the company.

In the UK, there are two types of limited company:

Private limited companies (with 'Ltd' after their name) – these tend to be smaller businesses (though not always). They can be owned by individual people, trusts, associations and other companies. Their shares cannot be offered to the general public and are only traded privately.

Public limited companies (with 'plc' after their name) – these are often much larger businesses. Shares can be offered to the general public on public stock markets, meaning that there can be millions of different shareholders. This makes it easier for the company to raise finance, enabling further growth.

Not-for-profit organisations

Definition

Not-for-profit organisations (NFPs or NPOs) do not see profitability as their main objective. Instead, they seek to satisfy the particular needs of their members or the sectors of society that they have been set up to benefit.

Example

NFPs include the following:

- Government departments and agencies (such as HM Revenue and Customs)
- schools
- hospitals
- charities (such as The Red Cross and Doctors Without Borders)

The objectives of different NFPs will vary significantly:

- Hospitals exist to treat patients.
- Councils may see their mission as caring for their communities.
- Government organisations usually exist to implement government policy.
- A charity may have 'provision of relief to victims of disasters' as its main objective.

BUSINESS AWARENESS

Test your understanding 3

Which of the following are usually seen as the primary objectives of companies?

(i) To maximise the wealth of shareholders
(ii) To protect the environment
(iii) To make a profit

A (i), (ii) and (iii)
B (i) and (ii) only
C (ii) and (iii) only
D (i) and (iii) only

2.2 Public versus private sector organisations

Public sector organisations

Definition

The public sector is the part of the economy that is concerned with providing basic government services and is controlled by government organisations.

The organisations that make up the public sector vary from country to country, but generally include the police, military, public transport, primary education and healthcare for the poor.

Private sector organisations

Definition

The private sector consists of organisations that are run by private individuals and groups, rather than the government.

The private sector will therefore normally include businesses, charities and clubs. Within these will be both profit-seeking and not-for-profit organisations.

KAPLAN PUBLISHING

The business organisation: **Chapter 1**

 Test your understanding 4

Many schools run fund-raising events such as fêtes, where the intention is to make a profit. This makes them 'profit-seeking'.

Is this statement:

A   True

B   False

Non-governmental organisations (NGOs)

 Definition

A non-governmental organisation is one which does not have profit as its primary goal and is not directly linked to the national government.

NGOs often promote political, social or environmental change within the countries they operate.

NGOs include the Red Cross, Doctors Without Borders, Greenpeace, Amnesty International.

2.3   Sectors in which organisations operate

A further difference between organisations is the market in which they operate. There are a large number of different sectors, which include:

- **Agriculture** – production, processing and packaging of foodstuffs.
- **Mining** – extraction and processing of minerals.
- **Finance** – this includes banks and other companies that profit through investments and the lending of money to others.
- **Retailers** – sale of goods produced by manufacturers to consumers.
- **Service** – production of intangible goods and services.
- **Transportation** – movement of goods between locations.

This is not an exhaustive list, but it should give you some idea of the wide range of activities that support organisations.

2.4   Service versus manufacturing operations

There are many similarities between businesses operating in the service sector and those in the manufacturing sector. Key issues are similar in both: the needs of the market should be identified and understood as well as its customers and users, and financial performance at a given cost or price should be ensured.

BUSINESS AWARENESS

Manufacturing business

Manufacturing businesses make a physical product to sell to customers. This will often involve inputs including direct materials and direct labour to make the finished good.

Revenues and costs are often easy to identify due to the physical tangible nature of the good produced.

Service business

Organisations in the service industry are focussed on provision of an intangible service, for example accountancy or cleaning services. This differs from a tangible good in the following ways (which can be remembered using the SHIP mnemonic):

- Simultaneity – The production and consumption occur at the same time.

- Heterogeneity – Quality and consistency is likely to vary, as a service is likely to involve less automation and be more tailored to the needs of the customer.

- Intangibility – There is no physical tangible product, which can sometimes make it harder to separate out the different elements of a service.

- Perishability – A service cannot be stored for future use. Service companies often have low levels of inventory in their accounts.

3 Separation of ownership and control

Separation of ownership and control refers to the situation in a company where the people who own the company (the shareholders) are not always the same people as those who run the company (the Board of Directors).

This situation tends to occur in larger companies, where there may be many external shareholders who play no role in the day-to-day running of the company.

This separation can bring benefits for both parties:

- Specialist managers can often run the business more efficiently than those who own the company.
- Managers cannot personally contribute all the capital needed to run the business, so they have to bring in external capital from investors who often have no interest in being involved in the day-to-day operations of the company.

Ownership and management of larger organisations is often separated. This is especially common in larger companies, where the owners (shareholders) elect directors to run the company on their behalf. Many safeguards and controls should be put in place in order to ensure that directors are running the business in the best interests of the owners.

Directors may lack the time to deal with every issue that arises in the day-to-day running of the organisation. They will therefore appoint managers to undertake these tasks for them. This leaves the directors free to focus on creating and managing the high level strategies for the organisation, while the managers focus on the day-to-day operational issues. For example, the directors may decide that the organisation is going to launch a new product, or will open a chain of new stores. The managers will be in charge of decisions such as hiring and firing junior staff, and dealing with customer complaints.

However, there is a risk that the directors may run the business in their own interests, rather than those of the shareholders and other stakeholders. This is referred to as the 'agency problem'.

BUSINESS AWARENESS

Example: The agency problem

The directors of a large quoted company may have a short-term profit target which is tied to their bonus. Directors may act in their own best interest by cutting the quality of the inputs used. This would reduce costs and help achieve their profit targets and therefore a higher bonus. However, this could have a detrimental effect on the reputation of the company, and therefore the long-term prospects of the company, which with be detrimental to the shareholders long-term wealth. This is an example of the agency problem.

The problem of directors not operating in the company's best interests can be solved by aligning the interests of the directors and the interests of the company. For example, the directors could be paid a small basic salary and bonuses depending on the growth in the share price, which is linked to the longer term prospects of the business. Directors could be paid partly in shares to make them shareholders so that they have a direct interest in the share price and level of dividends. Adopting such procedures would reduce the agency problem of the directors acting as agents of themselves rather than as agents for the shareholders.

Note that smaller companies often do not have this issue, as in these organisations the directors are also likely to own all of the shares in the company, meaning that there is no separation of ownership and control.

Test your understanding 5

The 'separation of ownership and control' refers to the fact that the owners of a company are always different people to the directors of the company.

Is this statement:

A   True

B   False

4 Types of funding used by businesses

The organisation may need additional funding to allow it to grow and invest in new projects. It may therefore need to raise finance from internal and/or external sources.

In terms of sources of funding, public sector organisations will tend to raise money from the central government. Private sector organisations, such as companies and co-operatives, are more likely to have to raise funds from their owners. Charities are usually funded by donations.

Also, businesses must finance both their day-to day-operations and their longer term aspirations. The shorter term operational needs of a business include paying for goods, services and wages as they fall due. Longer term requirements include the purchase of non-current assets for ongoing use in the business and financing growth, which involves in the medium term, increasing inventory and receivable levels.

4.1 Short- and long-term finance

The most common approach to financing is that short-term needs should be financed by short-term funds. This is basically determined by the working capital of a business (the balance of inventories, payables, receivables and cash). Better management of working capital releases the necessary short-term funding, for example squeezing trade credit by shortening customer credit periods.

Long-term assets should be financed by long-term funds, essentially debt and equity. The treasury and finance function will weigh up which source of finance best suits the circumstances of the business.

Debt finance, for example money lent from banks, require interest returns to be paid to the debt investor, the level of which is dependent on the amount of risk they face.

Equity finance, for example finance raised from selling ordinary shares, will expect high returns due to the risk of business failure.

Long-term finance is more expensive due to higher levels of risk and uncertainty that the investor faces over longer periods. However, it is more predictable and assured for the company.

4.2 Equity

Equity finance is the investment in a company by the ordinary shareholders, represented by the issued ordinary share capital plus reserves. This can be internally-generated funds (retained earnings), or new external share issues.

Internally generated funds

Retained earnings arise as a result of a company retaining their profits rather than paying them out to the owners (e.g. in the form of dividends)

Such finance is cheap and quick to raise, requiring no transaction costs, professional assistance or time delay.

Retained earnings are also a continual source of new funds, provided that the company is profitable and profits are not all paid out as dividends.

- Profits can either be paid out in the form of dividends or reinvested in the business.

- Shareholders expect a return on the funds re-invested in the business (i.e. an increase in their wealth).

- Profits which are re-invested in the business may lead to business growth and a resulting increase in the share price. This involves selling a stake in the business in order to raise cash. For companies, this involves selling shares to either new or existing shareholders.

Benefits of Equity finance

Raising equity finance has the following advantages:

- There is no minimum level of dividend that must be paid to shareholders. This means that dividends can be suspended if profits are low and the company cannot afford them. Interest payments on debt finance **must** be paid each year.

- A bank will normally require security on the company's assets before it will offer a loan. Some companies may lack quality assets to offer, making equity more attractive as it does not require security.

Equity shareholders are the owners of the business and exercise ultimate control through their voting rights.

The business organisation: Chapter 1

4.3 Long-term Debt

This involves borrowing cash from a third party and promising to repay them at a later date. Normally, the company will also have to pay interest on the amount borrowed.

There are various sources of debt that an organisation can raise funds from, including bank loans, venture capitalists and through selling bonds or debentures.

The main advantages of raising cash through debt finance are:

- Interest payments are allowable against tax. Note that dividend payments made to shareholders, by contrast, are not an allowable deduction.

- Raising debt finance does not change the ownership of the organisation.

- Debt tends to be cheaper to service than equity, as it is often secured against the assets of the company and takes priority over equity in the event of the business being liquidated. This means it is less risky to the investor.

4.4 Working capital and short-term finance

Organisations need cash to pay for all their day-to-day activities. They have to pay wages, pay for raw materials, pay bills and so on. The money available to them to do this is known as their working capital.

The main sources of working capital are the current assets as these are the short-term assets that the firm can use to generate cash. However, the organisation also has current liabilities and so these have to be taken account of when working out how much working capital the organisation has at its disposal. The total value of working capital will be the total of current assets less the total of current liabilities.

Working capital measures how much in liquid assets a company has available to build its business. The number can be positive or negative depending on how much debt the company is carrying. In general, companies that have a lot of working capital may be more successful since they can expand and improve their operations. Companies with negative working capital may lack the funds necessary for growth.

Different industries have diverse working capital profiles, reflecting their methods of doing business and what they are selling.

- Businesses with a lot of cash sales and few credit sales should have minimal trade receivables. Supermarkets are good examples of such businesses.

BUSINESS AWARENESS

- Businesses that exist to trade in completed products will only have finished goods held in inventory. Compare this with manufacturers who will also have to maintain stocks of raw materials and work in progress. Businesses in the service industry will often have very low levels of inventory as they are not producing a physical product.

- Some finished goods, notably foodstuffs, have to be sold within a limited period because of their perishable nature, which will result in lower inventories.

- Larger companies may be able to use their bargaining strength as customers to obtain more favourable, extended credit terms from suppliers. By contrast, smaller companies, particularly those that have recently started trading (and do not have a track record of creditworthiness) may be required to pay their suppliers immediately.

- Some businesses will receive their monies at certain times of the year, although they may incur expenses throughout the year at a fairly consistent level. This is often known as 'seasonality' of cash flow. For example, travel agents have peak sales in the weeks immediately following Christmas.

Working capital needs also fluctuate during the year:

- The amount of funds tied up in working capital would not typically be a constant figure throughout the year.

- Many businesses operate in industries that have seasonal changes in demand. This means that sales, inventory, receivables, etc. would be at higher levels during some predictable times of the year than at others.

5 Summary

In summary, there are a number of key differences between the various types of organisations. These include (but are not limited to):

- **Ownership** – private sector organisations are likely to be owned by individual owners or shareholders (depending on the type of organisation). Public sector organisations will be controlled by the government, while co-operatives will be owned by their members.

- **Objectives** – as mentioned, each organisation has very different goals. This can range from the provision of social services (for charities and public sector organisations) to the maximisation of owner wealth (for profit-seeking organisations).

- **Sources of funding** – public sector organisations will tend to raise money from the central government. Private sector organisations, such as companies and co-operatives, will most likely have to raise funds from their owners or debt investors. Charities are usually funded by donations.

- **Size** – organisations vary in size from large, multinational companies to sole traders consisting of only one person.

- **Liability** – the owners of sole traders or partnerships are liable for any losses their businesses make. Owners of companies enjoy **limited liability**.

In spite of these differences, the different types of organisations often face similar issues to each other. For instance, most will have employees that need to be motivated. Many organisations will need to design strategies for the future, or will need to consider what systems should be put in place to ensure the accurate recording of transactions.

These common issues will be examined in more detail in the coming chapters.

Test your understanding answers

Test your understanding 1

The correct answer is C

There would be no collective goals for an individual running a company with no employees, so this does not satisfy the definition given.

Test your understanding 2

The correct answer is A

Statement (iv) would not be true: organisations (which this committee could be classified as) allow for specialisation. Not all of the members would have to be skilled at performing all of the necessary tasks.

Test your understanding 3

The correct answer is D

Protecting the environment is to be encouraged and is reinforced within statute to some degree, but it is not a primary objective of the company. Companies exist primarily to maximise the return to their owners.

Test your understanding 4

The correct answer is B – false

Schools run fund-raising activities to help pay for extra books, e.g. to improve the quality of education given to pupils. The primary objective is educational, not profit. The money made at the fete is thus a means, not an end.

Test your understanding 5

The correct answer is B – false

In a small company the directors of the company (perhaps a husband and wife) are often the sole shareholders of the company, so the agency problem does not arise. The problem is potentially most serious in a large quoted company where there is a professional board of directors and many (perhaps thousands or even millions) external shareholders.

BUSINESS AWARENESS

The legal framework for companies and partnerships

Introduction

Upon completion of this chapter you will have an understanding of the legal environment companies and partnerships operate in. This section introduces you to the main authorities governing companies' activities, as well as the key elements of the law that must be adhered to when drafting financial statements.

This is an important chapter that sets the scene for the various actors of corporate life, the main ones being the directors (we'll explore their duties here) and the shareholders (whose roles and responsibilities will also be covered).

The chapter ends with an introduction to unlimited liability partnerships and their key features.

ASSESSMENT CRITERIA	CONTENTS
The legal framework for companies and partnerships (1.2)	1 Authorities to whom companies are accountable
	2 Legislation governing financial statements
	3 Directors
	4 Shareholders
	5 Unlimited liability partnerships

The legal framework for companies and partnerships: **Chapter 2**

1 Authorities to whom companies are accountable

1.1 Regulatory bodies

In most countries, there is a government department set up to oversee the regulation and accounts of companies. In the UK, this is known as Companies House, but it goes by various names in other countries (such as 'Companies Commission' in Malaysia).

Companies are usually required to submit their financial statements to these bodies so that interested parties can inspect them.

In addition to their financial statements, companies may also have to retain and submit certain key documents, such as a Register of Shareholders and a Register of Directors.

1.2 Tax authorities

Companies, as well as individuals, are accountable to the tax authorities in the countries in which they are based. They have to prepare tax returns each year, showing the amount of taxable profits they have earned in the period.

In many countries, businesses also have to submit returns showing the amount of sales tax (value added tax or VAT) that they owe to the tax authorities.

1.3 Other authorities

Companies and other organisations may be accountable to other regulatory authorities.

For example, in the UK:

- Most businesses in the financial services industry handle client money. The FCA (Financial Conduct Authority) and the PRA (Prudential Regulation Authority) are public bodies that monitor and control the activities of organisations within this industry, to protect clients against failure or poor advice.

- Charities have access to public money, so the Charity Commission is a public body that registers all charities and monitors their activities.

- Utilities, such as gas and electricity providers, need to offer a reliable, fair and safe service across the country. OFGEM is a public body in the UK that regulates the activities of these organisations. Regulated industries normally have to produce some form of accounting information for the regulator.

BUSINESS AWARENESS

In order to satisfy the relevant authorities, most organisations have to retain their accounting records and information for a minimum period (usually seven years), in case the authorities wish to verify information at a future date.

2 Legislation governing financial statements

For companies, legislation covers not only the need to prepare financial statements, but also how they should be prepared – including issues such as frequency and format.

This helps to ensure that interested parties are able to access the financial statements of a company, as well as making sure that they have been prepared in an understandable way.

This legislation varies between countries, but in the UK it is known as the **Companies Act 2006** (or CA2006).

2.1 Typical requirements for financial statements

The CA2006 in the UK requires that financial statements are produced that give a true and fair view of the position and performance of the company. The term 'true and fair' is not defined in company law, but normally means that the financial statements:

- apply all appropriate accounting standards
- contain information of sufficient quantity to satisfy the reasonable expectations of the users – indicating that the information must be adequately detailed. For example, it would not be acceptable to list 'current assets' without showing the different categories of current assets
- follow generally-accepted practice
- should not contain any material misstatement – the information should be reasonably accurate, and should not contain errors that would be significant enough to alter the view of the company's affairs.

Companies are also required to maintain proper accounting records which are sufficient to show and explain the transactions. The content of these records is not defined, but a record of transactions, assets and liabilities would be required as a minimum.

Financial statements must be approved by the board of directors, in accordance with the Companies Act.

Test your understanding 1

State whether each of the following statements is true or false. If false, explain why.

If financial statements give a true and fair view it means they are accurate.

Is this statement:

A   True

B   False

If financial statements give a true and fair view it means there is no fraud.

Is this statement:

A   True

B   False

3 Directors

Under company legislation, directors are responsible for producing financial statements that give a true and fair view.

This is usually delegated within the company to the Finance Director (FD) or the Chief Financial Officer (CFO). The financial reporting function within the accounting department will assist the FD with this.

If the FD does not have the skills to prepare the financial statements, an external accounting firm may be asked to provide assistance.

3.1 Definition

Definition

The term **'director'** includes 'any person occupying the position of director, by whatever name called': A director must normally be aged at least 16.

3.2 Types of director

Managing director/Chief executive officer (MD/CEO)	• A director appointed to carry out overall day-today management functions. • The Board can delegate to the MD/CEO any powers they see fit. • The MD/CEO has a dual role – member of board and also executive officer. • The MD/CEO has the authority to enter into all contracts of a commercial nature on behalf of the company.
Executive director	• Likely to be a full-time employee involved in management. • Performs a specific role under a service contract. • May be distinguished by a special title such as 'Sales Director' or 'Finance Director'.
Non-executive director (NED)	• Part-time and not an employee. • Brings outside expertise to board. • Contributes an independent view. • Exerts control over executive directors. • Subject to the same duties, controls and potential liabilities as executive directors.
Chairman of board	• Chairs meetings of board. • Acts as spokesperson for the company. • Has a casting vote.

3.3 Directors' duties

General duties

Prior to the Companies Act 2006, common law rules, equitable principles and fiduciary duties made up the law on directors' duties. A fiduciary duty is a duty imposed upon certain persons because of the position of trust and confidence they are in.

These have now been replaced by the specific statutory duties provided in the Companies Act 2006. However, the old case law still has relevance in interpreting the new legislation and illustrating its application.

- **Duty to act within powers** – A director must act in accordance with the company's constitution and only use his/her powers for the purpose for which they were given. Directors have a fiduciary duty to the company to exercise their powers bona fide in what they honestly consider to be in the interests of the company.

- **Duty to promote the success of the company** – A director must act in good faith, in a way which promotes the success of the company and for the benefit of the members as a whole.

- **Duty to exercise independent judgment** – A director of a company must exercise independent judgment, and cannot delegate their powers to others.

- **Duty to exercise reasonable care, skill and diligence** – directors should act with the knowledge, skill and experience that could reasonably be expected of a director.

- **Duty to avoid conflicts of interest** – A director must avoid any situation which places him/her in direct conflict with the interests of the company or the performance of any other duty.

- **Duty not to accept benefits from third parties** – A director must not accept any benefit from a third party which arises by reason of him/her being a director or performing/not performing an act as a director, unless acceptance cannot reasonably be regarded as likely to give rise to a conflict of interest.

- **Duty to declare interest in proposed transaction or arrangement** – A director is required to declare the nature and extent of any interest, either direct or indirect through a connected person, that they have in relation to a proposed transaction or arrangement with the company. Even if the director is not a party to a transaction, the duty may apply if they are aware or ought reasonably to have been aware, of the interest.

3.4 Directors' powers

The division of power within a company is between the board of directors who manage the business on a day-to-day basis and the members who make major decisions about the running of the company's business in a general meeting.

Directors are required to exercise their powers in accordance with the company's constitution i.e. the articles, which usually authorise the directors 'to manage the company's business' and to 'exercise all the powers of the company for any purpose connected with the company's business'.

Note that the power to manage the business of the company is given to the board as a whole, not to the individual directors. Where a company's articles delegate the management of the company's business to the board, the members have no right to interfere in decisions made by the board. Directors are not agents of the members and are not subject to their instruction as to how to act.

The authority of directors

In common law, individual directors cannot bind the company without being given authority to do so. There are three ways in which this authority may be given:

- Express: Where authority is expressly given, all decisions taken are binding.
- Implied: Authority flows from a person's position. The person appointed as the managing director has the implied authority to bind the company in the same way as the board.
- Apparent: Such authority arises where a director is believed by the other board members as having the authority to bind the company in contracts. This is normal when there is a managing director.

Test your understanding 2

SDF is a large, multinational company. The Finance Director heads up the department that produces the annual accounts. They are helped by a large external accountancy provider. After the accounts were audited and published, it was discovered that the Finance Director had made a number of errors, meaning that the published accounts were significantly inaccurate.

Who is responsible for SDF's accounts failing to show a true and fair view?

A   The Board of Directors as a whole

B   The Finance Director, as they were incompetent

C   The accountancy provider as they failed to notice the errors

D   The external auditor

Test your understanding 3

Which of the following statement(s) is/ are correct?

(i) The Board of Directors is required to set the company's objectives.

(ii) The Board of Directors is required to contribute capital into the company as individuals.

(iii) The Board of Directors is required to recruit all members of staff.

A (i) only
B (i) and (ii) only
C (ii) and (iii) only
D (i) and (iii) only

4 Shareholders

4.1 What is a company?

Organisations might choose to incorporate themselves as a company. Companies must be formally registered and incorporated and will require formal agreements.

A company is a separate legal entity (i.e. separate from its shareholders, the part owners and its directors, the managers). There are a number of consequences of being a separate legal entity:

- Limited liability. A company is fully liable for its own debts. If a company fails, the liability of the shareholders is limited to any amount still unpaid on their share capital (or any amount they have agreed to contribute if the company is limited by guarantee). The consequence that a company's members have limited liability for its debts gives protection to the members from the company's creditors and from the risk of the business collapsing.

- A company enters into contracts in its own name and can sue and be sued in its own name.

- A company owns its own property.

- A company has perpetual succession, irrespective of the fate of shareholders.

- The management (i.e. the directors) of a company is separated from its ownership (i.e. the shareholders).
- A company is subject to the requirements of the Companies Act 2006 (CA06) and the Small Business, Enterprise and Employment Act 2015.

The members of a company are usually shareholders who own shares in the company.

4.2 Company formation

Companies cannot simply be set up in the same was as a sole trader; their existence is heavily regulated by the government. In order to be established there is a significant amount of administration that must be undertaken.

Registration

The following must be submitted to the Registrar of Companies (the official responsible for Companies House) in order to form a company.

- **Memorandum of association**

    Used to be a more important document under previous company legislation.

    Signed by all subscribers and stating that they wish to form a company and agree to become members of the company.

    In relation to a company limited by shares, the memorandum provides evidence of the members' agreement to take at least one share each in the company.

    Is not possible to amend or update the memorandum of a company formed under CA2006.

- **Application for registration**

    CA2006 sets out the information that must be delivered to the Registrar when an application for registration is made. In all cases, the application form must include:

    - the proposed name of the company
    - whether the members will have limited liability (by shares or guarantee)
    - whether the company is to be private or public
    - details of the registered office.

Articles of association

The articles of association form the company's internal constitution. They:

- set out the manner in which the company is to be governed and
- regulate the relationship between the company, its shareholders and its directors.

Accounting records

The company must keep accounting records containing sufficient information to show and explain the company's transactions and its financial position.

At any time it should be possible:

- to disclose with reasonable accuracy the company's financial position at intervals of not more than six months
- for the directors to ensure that any accounts that needs to be prepared comply with Companies Act 2006 and International Accounting Standards.

Accounting records must be kept for three years in the case of a private company and six years in that of a public one. They should be kept at the company's registered office or at some other place thought fit by the directors.

4.3 The rights of shareholders

Companies will hold regular, typically annual general meetings (AGMs) during which shareholders can vote on resolutions. Resolutions are the way in which companies take decisions. They are voted on by the members in person or by proxy (where the member nominates someone else to vote on his or her behalf).

This gives shareholders the rights to do things such as change the company name, wind up the company, and remove directors.

The shareholders have the right:

- **To be sent a copy of annual accounts and reports.** (These may be sent in an electronic form, provided the member has agreed.) Companies are required to distribute a copy of annual accounts and reports for each financial year to every shareholder.
- **To require the directors to call a general meeting.**
- **To attend general meetings** – notice must be given to members regarding any shareholder meetings.

- **To appoint a proxy to exercise their rights.** Shareholders are entitled to appoint another person as their proxy to exercise any relevant rights to attend, speak, and vote at a meeting of the company.

- **To inspect company information**, including the register of members and a record of resolutions and minutes without any charge.

- **To bring a derivative claim.** This is essentially a claim on behalf of the company in relation to a breach of duty, trust, negligence or default by a director.

- **To vote on certain company affairs** – subject to their class of shares and the articles of association, members have a right to vote on certain company resolutions.

- **To be issued with a share certificate** within two months of their shares being allotted. This does not necessarily constitute a paper certificate. In addition to issuing share certificates, companies must also add new members to their register of members.

- **To inspect directors' service contracts** – all members are entitled to inspect a copy of every director's service contract with the company or with a subsidiary of the company, or a written memorandum setting out the terms of their contract.

- **Petition the courts on the basis of unfair prejudice** – a company shareholder "may apply to the court by petition for an order […] on the grounds […] that the company's affairs are being or have been conducted in a manner that is unfairly prejudicial to the interests of members generally or of some part of its members.

4.4 Minority and majority shareholders

A company is ultimately controlled by its shareholders. Most decisions require a majority of over 50% (although some require 75%). Anyone who has less than 50% control is a minority shareholder.

The legal framework for companies and partnerships: Chapter 2

 Test your understanding 4

Identify whether each of the following statements about the financial statements of limited companies is TRUE or FALSE.

'The preparation of financial statements is the responsibility of the shareholders.'

Is this statement:

A   True

B   False

'Financial statements must be approved by the board of directors.'

Is this statement:

A   True

B   False

5 Unlimited liability partnerships

5.1 What is a partnership?

There are several key elements that define partnerships:

- **Two or more individuals**

A partnership includes at least two individuals (partners). In certain jurisdictions, there may be an upper limit to the number of partners.

- **Business arrangement**

A partnership exists to carry on a business. As it is a business, the partners seek to generate a profit. A partnership is an unincorporated business entity. That means that the reporting entity (business entity) principle applies to a partnership, so for accounting purposes, the partnership is a separate entity from the partners.

However, from a legal perspective, the partnership is not a separate legal entity from the partners: the partners have unlimited liability, and if the partnership is unable to pay its liabilities, the partners may be called upon to use their personal assets to settle the unpaid liabilities of the partnership.

5.2 The partnership agreement

It is good practice to set out the terms agreed by the partners in a partnership agreement. Whilst this is not mandatory, it can reduce the possibility of expensive and acrimonious disputes in the future. As a formal agreement is not mandatory, there is no definitive list of what it should contain, but key elements include:

- **Share of residual profit**

This is the profit available to be shared between the partners in the profit and loss sharing ratio, after all other appropriations have been made. The profit and loss sharing ratio is sometimes simply called the 'profit sharing ratio' or 'PSR'.

Therefore, there is a distinction to be made between the profit for the year (income minus expenses), which is calculated in exactly the same way as for a sole trader and residual profit (the remaining profit after profit for the year has been adjusted by the appropriations in accordance with the partnership agreement).

The 'appropriation account' is an additional accounting statement that is required for a partnership. For a sole trader, the profit for the year is simply transferred to the credit side of the proprietor's capital account (the double entry is completed by a debit entry in the statement of profit or loss, resulting in a nil balance on that statement). In the case of a partnership, the statement of profit or loss will still be debited, but the profit will be credited to the appropriation account, rather than the capital account.

- **Partners' salaries**

The term 'salaries' is a misleading description. The salaries of employees are business expenses that are written off to the statement of profit or loss, thereby reducing profit for the year. However, as partners are the owners of the business, any amounts that are paid to them under the partnership agreement are part of their appropriation or share of the profit. As the 'salary' is guaranteed, it must be dealt with through a credit entry in the partner's account (usually the current account) before the residual profit is shared.

- **Partners' authority**

The partnership agreement will set out the express authority that each partner has (for example, to hire staff, to enter into contracts on the partnership's behalf or to borrow money etc.). There does not have to be a formal agreement but having one will make it easier to resolve any partnership disputes.

Partners' authority is also set out in law, regardless of whether a formal partnership agreement exists. The Partnership Act 1890 s5, a key piece of legislation for partnerships which states that every partner is the agent of the firm and of the other partners. This means that each partner has the power to bind all partners to business transactions entered into within their express or implied authority.

Many of the Act's provisions apply, unless they are excluded by a partnership agreement. The PA 1890 provides that partners shall share profits equally, but in cases where partners contribute different amounts of capital this may not be appropriate and partners will need to agree specific profit sharing arrangements within their partnership agreement.

Implied authority

Every partner is presumed to have the implied authority to:

- sell the firm's goods
- buy goods necessary for, or usually employed in, the business
- receive payments of debts due to the firm
- engage employees
- employ a solicitor to act for the firm in defence of a claim or in the pursuance of a debt.

Trading partnerships

The above implied powers apply to both trading and non-trading partnerships. Partners in trading partnerships have additional powers, such as to borrow money.

In order to be acting within their implied authority, the individual partner must be acting within the usual scope of a partner's powers in the particular business concerned.

5.3 Dissolution of the partnership

A partnership can come to an end and be dissolved in various ways:

Without court order

The partnership will automatically end in the following situations:

- The expiry of a fixed term or the completion of a specific enterprise.
- One of the partners gives notice (unless the partnership agreement excludes this right).
- Death or bankruptcy of a partner (the partnership agreement will usually make provision for the partnership to continue if a partner should die).
- Where continuation of the partnership would be illegal.

By court order

Under the PA 1890, the court can bring a partnership to an end in any of the following situations:

- Partner has mental disorder or permanent incapacity.
- Partner engages in activity prejudicial to the business.
- Partner wilfully or persistently breaches the partnership agreement.
- Partner conducts themselves in a way that it is no longer reasonably practicable for the others to carry on in business with them.
- Business can only be carried on at a loss.
- It is just and equitable to do so.

Distribution of assets

In the event of dissolution the assets of the partnership will be used to pay off the debts of the partnership. As a partnership normally does not have the advantage of limited liability status, if the proceeds on the sale of the assets does not cover the debts then the partners' personal wealth will be called upon to make up the shortfall.

The proceeds from the sale of the assets will be applied in the following order:

(i) paying debts to outsiders

(ii) paying the partners any advance they made to the firm beyond their capital contribution i.e. a loan

(iii) paying the capital contribution of the partners.

If there is a residue remaining this will be divided between the partners in the same proportion in which they share the profits of the partnership.

In the event that the assets are insufficient to meet the debts to outsiders then profits held back from previous years or partners' capital will be used to make good the shortfall. If these are also insufficient then the partners will individually contribute in the proportion to which they shared in the profits.

Effect of a change in partner

When a new partner is admitted to the partnership the old partnership is dissolved and a new partnership is created. The new partners effectively buy the assets of the old partnership from the old partners.

5.4 Goodwill

Goodwill is defined as the amount by which the fair value of the net assets of the business exceeds the carrying amount of the net assets. In simple terms, 'fair value' can be thought of as being the same as 'market value'. Goodwill arises due to factors such as the reputation, location, customer base, expertise or market position of the business.

When a new partner joins a partnership they will not be entitled to any goodwill created by the old partnership. So the goodwill value at that point needs to be allocated to the old partners:

- The first step for dealing with goodwill is to recognise an asset. This is a debit entry for the value of the goodwill in the goodwill account.

- The double entry is completed with credit entries in the old partners' capital accounts.

- The value of each entry is calculated by sharing the value of the goodwill between the partners in the old profit and loss sharing ratio.

- If goodwill is to be retained in the partnership (sometimes referred to as 'carried in the books') no further entries are required.

- If goodwill is not to be carried in the books, it is eliminated by a credit entry in the goodwill account. The double entry is completed with debit entries in the partners' capital accounts. The value of each entry is calculated by sharing the value of the goodwill between the new partners in the new profit and loss sharing ratio.

A person joining a partnership will normally be expected to contribute capital to the partnership. A partner leaving a partnership would want to withdraw their capital (which will include any goodwill accumulated to the date of departure).

If a partner is contributing (or withdrawing) capital, the relevant amount will be recorded in both the partner's capital account and the bank account. A contribution will be a credit entry in the capital account and a debit entry in the bank account, and a withdrawal will be a debit entry in the capital account and a credit entry in the bank account.

5.5 Unlimited liability partnerships

Definition

A partnership describes 'the relationship that subsists between persons carrying on a business in common with a view to profit'. A partnership is not a separate legal entity, and each partner has full personal liability for the partnership debts (liabilities).

When joint owners of a business are mutually responsible for the company's debt and liabilities and their personal liability isn't capped, this is known as an unlimited liability partnership.

Liability occurs when the entire business has a legal responsibility to come up with the funds in compliance with court requirements, expenses and third party contracts. This liability can be paid off through the release of money from the business owners' personal assets, as opposed to a limited liability business where personal assets are protected.

As an alternative to a limited liability company, many partnerships are established as limited liability partnerships (LLP) instead of potentially risking the loss of personal assets of the partners, which can be seen as too much of a financial burden.

The Limited Liabilities Partnership Act 2000 was created in order to set out the rules for LLPs. It states that, unlike normal partnerships, each partner is only liable for the amount of capital they put into the LLP, and as such they have limited liability. Many accountancy and law firms are set up as LLPs.

It is also possible to have an unlimited liability company. Advantages of unlimited liability in business include more freedom (there are usually fewer compliance regulations to adhere to with unlimited liability) and potential tax savings – depending on the level of profit, there could be some tax advantages to having unlimited liability using non-disclosure. The disadvantages of unlimited liability in business are that personal assets are at risk if the business sees high levels of liability, and securing a loan could be more difficult due to the increased risk.

Unlimited liability for debts

In most business partnerships, the partners all have unlimited liability and so are personally liable for any business debts. In a sole proprietorship business the one individual – known as the sole proprietor – has the entire responsibility for all debts, accountability and duties.

The legal framework for companies and partnerships: Chapter 2

What is the difference between unlimited liability and limited liability in business?

It depends on how a business is structured, but the owners may be responsible for whole debts or a certain percentage of debt.

'Limited' by definition means restriction, therefore owners are restricted with how much money they can lose. Companies such as a private limited company or a public limited company will have limited liability which means that owners can simply lose the money that they invested in the business whilst their personal assets are protected. Limited liability offers important protection for shareholders. This is because the company has a separate legal identity – the shareholders are distinct from the business.

'Unlimited' on the other hand, essentially means there are infinite ways in which a business owner might incur a loss. Unlimited liability means that the business owners are personally liable for any loss the business makes. Sole traders and partnerships often have unlimited liability.

Owners would choose to set up an unlimited company if they do not want to publicly file financial reports and annual accounts. Unlimited liability is suited to a business where the risk of insolvency is extremely low.

Test your understanding 5

Complete each of the following definitions about unlimited liability partnerships by selecting ONE option.

Goodwill in a partnership can be defined as:	Gap 1	The ownership proportions, salary and distribution of profits is defined by:	Gap 2

Gap 1	✓	Gap 2	✓
The partnership agreement		The partnership agreement	
The partnership contract		The partnership contract	
The amount by which the business's total value exceeds the value of its separately identifiable net assets		The amount by which the business's total value exceeds the value of its separately identifiable net assets	
The amount paid for the brand		The amount paid for the brand	

BUSINESS AWARENESS

6 Summary

In summary, we now understand the legal obligations companies and partnerships must operate under, the authorities to whom they are accountable, the rules they must follow when drafting financial statements, and the respective roles of directors and shareholders.

We also are now more familiar with the characteristics of unlimited liability partnerships.

Test your understanding answers

Test your understanding 1

'If financial statements give a true and fair view it means they are accurate.' This is **false**. It means that the financial statements are reasonably accurate, not materially misstated, but does not mean that the financial statements are totally accurate. Some errors in financial statements are inevitable, so they will never be totally accurate. Numbers which are estimates, such as depreciation or allowances for bad debts, are more at risk of error.

'If financial statements give a true and fair view it means there is no fraud.' This is **false**. As stated above, true and fair requires that the financial statements are reasonably rather than totally accurate. If a fraud is not material, then it will not cause a material misstatement.

Test your understanding 2

The correct answer is A

Remember that the Board of Directors is responsible for the financial statements giving a true and fair view. This responsibility cannot be delegated to others.

Test your understanding 3

The correct answer is A

Test your understanding 4

False, true

BUSINESS AWARENESS

Test your understanding 5

| Goodwill in a partnership can be defined as: | Gap 1 | The ownership proportions, salary and distribution of profits is defined by: | Gap 2 |

Gap 1	✓	Gap 2	✓
The partnership agreement		The partnership agreement	✓
The partnership contract		The partnership contract	
The amount by which the business's total value exceeds the value of its separately identifiable net assets	✓	The amount by which the business's total value exceeds the value of its separately identifiable net assets	
The amount paid for the brand		The amount paid for the brand	

BUSINESS AWARENESS

Business stakeholders' interactions and needs

Introduction

Upon completion of this chapter, you will be able to explain who the stakeholders of an organisation are, and to categorise those stakeholders as internal/connected/external stakeholders, and primary/secondary stakeholders.

You will also be able to identify the needs of different stakeholders and resolve stakeholder conflicts using Mendelow's matrix.

Finally, you will consider the different risk attitudes of different stakeholder groups.

ASSESSMENT CRITERIA	CONTENTS	
Business stakeholders' interactions and needs (1.3)	1	Who are stakeholders?
	2	Stakeholder needs analysis
	3	Stakeholder conflict
	4	The risk attitude of stakeholders

1 Who are stakeholders?

Stakeholder theory argues that the tension or alignment between the interests of managers and shareholders is not the only relationship that is relevant to an organisation.

A business does not only have shareholders. It has stakeholders, and shareholders are only one group of stakeholder among many.

Definition

A stakeholder is an individual or group which has an interest in what the organisation does, or who affects, or can be affected by, the organisation's actions.

It will depend on the industry, business and circumstances as to which stakeholder(s) take priority, although the customer is often prioritised as the most important e.g. in retail.

Those who provide resources and help turn them into outputs (e.g. suppliers and employees) are key when creating value. They also receive value from the firm at the same time. Customers are the ones to whom value is delivered.

It is vital for managers to understand the varying needs of the different stakeholders in their organisation. Failure to do so could mean that important stakeholders do not have their needs met, which could be disastrous for the company.

Stakeholders can be broadly categorised into three groups: internal, connected, and external.

1.1 Internal stakeholders

Within an organisation, there are a number of internal parties involved in corporate governance. These parties can be referred to as internal stakeholders. Their objectives are likely to have a strong influence on how the organisation is run.

Each internal stakeholder has:

- an operational role within the company
- a number of interests in the company (referred to as the **stakeholder 'claim'**).

BUSINESS AWARENESS

Internal stakeholders include:

Stakeholder	Operational role	Main interests in company	Example
Directors and managers	Responsible for the actions of the corporation	• pay • performance-linked bonuses • share options • status • reputation • power • profit targets	If growth is going to occur, the managers will want increased profits, leading to increased bonuses
Employees	Carry out orders of management	• pay • performance-linked bonuses • job stability/job security • career progression • status • working conditions	If workers are to be given more responsibility, they will expect increased pay

Test your understanding 1

Which of the following statements is/are correct?

(i) Internal stakeholders have little influence over the way an organisation is run.

(ii) The needs and expectations of managers and employees will always tend to be the same as they are both internal stakeholders.

A (i) only
B (ii) only
C Neither
D Both

1.2 Connected stakeholders

Connected stakeholders either invest in, or have dealings with, the firm. They tend to have varied objectives.

Stakeholder	Need/expectation	Example
Shareholders	Steady flow of income, possible capital growth and the continuation of the business	If capital is required for growth, the shareholders will expect a rise in the dividend stream
Customers	Satisfaction of customers' needs will be achieved through providing value-for-money products and services	Any attempt to, for example, increase the quality and the price, may lead to customer dissatisfaction
Suppliers	Prompt payment	If a decision is made to delay payment to suppliers to ease cash flow, existing suppliers may cease supplying goods
Finance providers e.g. banks	Ability to repay the finance including interest Security of investment	The firm's ability to generate cash

1.3 External stakeholders

These stakeholders tend not to have a direct link to the organisation, but can influence or be influenced by its activities.

As with connected stakeholders, they will have very diverse objectives for the organisation to take account of.

Stakeholder	Need/expectation	Example
Community at large	The general public can be a stakeholder, especially if their lives are affected by an organisation's decisions	E.g. local residents' attitude towards out-of-town shopping centres
Environmental pressure groups	The organisation does not harm the external environment	If an airport wants to build a new runway, the pressure groups may stage a 'sit in'
Government and regulatory/ professional bodies	Company activities are central to the success of the economy (providing jobs and paying taxes). Legislation (e.g. health and safety) must be met by the company	Actions by companies could break the law, or damage the environment, and governments therefore control what organisations can do
Trade unions	Taking an active part in the decision-making process	If a department is to be closed the union will want to be consulted, and there should be a scheme in place to help employees find alternative employment

1.4 Primary and secondary stakeholders

This is a different method of categorising stakeholders, which is based on whether or not they have a contractual relationship with the organisation.

Primary stakeholders are those that have a **contractual relationship**, for instance employees, directors, shareholders – in fact any stakeholder who falls into the 'connected' or 'internal' categories which are examined above.

Secondary stakeholders are parties that have an interest in the organisation, but have **no contractual link**, such as the public. Any stakeholders in the 'external' category would fall into this group.

Example: Nike

Nike is one of the most famous global sportswear companies. Its slogan is 'Just Do It'.

Mostly famous for athletic shoes and clothes, Nike is also one of the major manufacturers of sport equipment.

Nike was founded in January 1962 in Oregon, United States by Philip Knight and Bill Bowerman. Nike has somewhere around 700 or more retail outlets spread all over the world, and has approximately 45 offices outside the United States. It employs 30,000 people all over the world. Nike had a revenue in excess of $37 billion in 2020. Nike's factories are mostly located in Asian countries like Pakistan, India, Malaysia, China, Indonesia, Philippines, Taiwan, Vietnam and Thailand.

The **primary stakeholders** of the company are the shareholders, business partners, the employees, and the customers/consumers. What the shareholders and the investors want from the company is that the company achieves profits. The employees expect job satisfaction and good pay. The customers are concerned with quality, safety and availability of products. If any primary stakeholder group is not satisfied the organisation's progress becomes questionable.

The **secondary stakeholders** of the company include the wider community. Most companies like Nike operate within the limits of safety laws, environmental protection and other laws and regulations. Socially responsible organisations should consider the effect of their actions upon all stakeholders. What all of these stakeholders want is that the company is ethically and socially responsible. When this secondary stakeholder group becomes dissatisfied, the reputation of the company is tarnished (for example, the debate of sweatshops tarnished the reputation of Nike).

Issues faced by Nike:

- Child labour and the sweat shop problem
- Workers given a very low wage, and overtime in countries like Vietnam, China and Indonesia under a subcontract
- Poor working conditions, squalid working conditions and forced labour in the factories that manufacture their products
- Environmental damage done to society by air and water pollution, noise, and change in the climate due to pollution. (Stockdale & Crosby, 2004).

BUSINESS AWARENESS

There are different kinds of guiding principles that can prevent Nike type scandals. This is what the company did:

- PR campaign: Nike decided to use a PR campaign to repair its social image due to the sweatshop debate. The PR campaign covered the following actions:

- Employment Practices: The management of Nike looked at its employment practices; they made sure that the company was following the policies on recruitment, training, health, safety and welfare. The management of the company also oversaw their environmental practices – to make sure that the company follows procedures that are responsible in terms of waste disposal and avoidance and energy inputs.

- Training Plan: They conducted and designed a training programme for the employees. The management remembered that training and development programs are not universal solutions to every need of the company. Effective job designs, selection, placement and other activities of the HR department are also very important.

- Assessing Performance: They set targets and identified performance measurement standards. If performance is to be rated accurately, the performance of the company requires the management to assess each and every relevant performance dimension.

- Ethical Responsibility: The management of Nike understood that ethical responsibility is needed within the company because it is the obligation of every organisation's management to make decisions and take actions that will grow the welfare and interest of the organisation and of society as a whole. It would include activities and commitments that are related to human rights, governance and ethics, development, working conditions of the employees, community involvement, customer satisfaction, relations with the company's suppliers and customers, and respect for diverse cultures and different people.

> **Test your understanding 2**
>
> Employees are _____ stakeholders, while finance providers are _____ stakeholders.
>
> **Which two words fill the gaps in the above sentence?**
>
> A   Internal, connected
>
> B   External, internal
>
> C   Connected, outsiders
>
> D   Internal, suppliers

2 Stakeholder needs analysis

Stakeholder needs analysis involves an organisation undertaking research to determine who its **key** stakeholders are, and what their **needs** are.

For example, if a company has £1 million in the bank earning modest interest, then the bank is probably not a key stakeholder. In another company with a £100 million debt to the bank and large interest payments, the bank is clearly an extremely important stakeholder.

Once the organisation has identified its stakeholders, it needs to understand what their needs and wants are. There is no better way of accomplishing this than asking them directly. Possible methods include questionnaires, focus groups, direct interviews or interviews with representatives.

Example: Car manufacturer

As well as being sensitive to the requirements of customers with respect to factors such as price and performance, a car manufacturer should also consider public attitudes to pollution, and government policies on road tax and fuel tax.

As a result, it may choose to develop more environmentally-friendly vehicles as part of its long-term strategy even if current demand is for larger cars, say.

To some stakeholders, the company owes obligations arising from the law (e.g. to pay employees their salary each month, or to compensate them if they are made redundant).

However, other obligations arise voluntarily due to the company's commitment to corporate social responsibility (CSR) (e.g. to discuss their plans with interested pressure groups before a particular plan is adopted).

 Example: 888.com

888.com is an internet gambling site that is listed on the London Stock Exchange. It is headquartered in Gibraltar and operates under a licence granted by the Government of Gibraltar. It has responsibilities to the following stakeholders:

- Shareholders – since it is listed on the London Stock Exchange it must comply with the rules of that exchange, including adopting the Corporate Governance Code.

- Employees – to be a good employer to all its members of staff.

- Customers – to offer a fair, regulated and secure environment in which to gamble.

- Government – to comply with the terms of its licence granted in Gibraltar.

- The public – the company chooses to sponsor several sports teams as part of strengthening its brand. The company also tries to address public concerns about the negative aspects of gambling e.g. by identifying compulsive gamblers on their site and taking appropriate action.

3 Stakeholder conflict

An organisation can have many different stakeholders, all with different needs. Inevitably, the needs of some stakeholders will come into conflict with the needs of others.

Some of the most common conflicts include:

Stakeholders	Conflict
Employees versus managers	Jobs/wages versus profit-linked bonus (improved by cost efficiency)
Customers versus shareholders	Product quality/service levels versus profits/dividends
General public versus shareholders	Effect on the environment versus profit/dividends
Managers versus shareholders	Independence versus growth

Example: Car manufacturer

In an attempt to reduce costs and boost profits, a car manufacturer could consider using cheaper components in its engines.

The cheaper components are expected to fail after 4 years whereas the current components usually last the life of the car.

This is an example of prioritising the needs of shareholders over those of customers.

But it could harm the company in the long term if it creates a backlash from customers and wider society.

Test your understanding 3

How could a conflict arise between shareholders and bankers?

3.1 Mendelow's matrix

In the event of conflict, an organisation will need to decide which stakeholders' needs are more important. This will commonly be the most dominant stakeholder (in other words, the one with the most power).

If an organisation is having difficulty deciding who the dominant stakeholder is, it can use **Mendelow's power-interest matrix**.

The matrix was designed to track interested parties and evaluate their viewpoint in the context of some change in business strategy.

In strategic analysis, stakeholder influence is assessed in terms of each stakeholder's **power** and **interest**, with higher power and higher interest combining to generate the highest influence.

By plotting each stakeholder according to the power they have over the organisation and the interest they have in a particular decision, the dominant stakeholder(s) i.e. the key player(s), can be identified. The needs of the key players must be considered during the formulation and evaluation of new strategies.

		Level of interest	
Level of power		**Low**	**High**
	Low	Minimal effort	Keep informed
	High	Keep satisfied	Key players

3.2 Interpretation of Mendelow's matrix terminology

Level of power relates to the amount of influence (or power) that the stakeholder group can have over the organisation. However, the fact that a group has power does not necessarily mean that this power will be used.

Level of interest indicates whether the stakeholder is actively interested in the performance of the organisation.

Assessing the power and interest of each stakeholder group results in stakeholders being categorised into one of the following four groups:

- **Low interest – low power**

    These stakeholders typically include small shareholders and the general public. They have low interest in the organisation primarily due to lack of power to change strategy or influence corporate governance.

- **High interest – low power**

   These stakeholders would like to affect the strategy or influence corporate governance of the organisation but do not have the power to do this. Stakeholders include staff, customers and suppliers, particularly where the organisation provides a significant percentage of sales or purchases for those organisations. Environmental pressure groups would also be placed in this category as they will seek to influence company strategy, normally by attempting to persuade high power groups to take action.

- **Low interest – high power**

   These stakeholders normally have a low interest in the organisation, but they do have the ability to affect strategy and/or influence corporate governance should they choose to do so. Stakeholders in this group include the national government and in some situations institutional shareholders. The latter may well be happy to let the organisation operate as it wants to, but will exercise their power if they see their stake being threatened.

- **High interest – high power**

   These stakeholders (such as directors, major shareholders and trade unions) have a high interest in the organisation and have the ability to affect strategy and/or influence corporate governance.

Be aware that stakeholder groups can move from quadrant to quadrant as a result of specific events or new strategies, so Mendelow's matrix should not be seen as a static record of power and interest.

3.3 Resolving stakeholder conflicts using Mendelow's matrix

Whenever a company makes a strategic decision, the directors should consider the competing needs of stakeholders. To make sure any conflicts between stakeholder needs are identified and addressed, the following steps should be followed:

- **Identify** the stakeholders who will be affected by the decision.

- **Assess** each stakeholder's power and interest, and place each stakeholder in one of the categories on Mendelow's matrix.

- **Prioritise** the stakeholders (for example high interest – high power stakeholders are the key players).

BUSINESS AWARENESS

- **Identify** the needs of the high priority stakeholders.
- **Formulate a strategy** that meets the needs of the high priority stakeholders, but also follow Mendelow's guidance for other stakeholder groups (i.e. keep satisfied the 'low interest – high power' stakeholders; keep informed the 'low power – high interest' stakeholders).

Test your understanding 4

Chop Ltd is a forestry business, which leases several large woodlands from the central government of country Z. It currently employs 2,000 members of staff across the country.

Chop supplies over three hundred small businesses with wood across country Z. However, recently its profitability has been poor and it has been struggling to pay any dividends.

This has angered the company's three largest shareholders, who each own around twenty percent of Chop's share capital. The remainder is owned by the public, with no other investor owning more than one percent of the total share capital.

The three main shareholders have asked the Board of Directors to consider making 200 employees redundant. The employees are not heavily unionised.

Required:

State the appropriate strategy from Mendelow's matrix for each of the following stakeholders:

A   Chop Ltd's customers
B   Major shareholders
C   Employees
D   Government of country Z

Test your understanding 5

The LKJ Company is a distributor of electricity in a large country. LKJ purchases electricity from companies making electricity and then distributes this through a network of cables to companies and private individuals throughout the country. Electricity is generated from a variety of sources including burning coal and natural gas, nuclear power and a small amount from renewal resources such as wind and wave power.

LKJ's shares are owned by three other companies, who take an active interest in the profitability of LKJ. There are three other electricity distribution companies in the country LKJ operates in.

The directors of LKJ are currently considering the proposal to purchase electricity from another country. This source of supply is quoted as being cheaper from those within LKJ's home country, although the electricity is generated by burning coal. If this supply is taken, LKJ will stop purchasing electricity from an old nuclear power station and some of the expensive wind power plants.

The Clean-Earth environmental group has learnt of the proposal and is currently participating in a media campaign in an attempt to block the change by giving LKJ bad publicity.

The directors, managers and employees in LKJ appear indifferent, although changing the source of supply will provide a price advantage over LKJ's competitors, effectively guaranteeing their jobs for the next few years.

Required:

Identify the stakeholder groups who will be interested and/or affected by the decision of the LKJ Company to change electricity suppliers, evaluating the impact of that decision on the group.

Discuss the actions the board can take with respect to each stakeholder group.

4 The risk attitude of stakeholders

As well as assessing the power and interest of the various stakeholder groups, it is important for a business to understand the risk attitudes of its main stakeholders.

The risk attitude of the stakeholders determines how much risk the stakeholders consider acceptable, and hence when they will decide to take actions to mitigate potential adverse impacts of risks.

Not all stakeholders will have the same attitude towards risk.

4.1 Different risk attitudes

There are three main types of stakeholders:

- **Risk seekers** are likely to favour the strategy with the best possible outcomes, regardless of the likelihood that they will occur. These stakeholders are willing to accept risk even if it only delivers a marginal increase in return.

- **Risk averse** stakeholders try to avoid risk. They would rather select a lower, but certain, outcome than risk going for a higher pay-off that is less certain to occur. These stakeholders are unwilling to accept risk, no matter what the anticipated benefit or opportunity.

- **Risk neutral** stakeholders consider all possible outcomes and will favour the strategy that maximises the expected value or benefit. The stakeholder is neither risk averse nor risk seeking, and any given decision is not affected by the level of uncertainty of the outcomes. When two possible scenarios carry the same level of benefit, the risk neutral stakeholder will not be concerned if one scenario is riskier than the other.

Risk attitude is influenced by the following three factors:

- **Risk appetite** refers to how much uncertainty the stakeholder is willing to take on.

- **Risk tolerance** indicates the degree, amount, or volume of risk stakeholders will withstand.

- **Risk threshold** refers to the level at which a risk is acceptable to the stakeholder. A risk will fall above or below the risk threshold. If it is below, then the stakeholder is more likely to accept the risk.

The risk appetite, risk tolerance and risk threshold of key stakeholders of an organisation will differ depending on their personal circumstances.

Example: Stakeholder risk attitudes

Directors/managers compared to shareholders

Directors and managers of an organisation are likely to be more risk averse and shareholders are likely to be more risk seeking.

This is because directors and managers have much more to lose if a new strategy doesn't work out.

If the organisation is forced into liquidation, the directors/managers will lose their jobs, their income, their prestige and perhaps other assets (e.g. car, or even house in extreme cases).

The shareholders will lose the money they invested in the business, but that is the limit of their liability. If a shareholder is well diversified (with investments in many different companies), the impact of any one of those companies failing is negligible.

Therefore shareholders often try to encourage directors/managers to make more risky decisions than the directors/managers are happy with.

Shareholders compared to lenders

Lenders will also tend to be more risk averse than shareholders.

Lenders expect that payments of interest and repayments of principal should be made on time and without problems.

Shareholders, in theory, seek to maximise the value of their shares.

In seeking to maximise their wealth, shareholders might take actions that are detrimental to lenders. For example, shareholders (normally through their agents, the directors/managers) might use the finance provided by lenders to invest in very risky projects, which change the character of the risk that the lenders face. If the risky projects are successful, then the rewards flow primarily to the shareholders. If the projects fail then much of the cost of failure will fall on the lenders.

5 Summary

This chapter started by explaining who the stakeholders of an organisation are, and categorised those stakeholders as internal/connected/external stakeholders, and primary/secondary stakeholders.

It showed how important it is to recognise that different stakeholders will have different needs (and risk attitudes). Conflicts between stakeholders' requirements can be resolved using Mendelow's matrix.

Business stakeholders' interactions and needs: Chapter 3

Test your understanding answers

Test your understanding 1

The correct answer is C

Neither is correct. Internal stakeholders have a huge amount of influence over the running of an organisation.

In addition, just because they are in the same category of stakeholder does not mean that managers and employees have the same goals. For instance, managers will want to keep profits high to ensure they maximise their bonuses. This may encourage them to keep staff wages low, which is clearly not in the interests of employees!

Test your understanding 2

The correct answer is A

Internal stakeholders include employees and managers/directors; connected includes shareholders, customers, suppliers and finance providers. The third stakeholder group is external which includes the community at large, government and trade unions.

Test your understanding 3

The shareholders may be willing to take more risks in return for higher profits/returns, whereas the bankers will be more concerned with low risk/security.

Test your understanding 4

A   Minimal effort

Chop's customers are likely to have little interest in the staffing of their suppliers as long as it does not affect the service or products they receive. They will individually have little power as they do not form a significant part of Chop's revenue.

B   Key players

The board will see the three major shareholders as having high power due to their high proportion of voting rights in the business. They are clearly highly interested in their investment in Chop.

C   Keep informed

Employees are not heavily unionised, so have little collective power. They will be highly interested, however, as many of their jobs are at risk.

D   Keep satisfied

The government of country Z would have significant power over Chop, if it chose to exercise it, as it owns the forests that Chop leases. However, as long as Chop obeys the law, it is unlikely to take an active interest in the reduction of its workforce.

Test your understanding 5

The main strategy of the board regarding a large institutional investor is communication, with the need for change followed by participation in strategy determination. Most codes of corporate governance indicate the bi-lateral approach to be taken. The large investor is interested in the success of the organisation while at the same time having the ability to adversely affect the organisation if its shareholding is sold.

The organisation must therefore keep the stakeholder informed regarding important strategic decisions. Similarly, there is a responsibility on the part of the stakeholder to take an interest in the activities of the organisation and to use its influence responsibly.

The three investors in LKJ are likely to be keen for the electricity to be purchased from the different country, as this will increase the return on their investment.

A dialogue should be established between the chairperson and large shareholders, as a minimum by discussion at the annual general meeting. However, more frequent meetings throughout the year are also expected. The chairperson needs to ensure that the expectations of return from LKJ are congruent with the investing companies.

Environmental pressure group

The pressure group will attempt to influence other groups with high power to change the strategy of the organisation. The directors of LKJ therefore need to communicate with the group with the aim of explaining and educating them in respect of the actions being taken by LKJ.

Currently Clean-Earth is attempting to influence the strategy of LKJ by the media campaign. The basis of this campaign is likely to be the fact that obtaining electricity from coal is more harmful to the environment than renewable sources and possibly nuclear generation. Explanation of the reason for change in terms of increased profit may not, however, be acceptable.

However, the board must be prepared to learn from the pressure. Many pressure groups do have responsible and knowledgeable members. Ignoring these groups may mean that valuable advice and assistance is rejected on grounds of prejudice against this type of stakeholder. While it is likely that advice from the group will be biased towards renewable resources, they may have ideas regarding cost efficiency that LKJ can use.

Directors/managers/employees of LKJ

The directors of LKJ are stakeholders in the organisation. In terms of corporate governance, they have the responsibility to act in the best interests of the company and its shareholders. In this sense, there is no conflict in the decision to source electricity supplies from another country; LKJ profits are forecast to increase while there is job security for the directors. While the directors have high power and interest in LKJ, this power appears to be being used correctly.

Similarly, the actions of the directors appear to meet the requirements of the managers and employees of LKJ in that their jobs are protected.

However, the environmental impact of their action may be a cause for concern. If LKJ, and therefore the directors, are considered not to be acting ethically then customers may choose alternative suppliers. This action will mean that the profit forecasts are incorrect and the directors may need to consider alternative courses of action.

BUSINESS AWARENESS

Organisational structure and governance

Introduction

Upon completion of this chapter you will be able to describe the different ways in which formal organisations may be structured: entrepreneurial, matrix, functional, divisional.

You will also be able to explain basic organisational structure concepts (span of control, tall and flat organisations), as well as the characteristics of the strategic, tactical and operational managerial levels in the organisation.

Finally, you will understand the principles of governance for an organisation and how this is impacted by organisational structure and size. You will also be able to explain and evaluate centralisation and decentralisation of decision making.

ASSESSMENT CRITERIA
Organisational structure and governance (1.4)

CONTENTS	
1	Organisational structure
2	Tall and flat organisations
3	Governance
4	Management hierarchy
5	Structure and governance

KAPLAN PUBLISHING

1 Organisational structure

> **Definition**
>
> Organisational structure is concerned with the way in which work is divided up and allocated. It outlines the roles and responsibilities of individuals and groups within the organisation. There are several possible ways in which an organisation can be structured.

The structure of most organisations will change over time as the company grows. This will involve more levels of authority, more decentralisation (explained later) and more specialisation (where staff focus on a particular specialist task such as accounting rather than having to be involved in a wide range of tasks).

1.1 Entrepreneurial structure

This structure is built around the owner-manager. It is typical of small businesses in the early stages of their development. It is also often found where the entrepreneur has specialist knowledge of the product or service that the organisation offers. There is typically only one level of authority (all staff report directly to the entrepreneur), there is no decentralisation (all decisions are made centrally by the entrepreneur) and there is very little specialisation of tasks (staff work collectively as a team to achieve tasks).

Below is a table that compares the advantages and disadvantages of having an entrepreneurial structure:

Advantages	Disadvantages
Fast decision making: There is only one person making decisions – this leads to decisions being made quickly.	Lack of career structure: This type of structure is usually suited to small companies where due to the size there is no career path for the employees.
More responsive to market: As soon as an element of the market alters, the entrepreneur should recognise it and act quickly.	Dependent on the capabilities of the manager/owner: there is a lack of specialist skills and the entrepreneur must multi-task.

Advantages	Disadvantages
Goal congruence, good control: A lack of a chain of command and the small size of the organisation means that the entrepreneur has control over the workforce and all decisions within the organisation, leading to better goal congruence.	Cannot cope with diversification/growth: If the organisation grows, one person will not be able to cope with the increased volume of decisions.
Close bond to workforce: A bond can be created between the entrepreneur and the workforce which enhances motivation, staff retention and loyalty.	

1.2 Functional/departmental structure

In a functional structure, work and employees are divided by specialisation. It forms departments such as production, sales, research and development, accounting, HR, and marketing. Each department has a separate function and specialises in that area. For example, all HR professionals are part of the same function and report to a senior leader of HR. The same reporting process would be true for other functions, such as finance or production.

This type of structure is often found in organisations that have outgrown the entrepreneurial structure. It is most appropriate for small organisations which have relatively few products or locations and which exist in a relatively stable environment.

A functional structure will depend on the functions of the organisation but the organisation will be structured along the following lines:

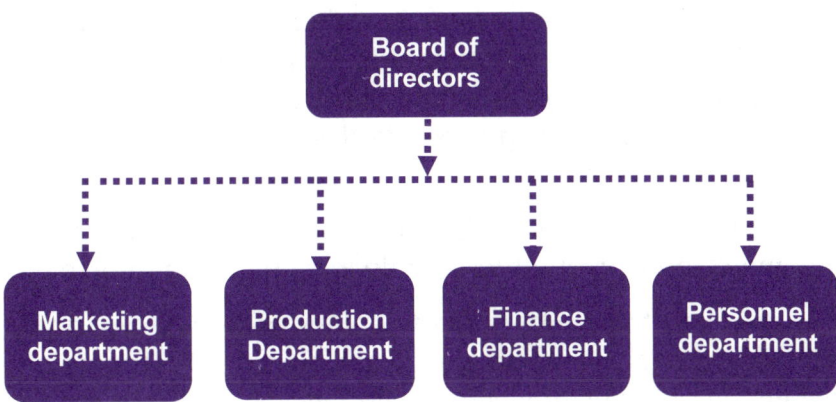

Below is a table that compares the advantages and disadvantages of having a functional structure:

Advantages	Disadvantages
Similar activities are grouped together, leading to: – lower costs – standardisation of output/ systems, etc. – people with similar skills being grouped together and so not feeling isolated.	Managers of the functions may try to make decisions to increase their own power or which are in the best interests of their function only, rather than working in the best interest of the company overall. This leads to empire building and conflicts between the functions.
Due to the larger size of the organisation and the grouping into functions, there is a career path for employees – they can work their way up through the function.	Due to the longer chain of command, decisions will be made more slowly.
There is an increased use of specialists such as specialists in accounting, marketing, HR, purchasing etc.	This style of structure is not suited to an organisation which is rapidly growing and diversifying. For example, the specialists may become so specialised in existing products and markets that they can struggle to adapt to new products or markets.

1.3 Divisional: product structure

This structure occurs where an organisation is split into several divisions – each one autonomously overseeing a product (for example, there might be separate divisions for cars and motor bikes), a geographic section (for example, having separate divisions for the US and Europe) or even by customer (for example, having separate divisions to look after corporate clients and private clients).

Each division is likely to have a functional structure, with all the departments it needs in order to operate in its particular market segment.

Divisions are likely to be run as profit centres, with their own revenues, expenditure and capital investments. Each division is a separately identifiable part of the overall organisation, which is often referred to as a strategic business unit (SBU).

An organisation chart for a divisional business might appear as follows:

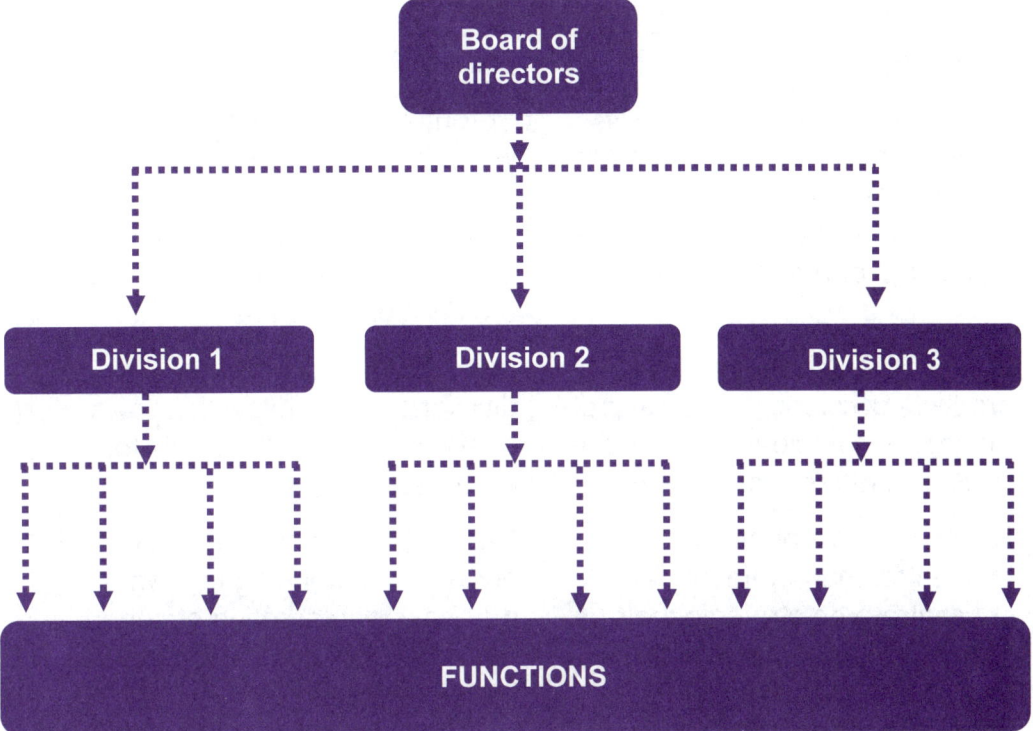

Divisions will have their own functions such as marketing, purchasing and production. But there may still be some centralised functions such as accounting and HR.

Example: divisional structure

A Ltd is a company that manufactures two different products – toasters and televisions. The products require different components and different advertising and sales.

A Ltd therefore operates a divisional structure, with a division for toasters and a division for televisions. Each division has its own sales, purchasing, HR and advertising divisions. This means that each division will deal with its own suppliers and customers, for example. The suppliers for the toaster division are likely to be very different to the suppliers for the television division.

The finance department, however, is still operated centrally. This function will prepare the financial statements for each division as well as for the company as a whole.

Organisational structure and governance: Chapter 4

Below is a table that compares the advantages and disadvantages of having a divisional structure:

Advantages	Disadvantages
A divisional structure makes it easier to grow into new markets or products: should the company want to diversify further, it is easy to 'bolt on' another division.	Potential loss of control: divisions will operate as mini-organisations, making their own decisions. This means that central management can lose some control over how the division operates.
Clear responsibility for products/divisions: the divisional managers can clearly see where their area of responsibility lies.	Lack of goal congruence: divisions might follow their own goals rather than the goals for the organisation as a whole.
Better strategic planning: top/central management can concentrate on strategic matters, rather than on the day-to-day operations of each division or function.	Duplication of activities: as each division will be doing its own purchasing, marketing etc. there will be a lot of duplication across the organisation.
Better performance appraisal: it is easier for central management to evaluate how each division is performing.	Specialists may feel isolated: specialists will now be split across a number of divisions rather than working together within one function. It may even be that a particular division has only one specialist who misses out on the teamwork and culture from working with other specialists in similar roles.
	Allocation of central costs: some functions, e.g. accounting, may be provided centrally. If this is the case, the cost of the centralised function could be recharged to divisions. There are different ways of calculating the recharge and divisional managers may complain if the profitability of their division is reduced by an amount that they perceive as being arbitrary.

1.4 Divisional: geographic structure

This is similar to the divisional structure (and has similar advantages and disadvantages), but involves each division covering a specific location.

For example, a global company may be split into different divisions based on geographic areas. There may be a division that looks after the organisation's Asian operations, one that covers Europe and another division for America.

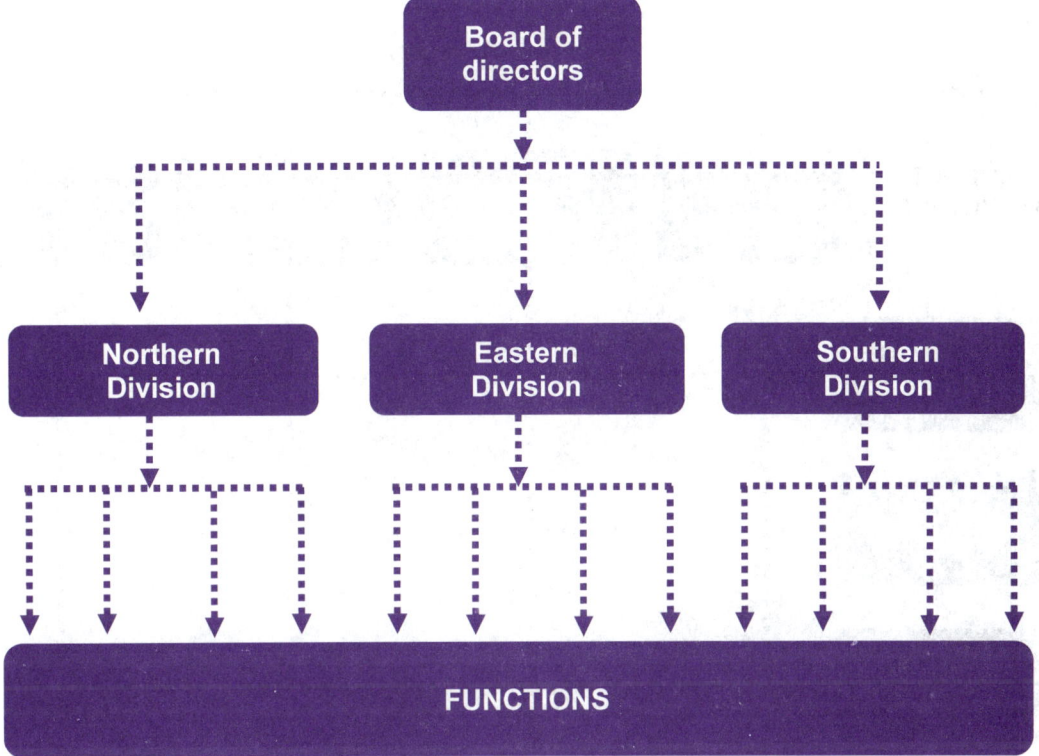

Example: Product vs geographic divisional structure

Product divisionalisation is generally preferred over geographic divisionalisation when the product is relatively complex and requires a high cost of capital equipment, skilled operators, etc., e.g. in the car industry.

A geographic structure is preferred when an organisation is spread over many geographic regions and is planning to grow into new geographic regions.

1.5 Matrix structure

Matrix structures are a combination of the functional and divisional structures (with an aim of achieving the advantages of both structures):

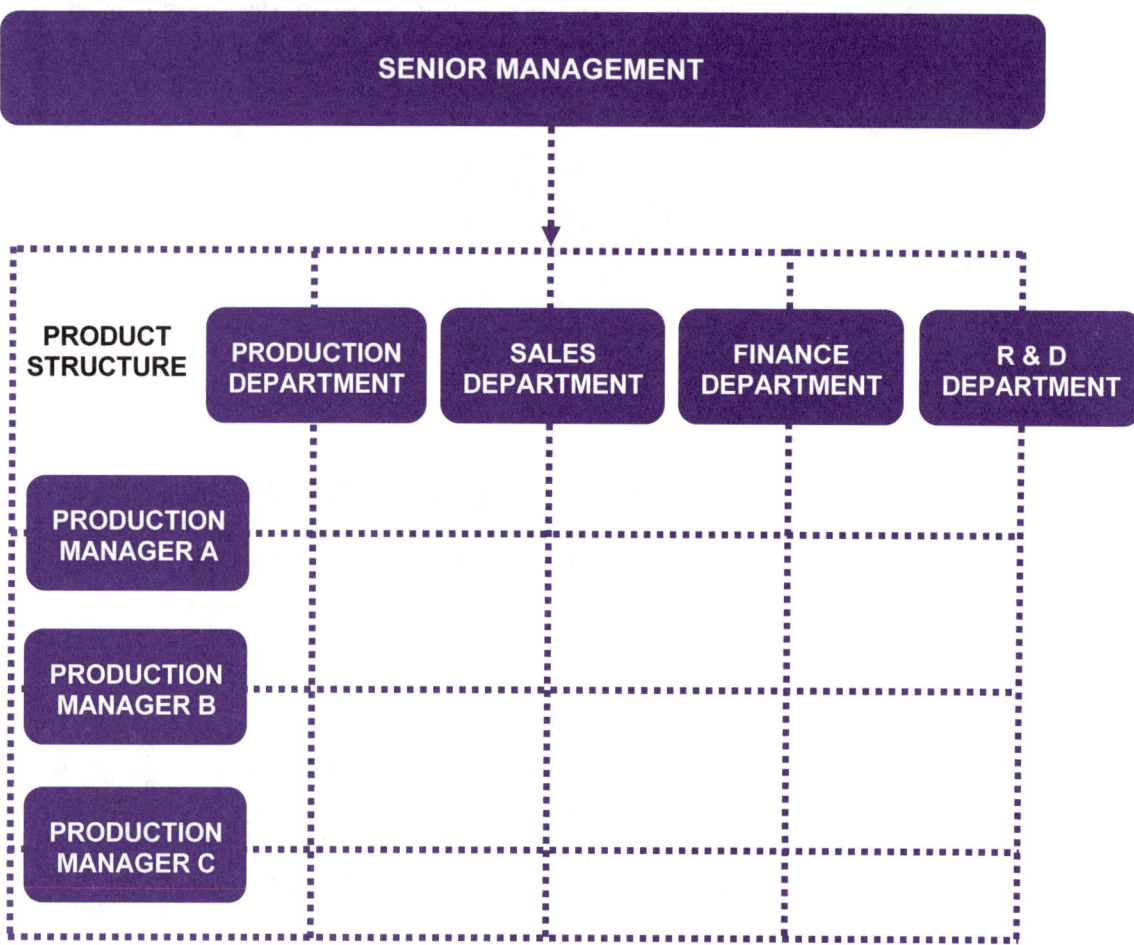

Matrix structures are common in heavily project-driven organisations, such as an accountancy firm. They are also increasingly common in high-tech organisations. Typically, employees from different functions form teams until completing a project, and then revert to their own functions.

The matrix requires dual reporting to two different managers. For example, looking at the diagram above, an employee manufacturing product A would have to report to the manager of the production department and the manager in charge of product A.

An organisation which runs regional projects often operates a matrix structure.

BUSINESS AWARENESS

Below is a table that compares the advantages and disadvantages of having a matrix structure:

Advantages	Disadvantages
Flexibility: In today's rapidly changing environment, there is a need for effective coordination in very complex situations. If a car manufacturer wants to design, produce and market a new model, the process involves most parts of the organisation and a flexible system is needed to achieve the objectives. The more rigid structure experienced in a divisional company would not have the flexibility to be able to coordinate the tasks and the people, whereas the matrix structure can cope.	Dual command and conflict: Where the matrix structure can cause difficulty is in the lines of control. These may become ambiguous and conflict with each other. A team member may be answerable to the product manager and to a functional head, and this may cause confusion and stress.
Customer orientation: The production managers could be replaced with customer managers, in which case the whole team will be focussed on meeting the needs of the customer. Customers can more easily achieve a bespoke product or service.	Extra administration: there is a need for more detailed planning and time-consuming meetings. This can increase administrative costs and make this structure an expensive one to operate.
Encourages teamwork and the exchange of opinions and expertise as employees will be regularly be working on different products, for different customers and within different teams.	Dilution of functional authority: staff are focused on the needs of the product manager and are working in product teams rather than functional teams. This means that the functional manager can lose some authority over functional staff and reduces the value of this role for both the organisation and the individual.

Test your understanding 1

Consider the following statements:

(i) Under the functional structure, each department operates as a strategic business unit.

(ii) The matrix structure will enable rapid decision-making within the organisation.

Which of the statements is/are correct?

A (i) only
B (ii) only
C Both
D Neither

Test your understanding 2

M plc is a large company that operates in country G. It manufactures several different products, each of which is highly complex and extremely specialised. Its sales have grown significantly over the last several years, with each of its products producing a roughly equal amount of M's overall revenue.

Which organisational structure is most likely to be appropriate for M?

A Geographic
B Divisional
C Functional
D Entrepreneurial

2 Tall and flat organisations

2.1 Span of control

A manager's span of control is the number of people for whom they are directly responsible.

The factors that influence the span of control include:

- the nature of the work – the more repetitive or simple the work, the wider the span of control can be.

- the type of personnel – the more skilled and motivated the managers and other staff members are, the wider the span of control can be.
- the location of personnel – if personnel are all located locally, it takes relatively little time and effort to supervise them. This allows the span of control to become wider.

2.2 Tall and flat organisations

> **Definition**
>
> A 'tall' organisation has many levels of management (a long scalar chain) and a narrow span of control.
>
> A 'flat' organisation has few levels of management (a short scalar chain) and a wide span of control.

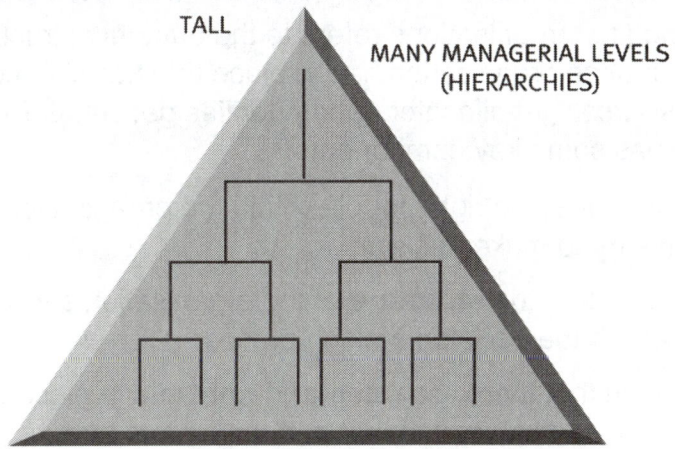

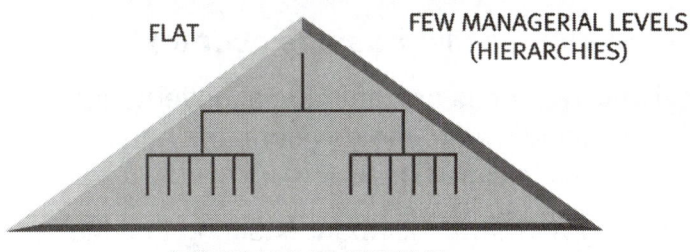

It is worth noting that tall organisations tend to be more bureaucratic and take longer to make decisions, due to the large number of levels of management that need to be involved.

Flat organisations tend to have weaker control and fewer chances for employees to progress or be promoted within the organisation.

Test your understanding 3

If a managerial structure has many levels of management, is it likely to have a narrow or wide span of control at each level of management?

3 Governance

Governance for organisations refers to the authority structures, processes, and rules that an organisation has in place to determine how decisions get made, resources get allocated, and priorities get set. Governance therefore has some key components:

- ensuring that the right people within the organisation have the **authority** to make decision

- ensuring that the **structure** of the organisation supports and enhances the decision making process

- ensuring that there are **rules and controls** in place which govern the limits to a person's authority and the factors that they should consider in making decisions.

3.1 Governance in a business context

In this syllabus we focus on commercial governance. Good commercial governance should lead to the development and achievement of the commercial organisational goals.

Commercial governance is about ensuring that the organisation can meet its commercial goals such as growing its market share, developing new products, improving services to customers, etc. It is important that there are structures in place to ensure that these goals are considered, that decisions are made that focus on the achievement of these goals, that authority is given to those in the best position to make those decisions, and that there are processes and controls in place to determine whether this commercial governance is working as it should.

Governance will therefore require the organisation to make decisions on the following areas:

- Specialisation: the extent to which an organisation's activities are divided into specialised roles.
- Standardisation: the degree to which an organisation operates under standard rules or procedures.
- Formalisation: the extent to which instructions and procedures are documented.
- Centralisation: the degree to which leaders at the top of the management hierarchy have authority to make certain decisions.
- Chain of command: the number of vertical levels or layers on the organisational chart (i.e. how tall the structure should be).
- Span of control: how wide or narrow this should be.

3.2 Other types of governance

Other types of governance that an organisation must consider are:

- **financial governance** – this focuses on financial viability of the organisation as well as ensuring that the financial performance and risks of the organisation meet the expectations of stakeholders (such as shareholders and lenders). This requires structures for measuring and reporting financial performance throughout the business, considering policies for how and when suppliers will be paid, ensuring that debt repayments can be met etc.
- **regulatory and legal governance** – this focuses on ensuring that the organisation complies with necessary regulation. Rules and processes will be supported by structures and the necessary authority to ensure that this is considered and managed within the organisation
- **corporate governance** – this is governance that is normally applied to companies that have a high level of public interest (such as those listed on stock exchanges). It is also important when there is a high risk of agency issues in an organisation (that is, where directors might follow their own goals and interests rather than meet the goals and consider the interests of other key stakeholders). Often this involves appointing non-executive directors to the board of the company who do not take part in functional decisions but ensure that the needs of a wide group of stakeholders are considered in the decision making process.

3.3 Centralisation and decentralisation

A key element of governance is determining who, within the organisation, has the authority to make decisions. This involves a decision on the amount of centralisation in decision making and whether any decision making should be decentralised.

In a **centralised** structure, the upper levels of an organisation's hierarchy (such as the board of directors of a company, the entrepreneur in an entrepreneurial structure or the board of trustees in a charity) retain the authority to make decisions.

- Decisions are said to be imposed in a 'top-down' manner. This allows the least amount of creativity and flexibility for staff. Staff are usually not involved in the decision making process that directly affects how they perform their jobs – front-line staff and managers are responsible for implementing the policies and procedures of executive management.

- Each person has very specific responsibilities and authority. Positions are also ranked according to supervisory level and importance. Those individuals who hold positions that are higher up in the organisation's hierarchy possess greater amounts of control and decision making ability. This means that the senior managers who make most of the decisions may rarely interact with the company's end consumer.

In a **decentralised** structure the authority to take decisions is passed down to units and people at lower levels (such as functional managers, divisional managers or team managers).

- Decisions are said to be made in a 'bottom-up' manner. Lower level employees have the authority to make decisions that directly impact the company's customer or the employees' job tasks. These staff do not have to go up the chain of command to get approval before acting. This will directly engage all employees in decisions that affect processes, procedures, and policies that might improve business conditions or job task efficiency. It is also likely to foster a more collaborative environment within the organisation.

The factors that will affect the amount of decentralisation are:

- **management style** – some managers want to be more involved and take more control and therefore more likely to use centralised decision making

- **ability of management/employees** – if employees have the skills and experience to make good decisions without close supervision then a more decentralised approach could be adopted

- **geographic spread** – when employees and managers are spread over long distances it can be very difficult to impose a centralised process
- **size of the organisation/scale of activities** – as organisations grow and become more complex decentralisation becomes more relevant as there are too many decisions for them all to be made centrally, especially as central managers may not have all of the relevant information required to make the best decision
- **predictability of the environment** – if the environment is very stable and predictable, and rarely changes, then centralisation can lead to standardisation and result in an elimination of waste and an adherence to the organisational goals. But when the environment is unpredictable, and changes rapidly, decentralisation typically leads to a leaner, flatter organisation that is better suited to reacting and adapting to a changing environment.

The advantages and disadvantages of **decentralisation** are:

Advantages	Disadvantages
Senior management are freed up to concentrate on strategy.	There is a loss of control by senior management as they are no longer involved in all decisions.
Decision making can be improved as 'local' decisions, made by local managers, will benefit from local expertise and knowledge.	There is the potential for poor decisions to be made if inexperienced managers are making decisions.
Decision making is quicker due to the smaller chain of command. This can make the organisation more flexible in reacting to local market or customer changes.	Managers may make decisions based on what is best for their area of authority (e.g. their product, function or division) but this may not be what is best for the organisation overall. These 'dysfunctional' decisions will occur when there is a lack of goal congruence (that is, where the managers goals don't align with those of the organisation).

Decision making managers have more authority and control which can increase their motivation and create a more attractive career path for all staff.	If local managers are to be involved in the decision making process they will require extra training which will take time and incur extra costs for the organisation.
	The process is slower (decisions often have to be approved by being passed up the chain of command) and more expensive (as more people are involved in making and approving the decision).

 Test your understanding 4

Which of the following is NOT a likely additional cost to an organisation caused by decentralisation?

A Additional training costs are often required in a decentralised organisation

B Duplication of roles, leading to higher personnel costs

C Extra costs of gathering information from various sources and locations

D Lost sales due to lack of local knowledge and expertise

BUSINESS AWARENESS

4 Management hierarchy

Another aspect of governance is to give consideration to the type of decisions that need to be made and who should be responsible for these.

4.1 A hierarchy of responsibilities

Business responsibilities can be split into three levels based on the types of plans that need to be considered within the organisation:

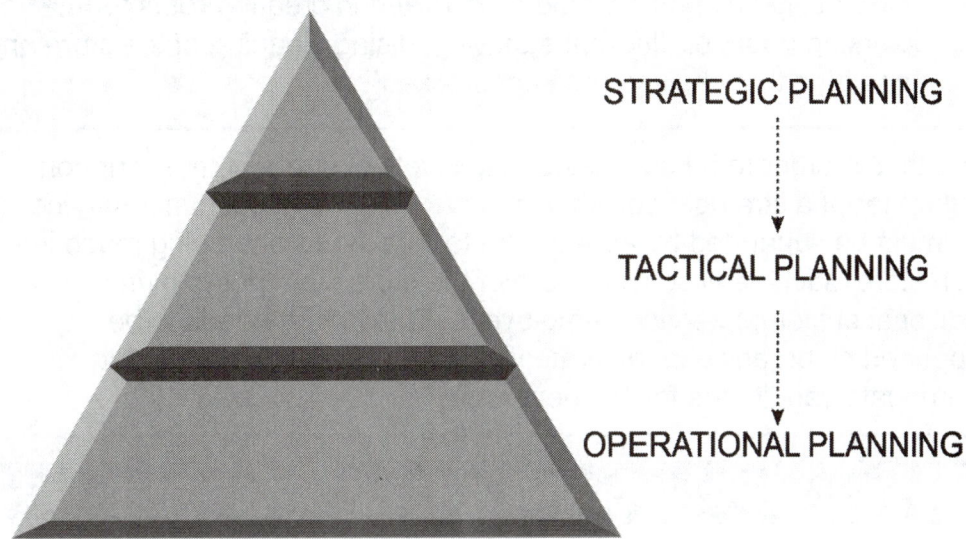

Different levels of planning

- **Strategic planning** involves making long-term decisions for the entire organisation, such as which products to launch, which markets to operate in or how the organisation will stand out from rivals.

- **Tactical (or business) planning** tends to look at plans for specific divisions or departments and specifies how to use resources, how to compete with rivals and how to achieve organisational goals.

- **Operational planning** is short-term, detailed and practical such as considering which staff will work on which jobs, when suppliers should deliver materials and hours of operations.

Example: Strategic, tactical and operational planning

The above planning levels could be applied to a supermarket as follows:

- Strategic planning would involve making plans for the whole business. This could involve which locations to open or close stores and whether to raise cash from investors.

- Tactical planning would be the creation of strategies for a particular supermarket. For example decisions about special offers, local advertising and which products should be stocked.

- Operational planning would be involved in creating rotas for the working hours of different staff, organising cleaning of the store and ensuring that shelves are kept stocked.

Note that in order to be successful, the levels of strategy must support each other. If a strategic decision is made to improve customer service, this must be supported by appropriate tactical decisions being made in each store, such as allocating more of the store's budget to hiring additional customer services employees. This in turn needs to be supported by organisational strategies such as selecting the most appropriate candidates for the new role.

 Test your understanding 5

H is a retail store selling electronics. It is currently deciding how many units of its products it will need to order next month in order to meet customer demand.

Which level of strategic planning does this relate to?

A   Strategic
B   Functional
C   Tactical
D   Operational

4.2 A hierarchy of management

The organisation might create a hierarchy of management as part of its governance, where each level of management within the hierarchy takes responsibilities for different types of decisions. So strategic managers would focus on strategic decisions whilst operational managers would focus on operational decisions, for example. This is especially the case when it comes to developing an organisational strategy, or plan for the future.

Most **governance structures** are comprised of a board of directors or executive management team, a middle level of management that might be responsible for a product, function or division and lower levels of supervisory management that might be responsible for a team of staff, a branch or a group of branches.

The board of directors usually represents the highest level of power, control, and authority in an organisation. They vote on company directives and help shape executive strategies. In terms of publicly owned corporations, the board of directors also acts as a sort of liaison between the company's executive management team and its shareholders. This corporate level of management is likely to take responsibility for strategic planning.

The lowest level of management, those responsible for a team of staff or a single branch, are likely to have the lowest level of power, control, and authority in the organisation. This operational level of management is likely to take responsibility for operational planning.

However, this will in turn be determined by the organisational structure chosen by the organisation.

5 Structure and governance

The structure of an organisation will have a significant impact on how it is governed. It will influence the roles, power and responsibilities of everyone within the organisation. It should be designed to meet the goals of the organisation as well as to ensure that the organisation can be governed in a way that is suitable to its environment.

5.1 How different structures relate to different governance

The structure of an organisation will have a significant impact on how it is governed.

For an **entrepreneurial structure** the governance might be as follows:

Governance consideration	How this might be applied in an entrepreneurial structure
Specialisation	None – the leader/entrepreneur/senior management team will make most decisions and staff will not be departmentalised or expected to have specialist skills.
Standardisation	None – activity levels will be low and processes and rules will constantly evolve. There will not yet be the scope for standardisation of tasks or processes.
Formalisation	Very little – work will be performed on an ad-hoc basis and the lack of standardisation will mean that activities will not yet be formailsed.
Centralisation	High – all decisions will be centralised around the entrepreneur.
Chain of command	Flat – there will be very few levels of authority.
Span of control	Wide – the entrepreneur will manage all staff.

The flatter chain of command will influence the levels of management and who makes the different types of planning decisions. In an entrepreneurial structure there is unlikely to be strategic, tactical and operational management teams. It is more likely that the senior management team (or the entrepreneur) will make all of the business planning decisions.

These additional levels of management, and the development of a hierarchy of management, is likely to occur with more complex organisational structures.

BUSINESS AWARENESS

As the organisation grows and moves through the other structures this governance will change. The governance for an organisation structured in a **divisional** way might be as follows:

Governance consideration	How this might be applied in a divisional structure
Specialisation	High – there will be specialist staff dedicated to particular tasks (such as accounting or purchasing).
Standardisation	High – tasks will be standardised to ensure that each unit or service is as identical as possible in order to provide consistency for customers and in production.
Formalisation	Very high – all work must be recorded and all tasks must be performed in accordance with formal rules and procedures.
Centralisation	Low – there will be too many decisions for central management to make and they will want to benefit from the better local knowledge that divisional managers might have.
Chain of command	Tall – there is likely to be many levels of authority and a clear career path for staff.
Span of control	Narrow – staff will work in smaller teams, often dedicated to particular tasks or customers.

A **functional structure** would lie somewhere between these two points, whilst a matrix structure is likely to have even more decentralisation, a narrower span of control and a more complex chain of command.

However, the **matrix structure** might actually be less formal, less standardised and have less specialisation. Staff will be expected to be flexible to changing customer and business needs, reducing the role of standardisation and formality of rules. Staff will work in cross-functional teams, reducing the need for specialisation.

Test your understanding 6

Which of the following is likely to be true?

A   The span of control in an entrepreneurial structure will be narrow

B   The chain of command for an entrepreneurial structure will be tall

C   The level of decentralisation in a matrix structure will be high

D   The chain of command in a matrix structure will be flat

 Test your understanding 7

Which of the following is likely to be true?

A   The chain of command in a functional structure will be flatter than in an entrepreneurial structure

B   The span of control in a functional structure will be wider than in an entrepreneurial structure

C   The level of specialisation in a functional structure will be less than in an entrepreneurial structure

D   The level of formality in a functional structure will be greater than in an entrepreneurial structure

6 Summary

There are a range of organisational structures available to an organisation. The most common of these are:

- **Entrepreneurial** – where all staff report to the senior management team.
- **Functional** – where staff are divided into specialist teams for each business function.
- **Divisional** – where the business is split up based on its products or geography.
- **Matrix** – where multi-function project teams are designed in order to provide greater flexibility for the business.

The organisation must also consider:

- Whether to have a tall or flat structure – a **tall** structure tends to be more bureaucratic but a **flat** structure removes career paths for employees.
- The level of decentralisation – **centralisation** ensures goal congruence, but **decentralisation** makes use of the better knowledge held by local managers.

Different structures will require different **governance** which will in turn be determined by factors such as the size of the company, the predictability of its environment and the capabilities of its staff.

Test your understanding answers

Test your understanding 1

The correct answer is D

The separate parts of the organisation operate as SBUs in a divisional structure – not a functional structure.

The matrix structure tends to require time-consuming meetings and has significant overlap of authority between managers. This tends to slow the decision-making process down.

Test your understanding 2

The correct answer is B

As M has several complex products, a structure that creates a separate division to look after each one seems the most logical. Functional and geographical structures would struggle to cope with the differing needs of the products. The level of work needed to run a large, complex organisation would also probably be beyond the capabilities of an entrepreneurial structure.

Test your understanding 3

Narrow

BUSINESS AWARENESS

Test your understanding 4

The correct answer is D

A decentralised business delegates decision-making to employees at a lower, or more local, level. This should allow for better local decisions to be made, hopefully maximising sales.

Note that another cost of decentralisation could be poor decisions or goal congruence leading to increased costs.

Test your understanding 5

The correct answer is D

This strategy is very detailed and practical. Note that functional strategy is another name for tactical strategy.

Test your understanding 6

The correct answer is C

In matrix structures there will be too many decisions to make for decision making to be centralised. Centralised decision making would also reduce the flexibility of the matrix structure which is a key component of the structure.

The other options are all false.

Test your understanding 7

The correct answer is D

There will be a greater amount of decentralisation and standardisation in a functional structure than in an entrepreneurial structure. This will require more formal rules than in an entrepreneurial structure.

The other options are all false.

The role of the finance function

Introduction

Upon completion of this chapter, you will understand the role of the finance function in an organisation.

In particular, the chapter looks at how the finance function contributes towards the operation of other business functions such as operations/production, sales and marketing, human resources, information technology, and distribution and logistics.

Effective interaction between the finance function and these other business functions is vital to the organisation's planning and decision making.

ASSESSMENT CRITERIA	CONTENTS
Organisational structure and governance (1.4) – in particular (1.4.4) "The role of the finance function in contributing towards the operation of the other business functions and the organisation's plans and decision making"	1 Introduction to the finance function 2 Operations/Production 3 Sales and marketing 4 Human resources 5 Information technology 6 Distribution and logistics

The role of the finance function: **Chapter 5**

1 Introduction to the finance function

1.1 The functions of an organisation

Before focusing on the finance function, it is useful to remind ourselves of the different functions that exist within an organisation.

The main functions of a business are:

- operations
- sales and marketing
- human resources (HR)
- IT and
- finance.

It is a major part of the finance function's work to look after the business's money. The finance function's role in managing the financial resources of the organisation and providing information to help economic decision making will be integral to the effectiveness of the finance function.

1.2 The roles of the finance function in organisations

The finance function plays **three key roles**. A finance function:

- **ENABLES** an organisation to create and preserve value though planning, forecasting and resource allocation:
    - **Planning:** the finance function will have an important role in preparing plans to assist the organisation in achieving its objectives and formulating relevant strategies. One of the main types of planning carried out at the operational level will be budgeting.
    - **Forecasting:** the preparation of forecasts, for example of future sales or material prices, will be an important role of the finance function at the operational level.
    - **Resource allocation:** an important role of the finance function will be to work out which resources (for example, labour, material, machinery, finance) the organisation will require to achieve its objectives.

- **SHAPES HOW** an organisation creates and preserves value through performance management and control:
  - **Performance management:** the finance function has an important role in the management of performance and the achievement of the organisation's plans and budgets.

    For example, it will help to prepare information for internal management such as performance measures. These measures will assist in monitoring the performance of the organisation. The performance measures may be quantitative, i.e. numerical (such as sales, profit or units produced) or may be qualitative, i.e. non-numerical (such as customer satisfaction or levels of innovation).
  - **Control:** this will be an important part of effective performance management; actual performance will be compared to planned performance to identify any differences. Variance analysis may be carried out as part of this role. The identification of these differences may result in a reassessment or amendment of the original plans, strategies or budgets.
- **NARRATES HOW** an organisation creates and preserves value through financial (corporate) reporting:
  - Financial reporting (also called corporate reporting): an important role of the finance function is in preparing comprehensive reports intended to give information to shareholders and/or other interested people about the organisation's activities and performance throughout the year.

If it plays these roles effectively, then finance professionals are valuable to organisations.

2 Operations/Production

2.1 Definitions

Definition

Operations are those activities concerned with the acquisition of raw materials, their conversion into finished products and the supply of that finished product to the customer. Or 'what the company does'.

Contemporary thinking has broadened the definition of 'what the company does' to include service operations as well as manufacturing operations.

INPUT RESOURCES → THE TRANSFORMATION PROCESS → OUTPUT PRODUCTS AND SERVICES → CUSTOMERS

Examples of operations

Organisation	Operations function	Operation
McDonald's	Kitchen and serving staff	Selling fast food
Vauxhall	Production line	Making cars
Dell	Production line, internet	Making and selling computers
Real Madrid	Football coaches, training facilities	Playing football

Definition

Operations management refers to the activities involved in designing, producing and delivering products and services that satisfy the customer's requirements.

Example: Operations management in IKEA

IKEA is the most successful furniture retailer ever. With over 400 stores in 25 countries, it has managed to develop its own special way of selling furniture. Innovations in its operations dramatically reduced its selling costs. These included the idea of selling furniture as self-assembly flat packs (resulting in reduced production and transport costs) and its 'showroom-warehouse' concept which required customers to pick the furniture up themselves from the warehouse (which reduced retailing costs). Both of these operating principles are still the basis of IKEA's retail operations process today.

IKEA's operations managers are involved in a number of activities. These include:

- Process design – arranging the store's layout to give smooth and effective flow of customers.
- Product design – designing stylish products that can be flat-packed efficiently.
- Job design – making sure that all staff can contribute to the company's success.
- Supply network design – locating stores of an appropriate size in the most effective place.
- Supply chain management – arranging for the delivery of products to stores.
- Capacity management – coping with fluctuations in demand.
- Failure prevention – maintain cleanliness and safety of storage area.
- Inventory management – avoiding running out of products for sale.
- Quality management – monitoring and enhancing quality of service to customers.
- Operations improvement – continually examining and improving operations practice.

These activities are only a small part of IKEA's total operations management effort but they do give an indication of how operations management can contribute to business success.

2.2 Areas of interaction between operations and finance

Operations management will be an important contributor to effective and efficient purchasing, production and delivery of customer specific goods and services. The operations function and the finance function should work in partnership to ensure this efficiency and effectiveness is optimised.

In this section, we will examine how specific parts of an organisation's operations (i.e. purchasing, production and service provision) interact with the organisation's finance function. The **focus here will be on the operational level** tasks performed by the finance function.

Purchasing (procurement)

Purchasing is an important part of the operations function. It is responsible for placing and following up orders. It co-ordinates with the finance function as follows:

Establishing credit terms	The finance function will work with purchasing to liaise with suppliers to obtain a credit account and to negotiate credit terms that are acceptable.
Prices	The finance function can advise purchasing on the maximum price that should be paid to maintain margins.
Payment	Payments may be approved by purchasing but are made by the finance function.
Data capture, for example, orders	Order details will be input by purchasing and details passed to the finance function.
Inventory	Purchasing will consult with the inventory section of the finance function to determine the quantity of items already in stock and therefore the quantity required.
Budgeting	The finance function will consult with purchasing on the likely costs in preparing budgets.

BUSINESS AWARENESS

 Example: Purchasing

XYZ Limited is a company manufacturing handbags.

Describe how purchasing liaises with the finance function when buying some leather to make handbags from DEF Limited, a new supplier.

Establishing credit terms	Purchasing will advise the finance function that the preferred supplier is DEF. The finance function contacts the credit controller at DEF and provides the information required to set up a credit account.
Prices	The finance function obtains the cost estimate for the handbag being produced. It discusses with purchasing how much can be paid for the leather in order to maintain margins.
Payment	The payment for the leather is approved by purchasing and then made by the finance function.
Data capture, for example, orders	Order details for the leather will be input by purchasing and details passed to the finance function to check that the price on the invoice is correct.
Inventory	Before placing the order, purchasing will consult with the inventory section to determine how much suitable leather is already in stock.

 Test your understanding 1

Which of the following is an example of coordination between purchasing and the finance function?

A   Establishing credit terms
B   Determining sales prices
C   Allocating costs
D   Calculating pay rises

Production

Production is a core part of the operations function. It plans and oversees the production of goods. It liaises with the finance function as follows:

Cost measurement, allocation, absorption	Production measures quantities of materials and time used; the management accountant gives a monetary value to them. Costs are then allocated and absorbed to calculate production costs based on advice given by production.
Budgeting	Production will decide how many items of what type are to be produced. The cost of producing these will be determined by the finance function and production together, and incorporated into the overall budget.
Cost v quality	Production and the finance function will discuss the features that can be included in products and the raw materials that should be used. They should agree which better quality materials and features justify the extra cost, and discuss how to maximise quality and profit.
Inventory	Production will liaise with the inventory section of the finance function to ensure that there are sufficient raw materials in inventory for the production that is planned.

Example: Production

XYZ Limited is a company manufacturing handbags. The company has commissioned a designer to design a new style of handbag and discussions are taking place about the materials to be used and the quantity to be produced. Describe how the finance function and production would liaise over this.

Cost measurement, allocation, absorption	Production estimates the quantity of raw materials required and (in conjunction with purchasing) their cost. Together with the finance function overheads will be allocated to determine the full cost of the handbag.
Budgeting	Production, the finance function and marketing will discuss how many bags are likely to be sold at what price and determine how many should be produced. A budget can then be produced.
Cost v quality	Production, the finance function (and marketing) will discuss the various grades of leather and the material that could be used, their costs, and the extra price that could be charged for better quality material. They will decide on the best combination of cost/quality/profit.

The role of the finance function: Chapter 5

Service provision (for non-manufacturers)

Service companies will not manufacture a product. The provision of the service will be core to their operation function. The finance function will co-ordinate with this function in many ways such as:

Chart out rates	Service suppliers typically charge a rate per service or a rate per hour of the service. The finance function will help in calculating this. For example, for a firm of accountants the finance function will help to determine how much to charge clients per hour for accountancy worked to ensure that employee salaries, overhead costs etc. are covered by the charge out rate. Or, for a firm that provides hairdressing services, the finance function might determine how much to charge per hair treatment.
Pricing for tenders	Many service contracts are won on the basis of tendering. A tender is where a price must be submitted for a job or service and the customer makes a decision on which supplier to use based on this tender. For example, a painter might submit a tender for painting a company's offices. Or a firm of auditors might tender for providing audit services to a potential client. The finance function will help the service function in pricing these tenders to ensure that all costs are covered and that a profit is made (if required).
Payment	There will be two parts to the payment support provided by the finance function. It will manage payments to staff and contractors as well as monitoring receipts from customers and identifying areas of risk from customers who might be paying later than expected.
Data capture	The operations department will record details of work completed, hours taken, staff used etc. and the finance function will use this to prepare profit and loss accounts. But the finance function will seek to capture additional data on key performance indicators such as cost per service undertaken, customer satisfaction and customer retention.
Budgeting	As with all functions, the finance department will help the operations function with its budgeting needs.

3 Sales and marketing

3.1 Finance interaction with Sales and Marketing

It is useful to begin by thinking about some basic ways in which finance interacts with sales and marketing:

Budgeting	Finance will discuss the likely sales volume of each product with sales and marketing, in order to produce the sales budget.
Advertising	Finance will help sales and marketing in setting a budget, and in monitoring whether it is cost effective. For example, they could help in measuring new business generated as a result of different advertising campaigns.
Pricing	Finance will have input into the price that is charged. Often products are priced at cost plus a percentage. Even if sales and marketing determine the price based on market forces they need to consult with finance to ensure that costs are covered.
Market share	Finance can provide marketing with information on sales volumes for each product, to help the marketing department in determining market share.
KPIs	Finance will establish and monitor the KPIs for the sales and marketing function.

- Finance, and sales and marketing should interact to achieve organisational goals and their own individual functional goals.

- Traditionally, there may have been antagonism between the two functions over issues such as pricing and cost control.

- The modern approach is for the two functions to collaborate and to work in partnership.

- Effective interaction will be based on close working teams that possess a shared vision for the organisation and an appreciation of each other's specialisms.

- Technology is assisting this collaboration through the use of tools such as cloud computing, data analytics and blockchain.

3.2 How finance helps to manage sales and marketing using Key Performance Indicators (KPIs)

- The sales and marketing function will identify its relevant Critical Success Factors (CSFs) (i.e. the vital areas where things must go right for the function in order for them to achieve their strategic objectives).

- The KPIs are the measures that indicate whether or not the sales and marketing function is achieving these CSFs. KPIs are essential to the achievement of these objectives since 'what gets measured gets done', i.e. the things that are measured get done more often than the things that are not measured.

- The finance function works with the sales and marketing function to:
    - **identify** appropriate KPIs
    - **assemble** KPI data and information
    - **analyse** this for insight
    - give **advice** to the sales and marketing function based on this insight and
    - **apply** what has been learned to impact the achievement of the objectives of the sales and marketing function and the organisation as a whole.

 Test your understanding 2

Which of the following is a way in which an organisation's marketing department would co-ordinate with its finance function?

A   Calculating charge-out rates for services provided by the organisation

B   Calculating the budgets for the number of units to be produced

C   Estimation of the costs of the raw materials required for the production

D   Decisions on the quality of raw materials that the organisation can afford to use

4 Human resources

The HR function is responsible for human resource management within the organisation. Human resource management (HRM) is the creation, development and maintenance of an effective workforce, matching the requirements of the organisation and responding to the environment.

4.1 Interaction between HR and finance

- **Traditionally**, the HR function and the finance function worked independently:
  - Finance viewed people as a cost whereas HR viewed people as an asset.
  - Collaboration between the functions was limited to, for example, establishing a budget for a reward programme.
- The **modern** approach is to view people as one of the greatest assets an organisation has. Finance and HR need to work more closely with 'people as assets' as their focus.
- Technology is freeing both functions from day-to-day duties in their respective fields. This combined with the increasingly competitive and fast-changing global environment is leading to the functions having an increased role in the strategic direction of the organisation and an opportunity to work in a more joined-up way.

Example: Artificial intelligence (AI) to replace doctors?

In the past, doctors were seen as one of the greatest assets in the medical world, with highly prized training, skills and experience.

However, there is a view that even in organisations that have previously viewed their employees as their key asset, technology will be able to replace many of the roles doctors previously carried out.

One example of this technology is the use of AI systems in medicine. AI systems simulate human intelligence by learning, reasoning and self-correction. Already this technology shows the potential to be more accurate at making diagnoses in specialist areas such as radiology and intensive care and at performing surgery.

Having said that, it is still widely thought that machines will never be able to fully replicate the human doctor-patient relationship and that doctors will still be viewed as the greatest asset in the treatment of patients.

- Both functions, HR and Finance, will have overlapping responsibilities. For example, they must consider:
  - the cost and benefit of recruiting and selecting new employees
  - the impact of HR policies, such as reward policies, on the profitability of the business.
- This requires data analysis and financial projections from the finance function. For example, an increase in salary, bonus payments or benefits will result in an increased cost for the organisation but this cost needs to be considered in the context of the increased benefit to the organisation due to, say, increased motivation and productivity and reduced staff turnover. The finance function can provide this 'information' and can then use it for 'insight', 'influence' and 'impact'.

Test your understanding 3

A large supermarket chain, Zedsa, employs a substantial number of employees in their many supermarkets and convenience stores.

Identify which TWO pieces of information Zedsa's Finance function would directly receive from the Human Resources function, not from the Operations function.

Information received ONLY from the Human Resources function	✓
New employee start date	
Overtime hours worked this week	
Hourly and overtime rate	
Travel expenses due for reimbursement	

5 Information technology

5.1 The need for information

Organisations need information systems to enable them to capture and generate the information that managers need for planning, control and decision making.

The hunger for information has never been greater than for today's organisations, likewise the value of information systems that deliver this information has never been so keenly felt. It follows that information technology (IT) and information systems (IS) assume increasing managerial importance within the modern organisation.

Definition – information systems (IS)

Information systems (IS) refers to the provision and management of information to support the running of an organisation. It often relates to the software used within an organisation (such as a Microsoft Excel spreadsheet that holds data on average customer spend).

Definition – information technology (IT)

Information technology (IT) is the supporting equipment (hardware) that provides the infrastructure to run the information systems.

IT is becoming a strategic weapon which many organisations are using to improve their competitive position. This can come in many forms. For example, using IT can improve efficiency and reduce costs in order to compete better, it can help the organisation react more quickly to the changing environment or it can create new opportunities etc.

5.2 Interaction between IT and finance

Given the central role that technology plays in supporting modern business and their finance functions, the finance function and the IT function need to form a productive partnership. Examples of why the two functions need to interact include:

- **Smarter investment in IT** – whether the business needs to implement a company-wide system or a solution that is for the finance function alone, the expert guidance of the IT function can help in determining which technology will help the company achieve its strategic goals and increase competitiveness. This will be of huge benefit to the finance function.

- **Information security and compliance** – when it comes to data privacy and security, the finance function can work with the IT function on many fronts, including creating access policies and minimising the threat of data theft and loss.

- **Data analytics** – organisations of all sizes are working to find ways to turn their data into actionable business intelligence. The finance function wants to make sure that only the most relevant and accurate data is used for decision making. This requires the business to apply the right combination of technologies, processes and strategies. The IT function is well equipped to lead and shape these activities.

Test your understanding 4

Which of the following statements is true?

A   The finance function will collaborate with the IT function on IT but not on IS

B   The finance function will collaborate with the IT function on IS but not on IT

C   The finance function will collaborate with the IT function on both IT and IS

D   The finance function will collaborate with the IT function on neither IT nor IS

BUSINESS AWARENESS

5.3 How finance helps to manage IT

The finance function will often help to create and monitor KPIs for IT. Examples of KPIs for IT include:

Type of activity	Possible KPIs
Operational activities – KPIs are used to monitor the day-to-day activity and effectiveness of the IT function.	• Ticket response rates for IT issues sent to IT support. • System/technology downtime.
Transformational activities – KPIs are used to measure the impact of IT initiatives in terms of better and more informed decision making.	• Cost of new technology. • IT spend per employee.
Strategic activities – KPIs are used to monitor the progress of the IT function towards long-term strategic goals.	• Revenue generated by using new technology. • Average age of IT systems.

You do not need to know these KPIs and you will not be asked to create KPIs. Nor do you need to know the categories of KPIs. But you may be given KPIs (which may be in the form of a chart or diagram [covered later in the syllabus]) and be asked to comment on them. This could apply to any function in the business, not just IT.

6 Distribution and logistics

Distribution and logistics are part of an organisation's supply chain.

Distribution concerns the physical provision of goods (or services) to the customer. **Logistics** relates to the overall planning and organisation of distribution, but will also concern itself with other elements of the supply chain such the storage and inventory control of goods.

Organisations with strong links between their finance function and supply chain teams are more likely to have effective supply chain management (SCM).

The role of the finance function: Chapter 5

6.1 Interaction between the finance function and the distribution and logistic function

The finance function and supply chain leaders are working increasingly together to understand, analyse and address supply chain issues. The finance function is drawing on its skills and unique view of the organisation to provide insight to deliver more informed decision making.

The finance function has a unique end-to-end view of the organisation and is considered a trusted advisor. As a result, there are a number of areas where the finance function has an opportunity to enhance performance through business partnering with the supply chain. These include:

- Stronger alignment between the supply chain and the broader strategy and consistency of strategy within the various parts of the supply chain.

- The finance function helps to set the right growth priorities and pace of growth; it supports and challenges the rationale for new investment, applies data analytics to support and challenge business decisions and ensures that tax is considered as part of operational decisions.

- Monitoring and enhancing performance through the establishment of appropriate KPIs that are aligned to the broader organisation.

- Managing risk and business continuity; the finance function has the opportunity to work with procurement to determine the extent to which risk is owned and managed by the company, and to what extent it is pushed to external elements of supply chain such as suppliers. For example, in determining what levels of inventory to hold; if high levels are held then the organisation is taking the risks associated with this, but it might instead expect suppliers to be more flexible and deliver with shorter lead times. This passes the inventory holding risk to the supplier.

 Test your understanding 5

Collaborating with its suppliers may bring a company added-value because it can:

A   Strike a harder bargain with suppliers

B   Work with a supplier to improve quality and reduce costs

C   Avoid transaction costs

D   Introduce price competition amongst suppliers

BUSINESS AWARENESS

7 Summary

The finance function is playing an increasingly important role within organisations. Not only should the finance function be focused on its own role in meeting organisational goals but it must also collaborate with other business functions to ensure that they can meet their organisational goals.

The finance function is unique in the organisation in that, firstly, it is more likely to play a role in developing and monitoring organisational goals than other functions within the business. Secondly, the finance function is likely to interact with other functions in matching their goals and performance with those of the organisation. The finance function will typically interact with:

Operations	–	this is concerned with producing/procuring the organisation's goods/service
Sales and marketing	–	this is concerned with acquiring new customers as well as retaining existing customers
HR	–	this is concerned with recruiting, training and motivating staff to meet the needs of the organisation's other functions
IT	–	this is concerned with ensuring that the other functions have the systems and technology required to achieve their goals
Distribution and logistics	–	this is concerned with the movement of goods across the organisation as well as the movement of goods into and out of the organisation.

For these functions the finance function will support and interact in numerous roles. The most commons ways are:

- Evaluating performance against organisational goals
- Providing information for decision making
- Evaluating the financial impacts of decisions
- Designing and monitoring key performance indicators.

The finance function (and those who work within it) can no longer focus only on its own goals and objectives. It must work together with other business functions to ensure the success of the business overall.

Test your understanding answers

Test your understanding 1

The correct answer is **A.** B relates to marketing, C relates to production and D relates to human resource management.

Test your understanding 2

Option A would most likely be a marketing or service provision crossover with the finance function. The other options relate to co-ordination between the production department and the finance function.

Test your understanding 3

Information received ONLY from the Human Resources function	✓
New employee start date	✓
Overtime hours worked this week	
Hourly and overtime rate	✓
Travel expenses due for reimbursement	

Test your understanding 4

The correct answer is option C

Whilst the primary collaboration between the finance function and the IT function will be on IT, they will also collaborate on IS. Not only will IS help the flow of information between these and other functions, but the finance function will also collaborate with the IT function in costing different systems when making purchasing decisions.

 Test your understanding 5

The correct answer is option B

Successful management of suppliers is based upon collaboration. A company should be able to improve quality and reduce costs as a result of this collaboration.

BUSINESS AWARENESS

Risk and risk management

Introduction

Upon completion of this chapter you will understand the nature of risk and why firms might choose to take risks. You will understand the difference between risk and uncertainty and the different types of risks that an organisation might face.

You will also understand the options available to organisations in determining how they should manage risks.

ASSESSMENT CRITERIA
The concept of risk and risk management (1.4)

CONTENTS	
1	What is risk?
2	Types of risk
3	Risk management

1 What is risk?

1.1 Definition

Definition

Risk, in business, is the chance that future events or results may not be as expected. Risk can be quantified by assigning probabilities to various levels of loss. For example, there is a 20% probability that this product launch will result in a net loss of greater than £1m.

There are many other ways of defining risk: 'Risk' is a condition in which there exists a quantifiable dispersion in the possible outcomes from any activity; 'Risk' can be defined as the combination of the probability of an event and its consequences.

1.2 Upside risks and downside risks

Risk is often thought of as purely bad ('pure' or 'downside' risk), but risk can also be good. Examples of pure risk are the risk of disruption to business from a pandemic, or the risk of losses from theft or fraud, the risk of damage to assets from a fire or accident, and risks to the health and safety of employees at work.

Not all risks are pure risks or downside risks. In many cases, risk is two-way, and actual outcomes might be either better or worse than expected. Two-way risk is sometimes called upside or speculative risk. In many business decisions, there is an element of upside risk – management will be aware that actual results could be better or worse than forecast.

For example, a new product launch might be more or less successful than planned, and the savings from an investment in labour-saving equipment might be higher or lower than anticipated.

1.3 The difference between risk and uncertainty

Definition

Uncertainty can be applied to a situation where there are several possible outcomes, but there is little past relevant experience to enable the probability of the possible outcomes to be predicted i.e. it cannot be quantified.

Risk is inherent in a situation whenever an outcome is not inevitable. Uncertainty, by contrast, arises from ignorance and a lack of information. For example, when launching a new product there is a risk that it might fail. This is known and a probability could be attached to it. However, there will be uncertainty on the actual levels of sales for this new product.

By definition, the future cannot be predicted under conditions of uncertainty because there is insufficient information about what the future outcomes might be or their probabilities of occurrence.

In business, uncertainty should be considered in decision-making. For example, there might be uncertainty about how consumers will respond to a new product or a new technology, or how shareholders will react to a cut in the annual dividend. Uncertainty is reduced by obtaining as much information as possible before making any decision.

Example: Risk and uncertainty

Risk: there are a number of possible outcomes and the probability of each outcome is known.

For example, based on past experience of digging for oil in a particular area, an oil company may estimate that they have a 60% chance of finding oil and a 40% chance of not finding oil.

Uncertainty: there are a number of possible outcomes, but the probability of each outcome is not known.

For example, the same oil company may dig for oil in a previously unexplored area. The company knows that it is possible for them to either find or not find oil but it does not know the probability attached to each of these outcomes.

One possible approach to risk is to deploy sophisticated modelling techniques in an attempt to improve the reliability of business forecasts. The aim is to develop a mathematical model to predict how future costs will behave based on past experience.

1.4 Risk and return

It is generally the case that firms must be willing to take higher risks if they want to achieve higher returns:

- To generate higher returns, a business may have to take more risks in order to be competitive.

- Incurring risk also implies that the returns from different activities will be higher – 'benefit' being the return for accepting risk.

- Benefits can be financial (e.g. decreased costs), or intangible (e.g. better quality information). In both cases, these will help the business in being able to gain competitive advantage.

- On the other hand, not accepting risk tends to make a business less dynamic, meaning that it fails to improve or innovate. For example, it might wait for rivals to release products first and take those risks. There is less risk of product failure from copying the innovations of rivals, but it is likely that the returns will be much smaller as it will be difficult to overcome the head start that rivals have achieved.

Test your understanding 1

Which of the following statements is true?

A   Uncertainty cannot be measured
B   Uncertainty can never be reduced
C   Risk can never be reduced
D   Upside risk can be ignored in decision making

2 Types of risk

Many organisations categorise risks into different types. The use of risk categories can help with the process of risk identification and assessment.

There is no single system of risk categories. The risk categories used by companies and other organisations differ according to circumstances. Some of the more commonly-used risk categories are described below.

2.1 Business risk

Definition

Business risk is the risk inherent in the nature of the company's operations.

BUSINESS AWARENESS

Business risk is the risk businesses face owing to the nature of their operations and products. Business risks can be categorised as follows:

- Strategic risk: this is the risk that business strategies (e.g. which markets the organisation chooses to operate in) will fail. For example, one company might decide to expand globally whilst another in the same industry focuses on its domestic market only. The former company will be taking more strategic risks than the latter. Strategic risks should be identified and assessed at senior management and board of director level.

- Environmental risk: this is the risk that the business fails to adapt to or recognise changes in its business environment. For example, the business might fail to react to changes in customer needs or to rivals launching new products with better technology. These risks are higher in environments that change rapidly, often and unpredictably such as those of high technology products. Environmental risk is explored in more detail when we look at the PESTLE model in a later chapter.

- Product risk: this is the risk that customers will not buy new products (or services) provided by the organisation, or that the sales demand for current products and services will decline unexpectedly. A new product might fail to achieve the expected volume of sales, or the take-up could be much slower than expected. For example, the demand for 'fifth generation' (5G) mobile communications services was much slower to build than expected by mobile service providers, due partly to the slower-than-expected development of suitable handsets.

- Market risk: this is the risk of changes in the market caused by actions of rivals, customers and suppliers. For example, rivals launching new/better products, customers no longer buying from the business and switching to rivals, failure of a supplier or a customer, or new entrants entering the market and taking market share from established rivals. Industries that are attractive based on their growth and level of profitability are likely to have higher market risks.

The examples above should illustrate that business risk is often outside the control of the business. It is influenced by factors such as the actions of rivals, the attitudes of customers and other changes in markets in which the organisation operates.

Business risk will also be related to the **industry** in which the business operates. Some businesses are inherently more risky than others.

Risk and risk management: **Chapter 6**

 Example: Business risks in different industries

Supermarkets are generally considered to have low business risk as they will always be used by consumers even in the worst of economic times. On the other hand, companies selling games consoles would be considered to have high business risk as their products will not be seen as a necessity and they might quickly go out of date when new technology becomes available.

Remember that with lower risks comes lower returns – if, for example, you were to buy shares in a supermarket or bank you are likely to make a lower return on your investment than you would do if you were to buy shares in, say, a company selling games consoles. But also remember that you would be taking more risk if investing in a company selling games consoles. Organisations face the same decisions when deciding which industries to operate in.

2.2 Operational risk

 Definition

Operational risk refers to potential losses that might arise in business operations. It is 'the risk of losses resulting from inadequate or failed internal processes, people and systems, or external events' (Basel Committee on Banking Supervision).

Examples of operational risk are:

- Business disruption risk: this is the risk that the organisation's operations cannot continue to operate as normal. This could be due to a staff strike, a pandemic, machine failures, loss of key staff, loss of a supplier, etc. Some organisations will experience higher risk than others. For example, if an organisation has only one type of staff, one machine, one supplier or operates in only one market then the business disruption risks will be higher.

- Regulatory risks: this is the risk that the business fails to meet regulatory standards or legislation. For example, it could refer to the risk that there is fraud carried out within the organisation, that there are health and safety breaches or that the organisation does not follow rules and laws set out for its industries. Failures in this area can lead to fines and penalties as well as potential compensation claims from injured parties. Organisations use internal controls, monitoring and training in an attempt to reduce this type of organisational risk.

- People risk: this is the risk of errors or problems caused by the people within the organisation. It includes errors by staff as well as issues caused by supervisors and management staff. If a manager has a poor management style that causes lots of staff to leave the organisation, for example, the organisation may no longer have enough staff with the necessary skills and experience to continue to operate.
- Process risk: this is the risk that processes are not efficient or fail. For example, a business offering a tax return service might have a process that requires employees to check that all boxes on the return have been completed. If employees ignore this process then this could cause major problems for the business.

Operational risks are generally within the control of the organisation. Risk assessment and risk management practices can help to reduce these risks. Organisations with poor risk management practices will therefore experience higher levels of operational risk.

Test your understanding 2

Which of the following would normally be classified as an operational risk? Select ALL that apply.

A   The risk that a new product will fail

B   The risk of competitors cutting costs by manufacturing overseas

C   The loss of an experienced supervisor

D   Raw materials being wasted during the production process due to untrained staff

2.3 Cyber risk

Cyber risk is a form of operational risk. As organisations embrace more technology and operate more digitally, cyber risks for most organisations are increasing.

Definition

Cyber risk is the risk of financial loss, disruption, or damage to an organisation caused by issues with the information technology systems they use.

Cyber security risks include:

- Malware is the term used for malicious software, regardless of the intended purpose. It can do any number of things, ranging from the stealing of credentials, other information or money to the general wreaking of havoc, or denial of service. There are various ways to execute malware, they include:

- Botnets are networks of private computers that are infected with a malware and controlled by a "botnet agent" designed to follow the attacker's instructions without the knowledge of the owner of the computer.

- Ransomware is malware designed to prevent a business from accessing its data, information or an entire computer system until a specified amount of money is paid.

Example: Ransomware

In July 2021, US IT firm Kaseya, was targeted in a ransomware attack that stole crucial operating files. The attack initially targeted Kaseya, before spreading through corporate networks which use its software. Kaseya estimated that between 800 and 1,500 businesses were affected, including 500 Swedish Co-op supermarkets and 11 schools in New Zealand. Criminal ransomware gang REvil demanded $70m worth of Bitcoin in return for a key that would unlock the stolen files.

- Trojans are named after the Trojan horse in an ancient Greek story where a wooden horse was allowed into the city as it was deemed harmless but which concealed soldiers inside ready to attack the city. This type of malware does a very similar thing: it pretends to be a useful piece of software whilst secretly releasing malware into the system, usually with the capability to be controlled by the attacker from a different location (known as a remote access trojan or RAT).

- Malvertising is when online advertisements have malware written into their code. It can involve hiding the malicious code in legitimate online advertising networks and web pages. The code may direct the victim to a malicious site where the malware can be installed or it may directly infect the victim's computer when they visit the page that contains the advert, even if the user does not click on anything to do with the online advert. Malvertising is a serious threat that requires little or no user interaction.

- Viruses are designed to endlessly replicate themselves and infect programs and files to damage or destroy data. Worm viruses spread across networks to infect other devices.
- Spyware is designed to spy on the victim's systems without being detected and gather information to send to the hacker. Keyloggers are similar – every keystroke typed by the victim is recorded and forwarded to the hacker.

Test your understanding 3

Which of the following are true of cyber risk? Select ALL that apply.

A It is a type of operational risk.

B It could be a deliberate and unauthorised breach of security to gain access to information systems to embarrass, extort or spy on a firm.

C It could manifest itself through IT issues from poor systems integrity or other factors.

D It is a strategic risk.

E The likelihood and impact are reducing all the time.

F Anti-virus software will stop all cyber risks.

2.4 Reputational risk

Reputational risk is another operational risk.

Definition

Reputational risk is the likelihood of losses occurring due to a deterioration in the belief or opinion held about someone or something.

Reputation is an area that organisations are increasing their focus upon, partially because there have been some high profile instances of reputational damage in recent times, and partially because of the rise in social media giving more customers a voice.

Reputational damage can be caused by many factors such as dishonesty, incompetence, activities that do unnecessary harm to the environment or unethical behaviour. It can be caused by an individual or by the behaviour of company as a whole.

Many large organisations are aware of the potential damage to their business from events affecting their 'reputation' in the opinion of the general public or more specific groups (such as existing customers or suppliers).

Some organisations succeed in being perceived as 'environmentally-friendly', and use public relations and advertising to promote this image.

For many organisations, however, reputational risk is a down-side risk as the better the reputation of the business the more risk there is of losing that reputation. A good reputation can be very quickly eroded if companies suffer adverse media comments or are perceived to be untrustworthy.

The risk can be particularly significant for companies that sell products or services to consumer markets. There have been cases where a company's reputation has been significantly affected by:

- employing child labour in under-developed countries or operating 'sweat shops' in which employees work long hours in poor conditions for low pay
- causing environmental damage and pollution
- public suspicions about the damage to health from using the company's products
- investing heavily in countries with an unpopular or tyrannical government
- involvement in business 'scandals' such as mis-selling products
- management announcements about the quality of the product a company produces
- becoming the victim of cyber attacks. Cyber risk is having a knock-on impact on reputation risk. Organisations that have suffered from cyber attacks lost the trust of customers regarding the safety of their data and the efficiency of the organisation's procedures and defences against cyber attacks.

Managing reputation risk can be complicated by the fact that many of these factors lie outside the control of the organisation. For example, many companies outsource production to third parties who operate in countries where labour costs are cheaper. Such arrangements can work well, although major multinational corporations have had their reputations tarnished by being associated with third parties who used dubious employment or environmental policies in order to keep costs down.

BUSINESS AWARENESS

 Example: Johnson & Johnson – good and bad reputation

In 1982, Johnson & Johnson was widely praised for its handling of a series of deaths that were caused by poisoned Tylenol (a product Johnson & Johnson made).

The CEO made the decision to recall all Tylenol products. The decision raised some eyebrows amongst analysts as it reduced Johnson & Johnson's market share from over 30% to under 10% and the view was Johnson & Johnson would never recover.

However, it transpired that the company was subject to a sabotage and was seen as one of the victims. As a result of its prompt actions, and the ensuing investigations, its reputation was enhanced and it regained a market share of over 30%.

In 2010, the company was in the news again, once again related to Tylenol. Customers started to complain of a musty, mildew smell from the product in 2008 and there were complaints of stomach pains. This time, the company decided not to report the concerns.

In 2009 it started to recall certain batches of Tylenol. As the number of recalled batches started to increase, anxiety grew amongst customers about what was wrong and whether they were impacted. At a similar time a rival started to give away bottles of their own version of the medicine and Johnson & Johnson lost significant market share as a result of their slow response.

Johnson & Johnson's response was widely derided and held up as a perfect example of how to damage the reputation of a company.

The sources of reputational risk are many and very diverse. It could manifest itself in anything from accounting deficiencies, poor customer service, lack of IT security or failure to meet expected standards of quality. All of these could lead to media coverage resulting in negative perceptions of the brand and company. These negative perceptions can then lead to investors and customers going elsewhere.

Example: Tesco accounting issues

In 2014 Britain's biggest supermarket chain revealed it had overstated its profits by around £250 million. In August that year it told the market half year profits would be £1.1 billion, but 4 weeks later it announced the overstatement. The issue related to discrepancies between when profits from deals with suppliers were accounted for and when costs were paid.

This led to over £214 million in fines and compensation claims, but also reputational damage. Investors no longer trusted the company and started to sell their shares – the share price fell by over 50% in a year.

2.5 Financial risk

 Definition

Financial risk is the risk of a change in a financial condition such as an interest rate, credit rating of a customer, or price of a good.

Financial risk is a major risk that affects businesses. Financial risks relate to the possibility of changes in financial conditions and circumstances. The main types of financial risk are:

- Credit risk: this is the risk of non-payment by customers. The exposure of a company to credit risks depends on factors such as the total volume of credit sales, the organisation's credit policy, credit terms offered (credit limits for individual customers and the time allowed to pay), and the credit risk 'quality' of customers (some types of customer are a greater credit risk than others).

- Interest rate risk: this is the risk that results from unexpected gains or losses arising as a consequence of a rise or fall in interest rates. Organisations with high levels of debt will face higher costs when interest rates rise.

- Gearing risk: this is the risk created by the way a business is financed (debt vs. equity). Organisations with high levels of debt are at greater risk of bankruptcy, and have higher levels of fixed obligations which have less flexibility.

- Financing risk: this is the risk that the organisation cannot raise the necessary financing to support its short-term and long-term needs. If financing (which is available from a wide range of sources) cannot be raised then the organisation will not be able to meet its financial obligations or finance its future strategies and plans.

BUSINESS AWARENESS

Test your understanding 4

Arthur Andersen (chartered accountants and registered auditors) failed to identify serious irregularities in the operations of major companies that it was auditing. This ultimately led to the closure of the Arthur Andersen business.

This was mainly due to which ONE of the following?

A   Business risk
B   Political risk
C   Environmental risk
D   Reputation risk

Test your understanding 5

Determine whether the following risks are business, operational or financial risks:

	Business risk	Operational risk	Financial risk
Exceeding an agreed overdraft limit			
Loss of a key customer to a rival			
Loss of a key manager to a rival			
New legislation which increases costs			

Risk and risk management: **Chapter 6**

> **Test your understanding 6**
>
> Jockey is a charity that employs 4,000 staff in various roles and has locations across the country. Half of all staff work remotely in their homes and are employed to take donations to the charity from members of the public. All staff are provided with laptop computers which are linked together through Jockey's IT systems. Jockey is considering making 10% of its staff redundant and moving 20% of all remaining staff to an office-based role in London.
>
> Identify ONE operational risk that Jockey will face.
>
> _____
> _____
> _____
> _____
> _____

3 Risk management

Risk management is the process of understanding and managing the risks that the organisation is inevitably subject to in attempting to achieve its corporate objectives.

3.1 Risk identification and evaluation

The first step in risk management is to identify risk. This can be done by considering categories of risks as previously described (i.e. considering what business, operational and financial risks the organisation will be facing).

The next step in the risk management process is to evaluate each of these risks. The most common way to do this is to evaluate the risk across two criteria:

- likelihood – this considers the likelihood of the risk materialising (for example, how likely is it that a major customer will take its business elsewhere?)

- impact – this considers the impact that the risk materialising could have on the business (for example, how damaging would it be to the business if a major customer was to take its business elsewhere? Could the business continue to make a profit?).

Risks are then evaluated as being either high or low under each of these categories.

Some organisations choose to plot risks on a diagram or map called a 'risk map'. A risk map is simply a 2 × 2 table or chart, with one axis for the impact of the risk and another for the likelihood of the risk occurring. This makes it easier to determine how individual risks should be managed, which is the next step in the risk management process.

Example: Risk map for an auditor

The following simple risk map might be prepared for a firm of auditors:

		Impact/consequences	
		Low	High
Probability/likelihood	High	New audit regulations for the profession	Loss of non-audit work from existing clients
	Low	Increases in salaries above the general rate of inflation	Loss of audit clients within the next two years

A risk map immediately indicates which risks should be given the highest priority.

3.2 The TARA framework

The TARA framework is used to determine how individual risks should be managed. TARA is a mnemonic for the four possible actions that can be applied to individual risks:

- **Transfer.** In some circumstances, risk can be transferred wholly or in part to a third party, so that if an adverse event occurs, the third party suffers all or most of the loss. A common example of risk transfer is insurance. Businesses arrange a wide range of insurance policies for protection against possible losses.

    Another example is outsourcing, using a third party to undertake part of the operations and hence taking on the risk.

    This strategy should be employed on risks that are **low likelihood, high impact**.

- **Avoid.** An organisation might choose to avoid a risk altogether. However, since many risks are unavoidable in business ventures, they can only be avoided by not investing (or withdrawing from the business area completely).

    This strategy should be employed on risks that are **high likelihood, high impact**.

- **Reduce/mitigate.** A third strategy is to reduce the risk, either by limiting exposure in a particular area or attempting to decrease the adverse effects should that risk actually crystallise. This can be done by using internal controls. For example, if there is a risk that a machine might break down a business could ensure that there are regular checks and maintenance carried out on the machine.

    This strategy should be employed on risks that are **high likelihood, low impact**.

- **Accept.** The final strategy is to simply accept that the risk may occur and decide to deal with the consequences in that particular situation. For example, there may be a risk that some staff cannot work due to illness. If there are lots of staff employed in the business then the impact on the business is likely to be low and the business may be willing to accept this risk.

    This strategy should be employed on risks that are **low likelihood, low impact**.

These approaches to risk can then be applied to a risk map as follows:

		Impact/consequence on business	
		Low	High
Likelihood	High	Reduce the risk	Avoid the risk
	Low	Accept the risk	Transfer the risk

BUSINESS AWARENESS

 Test your understanding 7

CC Freight is a freight forwarding business. It sends containers of freight from Heathrow to other airports around the world. It specialises in consolidating the freight of different shippers into a single container, in order to obtain the benefit of lower freight charges for large shipments. The price that CC charges its clients covers a share of the airline flight costs and insurance, and provides a margin to cover its running costs and for profit. To make a satisfactory profit, CC needs to fill its containers at least 75% full, and at the moment it is achieving an average 'fill' of 78%.

International trade and commerce has been growing in the past year, although at a slow rate. CC's management is aware that airline flight costs are likely to rise next year due to higher fuel costs. There may also be price increases from several major airlines. These airlines have experienced high losses recently despite making very high profits in the past.

Place each of the following risks in a cell of a risk map:

Risk 1: Downturn in international trade

Risk 2: Insufficient freight to fill containers

Risk 3: Higher airline flight costs

Risk 4: A major airline will go out of business

 Test your understanding 8

Following on from Test Your Understanding 7, explain how risk 4 should be managed by CC Freight.

 Test your understanding 9

Following on from Test Your Understanding 7, explain how risk 3 could be mitigated or reduced by CC Freight.

4 Summary

In order to assess and measure the risks that an organisation faces, a business must be able to identify the principal sources of risk.

Risks facing an organisation are those that affect the achievement of its overall objectives (which should be reflected in its strategic aims).

There are three key areas of risk:

- Business risk – this is the risk that the business fails and is largely from external environment

- Operational risk – this is the risk that the business operations fail and comes mainly from internal factors such as poor cyber security or poor staff management leading to strikes

- Financial risk – this is the risk that the business finances are not sufficient or well managed and the business enters into bankruptcy.

Risk should be managed and there should be strategies for dealing with risk. Risks should be evaluated based on their likelihood of materialising and their potential impact on the business.

The TARA framework gives guidance on how risks should be managed. Risks with a high impact and high likelihood should be avoided, whilst those with a low impact and low likelihood can be accepted.

BUSINESS AWARENESS

Test your understanding answers

Test your understanding 1

Answer A

The other options are all false. Risk can be reduced through good risk management whilst uncertainty can be reduced by gathering more information. Upside risk should be included in decision making otherwise decision making will only consider the worst case results from downside risks.

Test your understanding 2

The correct answers are C and D – A and B are business risks.

Test your understanding 3

The correct answers are A, B and C

While cyber risks can have very significant consequences for an organisation, they most commonly arise as a result of operational mistakes, so cyber risk is an operational risk.

Unauthorised breach of information systems is a cyber risk and it could manifest itself in the form of poor systems integrity.

As technology is utilised more and more, the likelihood and impact are increasing all the time.

Anti-virus software is a useful part of any defence, but cannot remove cyber risk completely.

Risk and risk management: **Chapter 6**

 Test your understanding 4

The correct answer is D – Arthur Anderson lost their reputation as being the number one accountancy firm in the world and consequently many of their customers.

 Test your understanding 5

	Business risk	Operational risk	Financial risk
Exceeding an agreed overdraft limit			✓
Loss of a key customer to a rival	✓		
Loss of a key manager to a rival		✓	
New legislation which increases costs	✓		

 Test your understanding 6

There are a number of operational risks that Jockey could face. Here are examples of some of them:

Jockey faces cyber risks from the extensive use of IT within its organisation. The IT system could be attacked and breached and give the hackers personal details of customers such as their bank details.

Making staff redundant could open Jockey up to reputational risk if this is seen by the public to either reduce the perceived service that the charity provides or to be unfair on those staff who are made redundant.

Making staff redundant may make it harder for Jockey to operate as normal and some key staff may be lost. This could reduce the level of service provided by Jockey or reduce the amount of donations it is able to process.

Moving staff to a permanent base in London may cause significant disruption to the charity's activities. This may impact on Jockey's ability to operate during this period.

BUSINESS AWARENESS

Test your understanding 7

		Impact	
		Low	High
Likelihood	Low	Risk 4: A major airline will go out of business	Risk 1: Downturn in international trade
	High	Risk 3: Higher airline flight costs	Risk 2: Insufficient freight to fill containers

Risk 1: A downturn in international trade would reduce the volume of business and reduce CC's profitability so its impact on CC could be high. But international trade is growing, and therefore the likelihood of a downturn is low.

Risk 2: The business will be affected if the average 'fill' of containers falls from its current level of 78%. Profits will be adversely affected if the fill is less than 75%, which does not give a large scope for a fall from the current level. Therefore this risk could be highly likely and also have a high impact on the business.

Risk 3: It seems inevitable that airlines will charge high prices but CC can pass these increases on to its own customers. Therefore the impact of this risk is low.

Risk 4: The collapse of a major airline is possible due to high losses, but it is unlikely. If an airline did go out of business, the impact on international freight would be low as business could be moved to other airlines.

Test your understanding 8

Risk 4: As a low impact and low likelihood risk CC should simply accept that this risk might arise. It should not change its operations in any way to try to reduce or avoid this risk.

Test your understanding 9

Risk 3 should be reduced or mitigated by CC. The easiest way for the company to do this is to ensure that its own sales prices are not fixed and that they can be increased as the airline costs increase. Flight costs should be monitored and changes in costs should immediately be reflected in higher prices being charged by CC.

BUSINESS AWARENESS

External Analysis – the PESTLE model

Introduction

Upon completion of this chapter you will understand what the PESTLE model is and how it helps an organisation understand its macro-environment.

You will be able to explore each element of the model and develop an understanding of the key factors in each area that might impact on a company and its industry. You can then apply these to particular industries and organisations when you have been given some relevant factors in each area of the model.

ASSESSMENT CRITERIA
The use of PESTLE model for analysing the external environment (2.1)

CONTENTS	
1	Introduction: the PESTLE acronym
2	Political factors affecting a business
3	Economic factors
4	Social factors
5	Technological factors
6	Legal factors
7	Environmental factors

External Analysis – the PESTLE model: Chapter 7

1 Introduction: the PESTLE acronym

With external analysis we are looking at factors which are outside an organisation's control but which may still impact on its operations and determine its future success and failure. It is critical that a business understands and 'best fits' the environment in which it is operating.

1.1 The business environment(s)

There are three levels to a business environment:

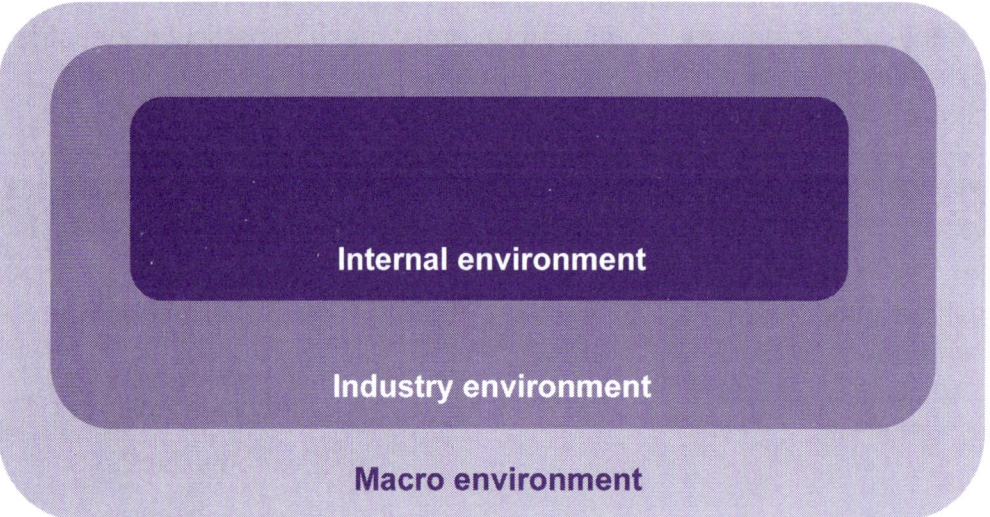

- **The macro environment** consists of external factors that affect the overall environment in which the business operates.

- **The industry environment** consists of external factors affecting the competitiveness of the industry in which the business operates.

- **The internal environment (internal capabilities)** consists of the organisation's own internal resources and capabilities (next chapter).

The PESTLE model looks at the macro-environment and its influence on organisational performance.

1.2 PESTLE analysis – definition

In order to fully understand an organisation, we need to examine the **macro environment** that it operates in – essentially, we need to learn about the world around it. PESTLE is an acronym used to help organise the macro environment into broad categories.

Definition

PESTLE analysis divides the business environment into political, economic, social (and cultural), technical, legal and ecological/environmental factors. Analysing these factors can help organisations understand the opportunities and threats within their macro environment.

This understanding is crucial in shaping the organisation's current and future strategic decisions, for example:

- **political** influences and events – legislation, government policies, changes to competition policy or import duties, etc.

- **economic** influences – a multinational company will be concerned about the international situation, while an organisation trading exclusively in one country might be more concerned with the level and timing of domestic development. Items of information relevant to marketing plans might include changes in the gross domestic product, changes in consumers' income and expenditure, inflation, interest rates, and oil prices.

- **social** influences – includes social, cultural or demographic factors (i.e. population shifts, age profiles, etc.) and refers to attitudes, value and beliefs held by people; also changes in lifestyles, education and health, amongst other factors.

- **technological** influences – changes in material supply, processing or production methods and new product development. For example the improvements in video conferencing technology have improved the ability for organisations to operate internationally without the need for regular travel.

- **legal** influences – changes in laws and regulations affecting, for example, competition, patents, sale of goods, pollution, working regulations and industrial standards.

- **ecological/environmental** influences – includes the impact the organisation has on its external environment in terms of pollution etc.

Example: Oil company

Oil company BP has explained on its website how it approaches the task of identifying and assessing country risk. BP carries out a country risk assessment whenever it faces a strategic decision about whether to invest in a new country. Country risk assessments are also made when the political or social environment changes, or if a significant change in the size of investment is under consideration.

This process culminates in an intensive discussion with active participation from outside experts and BP personnel with experience of the region and relevant BP operations. Over two days many strands of thinking and research are brought together to form a view of the country in question, which then informs all major decisions, including investment decisions, relating to BP's involvement in the country. The results of these assessments remain, by their nature, confidential to the business.

Example: Introduction to PESTLE analysis

For example, a haulage firm might monitor the following factors:

Political

- Fuel tax
- Government steps to reduce pollution from lorries
- Congestion charges in cities
- Plans to build new roads
- Road blockades due to strikes (e.g. in France).

Economic

- State of the economy – a downturn would result in less trade
- Fuel is a major cost so oil price movements will be seen as significant
- Most hauliers borrow to purchase trucks, so a rise in interest rates would increase costs.

Social

- Predicted car numbers and usage would affect likelihood of traffic jams and hence journey times
- Public concerns over safety could result in lorries being banned from certain routes or/and reductions in speed limits.

Technological

- Developments in route planning software
- Anti-theft devices
- Tracking systems to monitor driver hours
- Developments in tyre technology.

 Test your understanding 1

Ava is carrying out a PESTLE analysis for their employers. During this research, the aging of Europe's population has become apparent to Ava as a potentially important strategic issue for the company.

In which section of their analysis should Ava record this matter?

A   Political

B   Social

C   Technological

D   Legal

2 Political factors affecting a business

Political influences on businesses are dominated by the influence of government, which can and very often does have a profound effect on the structure of entire industries. Governments can affect organisations in a number of ways:

- government policy
- taxation
- imports and exports
- public spending.

2.1 Government policy

Each government will have principles and rules which help define how it will govern the country. A government might have principles or objectives concerning areas such as climate change or job creation, for example. Each time a different government is elected these principles might change and organisations will have to adapt accordingly.

Example: Areas government policy must consider

- Environmental: Targets on greenhouse gas emissions will affect major manufacturers. The government may also promote green initiatives that help meet carbon neutral targets.

- Town planning: National plans to build new roads could influence business location. On a local level, firms need to obtain planning permission for a new factory or to open new shops or build new houses.

- Employment: A government may use regional development grants to attract new employers to areas of high unemployment.

- Health: The government may promote initiatives that improve the health and wellbeing of the nation e.g. cycle to work schemes.

2.2 Taxation

Government taxation policy can impact on consumer spending, the willingness of organisations to invest and the price of products to consumers.

- Direct taxes (such as the tax consumers pay on their income) can reduce demand and hence supply.

- The tax system can offer capital allowances to encourage investment in equipment.

- Corporation tax affects how much businesses can invest or return to shareholders. Income tax and VAT affect how much consumers have to spend, hence their demand.

Example: Indirect tax on newspapers

Many countries treat newspapers in the same way as books and therefore do not apply sales tax (or value added tax) on their sales price. If government policy was to change and sales tax was added to the price of newspapers, this would make newspapers more expensive for consumers. This is likely to lead to a fall in the demand for newspapers.

2.3 Imports/exports

Government policy can discourage foreign firms from entering an industry, by restricting investment or competition or by making it harder or more expensive for foreign companies to trade in the country. This is typically done through the use of import quotas and tariffs.

Example: Import tariffs on paper

The government might decide that, in order to protect domestic paper manufacturers it will apply a tariff on overseas paper. This will make all overseas paper more expensive. If newspaper producers buy their paper overseas then they will experience an increase in their raw material (paper) costs.

Governments can also work to encourage exports for domestic products, for example by arranging trade deals with foreign governments that make it easier or cheaper for products to move between countries. This can boost domestic industries that export a lot of products abroad.

2.4 Public spending

The level of government spending on public projects affects those businesses that are suppliers to the government such as construction firms and IT consultants. It will also create employment in the economy in order to satisfy the staff requirements for such work.

Example: Areas of government public spending

- **Housing:** New housing developments can create new communities that will demand shops, leisure facilities, etc., giving opportunities for firms in these industries.
- **Crime:** Crime policy can affect firms that specialise in security.
- **Education:** Education policy can affect the availability of suitable potential employees for firms.
- **Defence:** Defence policy will primarily affect arms manufacturers. Closure of a military base could have serious implications for local suppliers.
- **Healthcare:** Healthcare policy has obvious implications for drugs and equipment manufacturers and private hospitals.
- **Infrastructure:** Governments will spend on roads and other distribution channels such as rail and bus networks. This might open up new sales channels for organisations or reduce distribution times to make products more attractive to customers.

Test your understanding 2

Which of the following would a transport company monitor under the political heading as part of a PESTLE analysis?

A   Tracker systems to monitor driver hours/anti-theft devices/ developments in tyre technology

B   State of the economy/oil price movements/a rise in interest rates

C   Fuel tax/congestion charges in cities/plans to build new roads

D   Predicted car numbers and usage/public concerns over safety

3 Economic factors

The economic environment is an important influence, both at local and national levels.

A multinational company will be concerned about the international situation, while an organisation trading exclusively in one country might be more concerned with the level and timing of domestic development.

Items of economic information relevant to the PESTLE might include changes in the Gross Domestic Product (GDP), changes in consumers' income and expenditure, and changes in inflation and interest rates.

3.1 Interest rates

Interest rates determine how much it costs to borrow money (the interest rate). This can affect cash flows for both businesses and consumers. They can therefore impact how much businesses and consumers can afford to spend. For example, a rise in interest rates will increase consumers' mortgage and other debt payments reducing the amount they have to spend on goods and services. A decrease in interest rates would have the opposite effect, and would discourage saving, so we may see an increase in consumption and spending.

3.2 Exchange rates

Changing exchange rates might affect how much a company has to pay to its international suppliers, or the value of receipts it makes from international customers. This can affect profit margins.

Example: Influence of exchange rates on newspapers

Most newspapers import their raw materials (paper, pulp etc.) and therefore they will suffer when their domestic currency weakens (this means the pound, for example, would be able to buy less paper per pound than previously).

3.3 Changes in disposable income

Overall growth or fall in wealth in the economy (measured using what is called the Gross Domestic Product or GDP), as well as rising standards of living, influences demand for goods and services. Disposable income refers to the amount of income that consumers have remaining after they have paid necessary expenses (such as rent, taxes, food, childcare, loan repayments etc.). The higher the level of disposable income in the economy the higher the spending will be on non-essential goods and services such as cinema tickets, personal technology, hairdressing services etc.

The level of disposable income in the economy will in turn be influenced by government policies on taxation, the level of rents/house prices, interest rates on debt etc. The wealthier the economy (the higher the GDP) the higher the levels of disposable income.

3.4 Business cycles

Wealth in the economy typically goes in cycles. When it is consistently increasing we are said to be in a boom period, when it is consistently decreasing we are said to be in a recession. Neither period is sustainable for a very long term and one tends to follow the other. Government policy can cause, exacerbate or mitigate such trends, but cannot abolish the business cycle.

In a recession consumers have less disposable income and therefore cut back on non-essentials and move 'downmarket' for essential items. This means that companies supplying downmarket (low priced) goods can do well in a recession.

But those selling upmarket (high quality) goods and those selling non-essential goods and services can suffer in a recession. As the economy moves to a boom period the opposite will become true. Industries which prosper when others are declining are called counter-cyclical industries.

Example: Business cycles for newspapers

In a recession, consumers may not see newspapers as an essential item. Therefore, the industry will go into decline (matching the business cycle of the economy).

3.5 Inflation

Inflation reflects the changing price of goods or services in an economy. There are two types of inflation that might be relevant to an organisation:

- demand-pull inflation – this is inflation caused by demand outweighing supply for a good or service. For example, it may be that more people decide that they want to buy rather than rent a home. As more people want to buy and bid higher prices, this increases asking prices. This demand will pull up prices. This would be very good for house-builders.

- cost-push inflation – this is inflation caused by substantial increases in the cost of important goods or services where no suitable alternative is available. For example, if there was a period of bad weather that harmed the supply of apples, this would increase the cost of apples even if there was no increase in demand. This would be bad for makers of apple juice, increasing the cost of apple juice production. Apple juice makers might increase their own selling prices in order to compensate for this, forcing the rising cost of apples to push up inflation in the apple juice market.

An economy that grows faster than its underlying growth in productivity risks inflation, which in turn can distort business decisions.

Test your understanding 3

Jop Limited is a high-end retailer of quality, gaming laptops.

Which of the following statements is likely to be true for Jop?

A   Jop is likely to do well in a recession
B   Jop will be unaffected by changes in interest rates in the economy
C   Jop can ignore demand-pull inflation
D   Jop will perform better if disposable incomes increase

3.6 Employment/Unemployment

The level of employment gives rise to factors that are important in a PESTLE analysis. It can impact on levels of disposable income as well as wealth in the economy. High unemployment is often an indicator that the economy is in a recession and rising unemployment might indicate that the economy is moving towards a recession.

The level of employment and unemployment might also provide information regarding the availability and likely cost of potential employees. When unemployment is low it can be difficult and expensive to attract new staff and this may impact on an industry's ability to grow in the future.

We should also consider changes to working methods. Many organisations are moving towards having a more flexible workforce; this could involve the use of more temporary staff or encouraging full time staff to work more flexible hours or in more flexible ways (such as working from home more often).

BUSINESS AWARENESS

4 Social factors

Social factors include social, cultural or demographic factors (i.e. population shifts, age profiles, etc.) and refers to attitudes, value and beliefs held by people. They also refer to trends in lifestyles, education and health.

4.1 Demographic changes

Demographics (that is, how a country's population is made up) give rise to factors that are important in a PESTLE analysis. These demographic factors include:

- Household and family structure: this refers to the average number of people in a household and the relationship between them.
- The rate of decline or growth in a national population and in regional populations.
- Age: changes in the age distribution of the population.
- Geography: the concentration of population into certain geographical areas.

 Test your understanding 4

Which of the following issues could result from an aging population? Select ALL that apply.

A   An increase in taxation levels

B   Increased demand for pension services

C   Cheaper healthcare

D   An increase in the retirement age

4.2 Trends

Social factors are also important in the context of society's changing values, preferences, fashions and attitudes to certain issues such as marriage, crime, the environment etc. Very often, these attitudes are influenced by advertising, the established media (newspapers, TV, radio) and social media (Twitter, etc).

Example: Newspapers

People want more up-to-date information – consumers are less inclined to wait for news than they were 20/30 years ago and may therefore switch to alternative sources of information, such as news websites and social media.

Multiple ethnicities increased social mobility around the world which might open new avenues of growth for newspapers through launching, for example, different language versions.

5 Technological factors

Organisations will always have to evolve to keep up with changing environments, for example with advances in technology, if they are to satisfy their rapidly changing expectations.

5.1 Changes in technology

There have been a number of significant changes in technology in recent years such as:

- Mobile and internet penetration – the increasing rate of mobile phone ownership, combined with access to the internet (with mobile beginning to exceed broadband). It is estimated that 5 billion people currently have a mobile device. This is providing organisations with new ways to communicate and interact with customers as well as presenting new avenues for sales.

- Data analytics and the cloud – cloud computing has increased the processing speed and capacity for many organisations when it comes to IT. This has facilitated the wider use of data analytics, analysing data such as customer information held on social networks, developing buying trends, actions of rivals etc. Many of these topics are discussed in a later chapter. Better data (and the analysis of this data) will improve organisational decision making (such as giving better data on the likely success of new product developments).

- User interfaces – advances in how human beings interact with machines (e.g. through voice recognition or motion-tracking systems) mean that carrying out tasks is quicker and more efficient. This can lead to reductions in cost and more efficient services for customers.

Example: The music industry

In the music industry, the accepted medium for listening to music was, for many years, vinyl and cassette. This changed in the 1980s to CDs, before the advent of the internet enabled consumers to purchase online and download or stream to mobile devices such as MP3 players. This progressed further to streaming instead of outright purchase. Each successive development lead to a decline in demand for the previous format (although, interestingly, there has been a recent resurgence in demand vinyl records and cassettes!).

Since the start of the new millennium, the rate of change has grown considerably, driven by two principal factors: organisations are adopting technologies that enable them to transform the experience that customers can enjoy; and customer expectations are changing at a much faster rate. The latter will likely continue, as present and future consumers embrace new technologies more quickly and expect to benefit from improvements to their lives as a result, meaning that organisations will find it much more difficult to surprise them.

- Global accessibility – rising living standards in developing economies means that more people are gaining access to the internet and increased connectivity.

 Example: Newspapers

There are many news sources available through technologies such as the internet, tablet computing, mobile apps and television – this is likely to adversely affect the sales of newspapers. However, the rising popularity of e-readers might present an opportunity for newspapers to provide daily digital content to these devices.

5.2 Impact on structure

Advances in technology and increasing globalisation have changed ideas about the best ways to do business. In recent years, the rapid increase in the development of new technologies, greater openness and escalating customer expectations are converging into a fundamental business change.

Customers have begun to experience individualised and integrated experiences in areas such as telephony and now expect similar experiences across all their interactions, regardless of whether they are in a business-to-consumer, business-to-business or consumer-to-government context.

BUSINESS AWARENESS

In essence, more and more people are connected to technology, enjoying the benefits that it delivers, and demanding that such benefits increase, across industries – there is no reason to believe that advances in one area of business cannot be transferred to other areas.

Technology impacts markets through its effect on productivity, efficiency and the production and delivery of new types of goods and services. Organisations are discovering that they need to become more flexible in reacting to and adapting to technology. This can mean the redesign of production, increased automation, new methods for interacting with customers and new ways of gathering and reporting information.

IT is therefore permeating entire organisations and having an impact at all levels of management. Organisations that fail to adapt or which remain inflexible in meeting the needs of customers are most likely to fail.

Test your understanding 5

H is a large vehicle manufacturing company in country F, which has recently decided to undertake a PESTLE analysis.

Which ONE of the following factors would most likely be identified under the 'technological' heading of a PESTLE analysis?

A   New computer-aided design (CAD) and computer-aided manufacturing (CAM) has recently become available for use in F's factories

B   Recycling is seen as being increasingly important by the residents of country F

C   Increased disposable income of consumers within country F

D   Changes in minimum wage legislation within country

6 Legal factors

Many legal issues can affect the growth and prosperity of an industry. Legal influences can include changes in laws and regulations affecting, for example, competition, patents, sale of goods, pollution, working regulations and industrial standards.

Organisations must comply with appropriate legislation. Failure to do so could result in fines, closure, bad publicity and/or loss of customers.

Example: Legal factors for newspapers

Limits on what can be published makes it harder for newspapers to differentiate themselves from each other and therefore harm growth prospects.

Most industries have specific legislation that they have to comply with (e.g. with food labelling in the food industry), but the general legal framework defines the basic ways of doing business for everyone.

Some pieces of legislation that apply to most organisations include:

- employment law: minimum and living wage, trade union recognition, diversity, unfair dismissal, redundancy, maternity, equality, gender pay gap

- data protection law: the use of information about employees and customers

- health and safety law: fire precautions and safety procedures

- consumer protection: laws to protect consumers (refunds and replacements, cooling off periods after credit agreements), advertising watchdog regulations.

BUSINESS AWARENESS

Test your understanding 6

X is a large logistics (parcel delivery) company. As part of its strategic planning process, X has identified several factors in its business environment that seem to be important.

Categorise each factor according to PESTLE analysis.

The government is planning a change to employment law, to prevent drivers working more than ten hours in any 24 hour period. This should be classified as ____1____.

The use of Global Positioning Systems (GPS) and smartphones are now becoming an industry threshold competence. This should be classified as ____2____.

The current government is unpopular with voters, and there may be an election soon. X is unsure of the impact this would have on their business. This should be classified as ____3____.

Use the options below to fill in the missing words in gaps 1 to 3.

A Political
B Economic
C Legal
D Social
E Technological

7 Environmental factors

Ecological/environmental influences include the impact the organisation has on its external environment. This could refer to areas such as the depletion of or damage to natural resources (such as wood or waterways), the impact on society as a whole, or the impact on the global climate.

Sustainability is an increasingly important concern under in this area. Sustainability of raw materials could affect how organisations source their raw materials, which in turn could affect production costs.

Sustainability can be analysed from a number of different viewpoints:

- Demand – consumers are increasingly demanding environmentally friendly products and disapproving of excessive packaging and other negative impacts on the environment

External Analysis – the PESTLE model: Chapter 7

- Resource inputs – organisations put more effort into managing physical resources sustainably (by replanting forests, for example)
- Manufacturing waste – organisations establish practices to minimise the generation of waste
- Government/legislation – more attention is paid to regulations on controlling pollution, as well as food hygiene and safety, reflecting the effect of transport on the natural environment ('food miles').

Example: Newspapers

Concern about the impact of carbon emissions from the use and production of paper – newspapers may be seen as being harmful to the environment due to their use of natural resources, their high production volumes and large distribution networks. Buyers might abandon newspapers in favour of carbon neutral news via modern technologies.

Test your understanding 7

BoCo runs a chain of restaurants within the country Zigma. It is considering extending its operations to neighbouring countries.

Match up the following macro-economic factors with the heading they would be analysed under in a PESTLE analysis (use a tick ✓ in the right column).

P = Political, Ec = Economic, S = Social, T = Technological

L = Legal, Env. = Environmental

	P	Ec	S	T	L	Env
Rules on the safe disposal of food waste						
Government tax on sales of food						
People's religious beliefs and attitudes towards certain foods						
The level of disposable income people have						

BUSINESS AWARENESS

8 Summary

The PESTLE model is part of the analysis of an organisation's external environment. It therefore focuses on the factors which the organisation can't control but which may still determine the organisation's future strategic success or failure.

PESTLE is an acronym to help us remember the sources of these external, macro-economic influences:

- Political factors
  - such as changes to government policy, taxation, import/export rules or levels of public spending
  - different political parties will have different policies and goals that will impact on these political factors
- Economic factors
  - such as changes in interest rates, exchange rates, disposable incomes, business cycles and inflation
  - different organisations will be impacted in different ways by economic factors (often dependent on whether they are upmarket or downmarket)
- Social factors
  - such as changes to demographics or trends in consumer habits
- Technological factors
  - such as changes in technology or a failure to adopt a structure that can react to changes in technology
- Legal factors
  - such as changes to legislation
- Environmental factors
  - such as increased concern about sustainability or potential impacts on wider society

Test your understanding answers

Test your understanding 1

The correct answer is B

Age is a demographic factor that falls under the **social** aspect of the PESTLE analysis.

Test your understanding 2

The correct answer is C

A = Technological heading, B = Economic heading, D = Social heading.

Test your understanding 3

The correct answer is D

In a recession, high-end, quality retailers are likely to do worse than in a boom. Interest rates will impact on levels of disposable income as well as Jop's own cash flows and cannot be ignored. Likewise, changes in inflation, just like any other economic factor, cannot be ignored.

Jop's products are likely to be non-essential luxury items and these types of items usually perform better when consumer disposable income increases.

BUSINESS AWARENESS

Test your understanding 4

The correct answers are A, B and D

We would expect taxation to go up so that governments can fund pensions and healthcare for the older population.

There would be a greater demand for pension services as we are likely to have a higher proportion of people over the retirement age.

Healthcare is likely to become more expensive due to a greater demand from elderly people.

Governments may need to fund pensions and benefits for the increasing elderly population by increasing the retirement age. This delays the need for pensions, and raises more tax revenue as people work for longer.

Test your understanding 5

The correct answer is A

B is an environmental factor, C is an economic factor, and D is a legal factor within PESTLE analysis.

Test your understanding 6

Gap 1 – C (legal), Gap 2 – E (technological), Gap 3 – A (political).

Test your understanding 7

	P	Ec	S	T	L	Env
Rules on the safe disposal of food waste					✓	
Government tax on sales of food	✓					
People's religious beliefs and attitudes towards certain foods			✓			
The level of disposable income people have		✓				

BUSINESS AWARENESS

The microeconomic environment

Introduction

In order to fully understand the environment in which an organisation sits and the potential for its products/services to prosper, you must have an understanding of the economic environment it operates in.

In this chapter, we will look at supply and demand for products and services and how these interact to determine prices and the allocation of resources by organisations.

An organisation cannot make decisions about its future without understanding the competitive environment it operates in, so we will also look at factors that determine competition levels.

ASSESSMENT CRITERIA	CONTENTS	
The microeconomic environment (2.2)	1	Microeconomics
	2	Demand
	3	Supply
	4	The price mechanism
	5	Competition

The microeconomic environment: **Chapter 8**

1 Microeconomics

Part of an organisation's external PESTLE analysis involves assessing the economic factors which will affect its industry. The goal is to identify potential opportunities and threats.

Economics can be defined in various ways, including:

Definition

Economics is the study of how society allocates scarce resources, which have alternative uses, between competing ends.

It is useful to distinguish between two aspects of economics:

Definition

Macroeconomics considers aggregate behaviour, and the sum of individual economic decisions – in other words, the workings of the economy as a whole.

Definition

Microeconomics is the study of the economic behaviour of individual consumers, firms and industries. It focuses on how these three individual parts of an economy make decisions about how to allocate scarce resources.

Microeconomics examines how supply and demand decisions made by individuals affects the selling prices of goods and services within an industry or market.

This chapter focuses on the **microeconomic** aspects of the economy.

BUSINESS AWARENESS

2 Demand

2.1 Individual demand

Individual demand shows how much of a good or service someone is willing and able to buy at different prices. When considering the level of demand at a given price, we assume that the 'conditions of demand' (i.e. other variables) are held constant, so the only element changing is the price.

Demand will be higher at a low price and lower at a high price for most goods and services.

When the demand for a good or service changes in response to a change in its price, the change is referred to as:

- an **expansion** in demand as demand rises due to a price fall.
- a **contraction** in demand as demand falls due to a price rise.
- The relationship between demand and price can be shown in a diagram and is referred to as a demand curve. We show the curve as a straight line, for simplification.
- In the diagram below, the downward-sloping demand curve D illustrates the demand for a normal good. Movements along this curve as the price changes would be called a contraction in demand (price is rising) or an expansion in demand (price is falling).

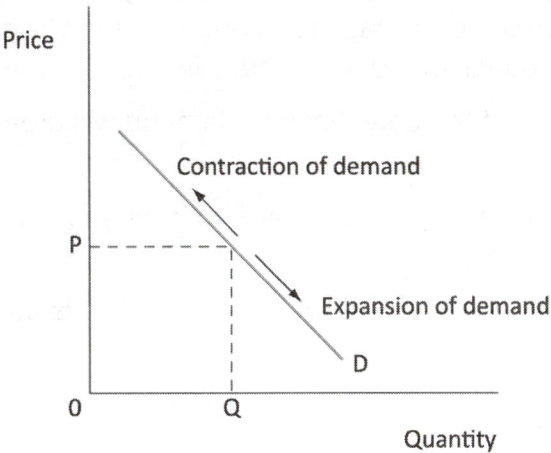

Example: Individual demand

K plc is a motor car manufacturer. It may find that if it raises the prices it sells its cars for, the demand for the vehicles, and therefore the number of cars the company sells, will fall.

This could be due to the **substitution effect**. There are a large number of car manufacturers that customers can choose between. If K raises its prices, it may become more expensive than its rivals, leading customers to switch to lower-priced alternatives.

K's sales may also suffer because of the **income effect**. Cars are normally relatively expensive, costing a high proportion of a consumer's income. If K prices its cars at too high a price, many of its customers may simply become unable to afford the product, leading to a drop in demand.

2.2 Market demand

Market demand shows the total amount of effective demand from all the consumers in a market. Market demand is usually shortened to demand and represented by a straight-line curve on a graph. The demand curve for most normal goods is negatively inclined, sloping downwards from left to right for the reasons explained in the previous section.

2.3 Conditions of demand

So far we have considered exclusively the influence of price on the quantity demanded, assuming other factors to be constant. Changes to these factors, termed the conditions of demand, will now be considered.

Any change in one or more of the conditions of demand will create shifts in the demand curve itself.

- If the shift in the demand curve is outward, to the right, it is called an **increase/rise** in demand.

- If the shift in the demand curve is inward, to the left, it is called a **decrease/fall** in demand.

It is important to distinguish between:

- increases and decreases in demand that result from a shift in the demand curve as a whole
- expansions and contractions in demand that result from price changes leading to movements along the demand curve itself.

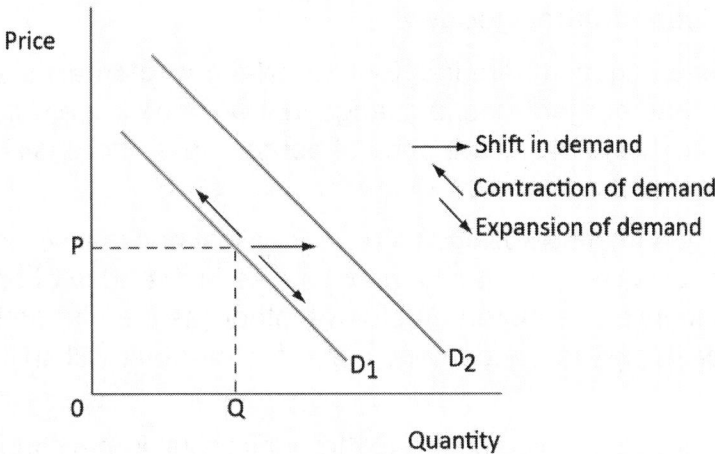

The main conditions that could shift the demand curve are:

- **Income**

    Changes in income often affect demand.

    For example, lower direct taxes would raise disposable incomes and, other things being equal, make consumers better off and able to spend more on discretionary expenditure. For normal goods, an increase in income leads to an increase in demand. Examples include cars, jewellery, fashion clothing and music streaming services.

    For inferior goods, however, a rise in income leads to a **lower** demand for the product as consumers, now being richer, substitute better quality and preferred goods and services for the original ('inferior') good or service. An example of this is public transport. Here, as incomes rise, the demand for public transport falls as consumers substitute more expensive, private transport such as cars.

- **Tastes**

    Tastes, in particular fashions, change frequently and this may make the demand for certain goods volatile.

    A good example of this is the rapid rise in demand for fidget spinners seen in 2017 followed by a decline as people's attention moved elsewhere.

Tastes can be manipulated through the use of advertising to 'create' markets. For example, this happened with air purifiers, a product which our ancestors survived perfectly well without. Some goods are in seasonal demand (e.g. cooked meat) even though they are available all year round, because tastes change throughout the year (e.g. more salads are consumed in the summer).

- **The prices of other goods**

    If goods are in joint demand, for example, **complements** such as burgers and burger buns, a change in the price of one will also affect the other. Therefore, if the price of burgers falls, there is likely to be an increase in demand for burger buns.

    Where goods are **substitutes** (e.g. Physical books vs e-books, trains vs cars, glasses vs contact lenses), a rise in the price of one will cause an increase in demand for the other (as the alternative is now less appealing) so the demand curve for the other will shift to the right.

    Sometimes, technological breakthroughs result in new substitute products coming into the market. For instance, the introduction of affordable streaming services for music and films has reduced the demand for CDs and DVDs (the latter leading to the closure of the Blockbuster chain).

- **Population**

    An increase in population creates a larger market for most goods, thereby shifting demand outwards. For instance, an influx of seasonal workers from other countries will raise the demand for most essential goods during the season in which they are working. Changes in population distribution will also affect demand patterns. If the proportion of old people relative to young people increases, then the demand for products such as pensions, healthcare and retirement homes will increase relative to that of gripe water, nappies and cots.

In the analysis of how the demand and supply model works, the distinctions between increase/decrease in demand and expansion/contraction in demand are very important. Remember:

- If a **price change** occurs, there will be a movement **along** the demand curve and the result will be either an **expansion or a contraction** in demand.

- If the **conditions of demand change**, there will be a **shift in the demand curve** and the result will be either an **increase** (curve moves outward to the right) **or a decrease** (curve moves inward to the left) in demand.

BUSINESS AWARENESS

> **Test your understanding 1**
>
> **Which one of the following would NOT lead to a shift in the demand curve for overseas holidays?**
>
> A   An advertising campaign by holiday-tour operators
> B   A fall in the disposable income of consumers
> C   A rise in the price of domestic holidays
> D   A rise in the exchange rate for the domestic currency

3 Supply

3.1 The supply curve of a firm

A supply curve shows how many units producers would be willing and able to offer for sale, at different prices, over a given period of time.

The supply curve of a firm is underpinned by the desire to make profit. It demonstrates what a firm will provide to the market at certain prices. If the prices that goods can be sold at increase, each unit will make more profit for the supplier, meaning that suppliers will be willing and able to manufacture, or supply, more units to the market. Therefore the supply curves tend to slope upwards.

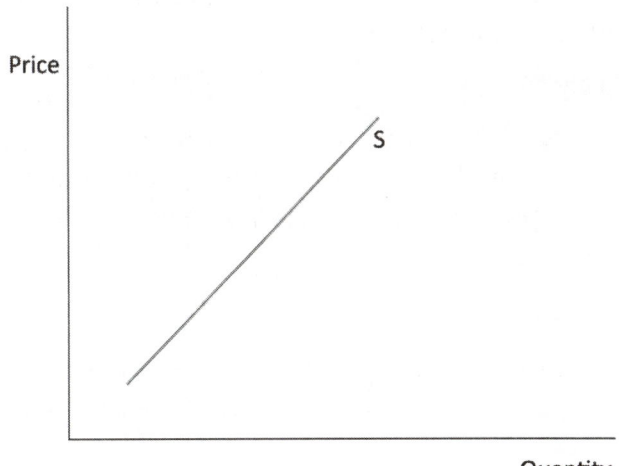

A movement along the supply curve is referred to as an **expansion** (if the prices rises so more is supplied) or a **contraction** (if the price falls).

KAPLAN PUBLISHING

3.2 Conditions of supply

A change in factors other than the price will move the supply curve itself.

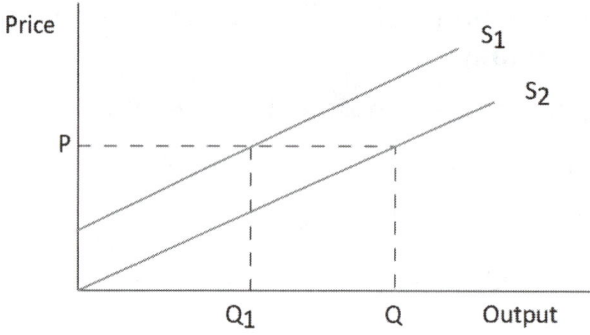

A decrease in supply

At existing prices, **less** will now be supplied, as shown on the upward-sloping, elastic supply curve. At price P, the quantity supplied falls from Q to Q1 as the supply curve shifts from S2 to S1, known as a leftward or upward shift. This means that the cost of supply has increased.

This results from:

- **Higher production costs.** The costs of production may increase because the factors of production become more expensive. Conditions such as higher wage costs per unit, higher input prices and increased interest rates will lead to reductions in supply.

- **Indirect taxes.** The imposition of an indirect tax, such as VAT, makes supply at existing prices less profitable. With an indirect tax, the costs of production are raised directly because the tax must be paid on each item sold. The profit margin is reduced (by some varying amount) as an indirect effect.

An increase in supply

A shift in the supply curve from S1 to S2 (a rightwards or downwards shift) illustrates an increase in supply with **more** being supplied at each price, showing that the cost of production has fallen or lower profits are being taken.

Lower product costs may arise from:

- technological innovations, for example, the advance of microchip technology lowered the cost of computers and led to large increases in supply

- more efficient use of existing factors of production (land, labour, capital funding and entrepreneurship). For example, introduction of a shift system of working might mean fuller use of productive capacity, leading to lower unit costs

- improvements in productivity that allow maintenance of output levels with fewer workers
- lower input prices, such as cheaper raw material imports and lower-priced components, could bring down production costs
- a reduction or abolition of an indirect tax or the application of or increase in subsidies.

Test your understanding 2

L makes a variety of different products, including windows.

Which TWO of the following would cause a decrease in the level of supply of L's windows?

A   An increase in the level of VAT charged by the government on windows

B   A new automated assembly system for L's products that reduces L's window manufacturing overheads

C   Staff negotiations, leading to window production staff adopting a shift-work approach which makes better use of L's production facilities

D   Staff negotiations, leading to a slight rise in the hourly rate paid to window production workers

The microeconomic environment: Chapter 8

4 The price mechanism

4.1 Equilibrium

Now we have looked at demand and supply in detail, let us consider how the price mechanism sets a price. The way to see how market forces achieve equilibrium is to consider what happens if the price is too high or too low:

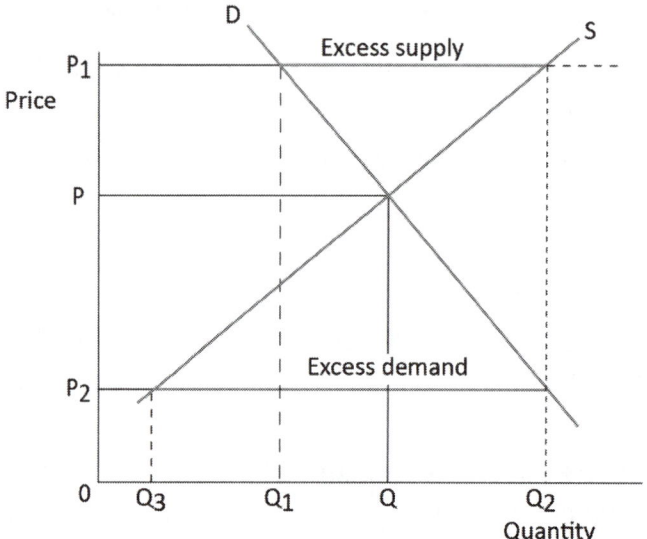

The graph shows the intended demand and planned supply at a set of prices. It is only at price P where demand and supply are the same. If the demand of consumers and the supply plans of sellers correspond, then the market is deemed to be in equilibrium. Only at output Q and price P are the plans of both sellers and buyers realised. Thus Q is the equilibrium quantity and P is the equilibrium price in this market.

There is only one equilibrium position in a market. At this point, there is no tendency for change in the market, because the plans of both buyers and sellers are satisfied. At prices and outputs other than the equilibrium (P, Q) either demand or supply aspirations could be fulfilled but not both simultaneously.

- For instance at price P1, consumers only want Q1 output but producers are making Q2 output available. There is a **surplus of supply**, the excess supply being the difference between the Q1 and Q2 output levels.

    Assuming the conditions of demand and supply remain unchanged, it is likely that the buyers and sellers will reassess their intentions.

BUSINESS AWARENESS

This will be reflected in the short term by retailers having unwanted goods, returns made to manufacturers, reduced orders and some products being thrown away and so suppliers may be prepared to accept lower prices than P1 for their goods.

This reduction in price will lead to a contraction in supply and an expansion in demand until equilibrium is reached at price P.

- Conversely, at a price of P2, the quantity demanded, Q2, will exceed the quantity supplied, Q3. There will be a **shortage of supply** (Q2 – Q3), demonstrating the excess demand.

This will be reflected in the short term by retailers having empty shelves, queues and increased orders. There may also be high second-hand values, for example on eBay or Gumtree. The supplier will respond by increasing prices to reduce the shortage.

This excess demand will lead to a rise in the market price, and demand will contract and supply will expand until equilibrium is reached at price P.

 Test your understanding 3

When the price of a good is held above the equilibrium price, the result will be:

A   excess demand for the good

B   a shortage of supply of the good

C   a surplus of supply of the good

D   an increase in demand for the good

4.2 Shifts in supply or demand

As well as signalling information in a market, price acts as a stimulant. Price information may provide incentives for buyers and sellers. For instance, a price rise may encourage firms to shift resources into one industry in order to obtain a better reward for their use.

The microeconomic environment: Chapter 8

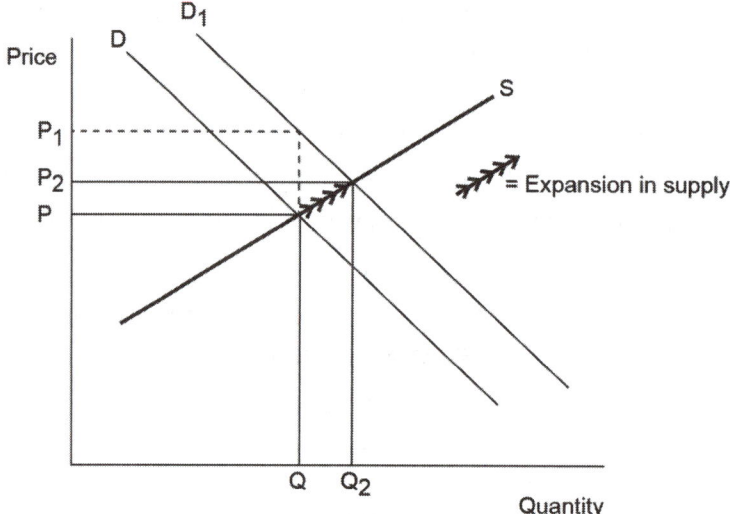

- For example, suppose the equilibrium is disturbed when the conditions of demand change. Consumers' tastes have moved positively in favour of the good and a new curve D_1 shows customers' intentions.

- Supply is initially Q, at the equilibrium, and it is momentarily fixed, so the market price is bid up to P_1.

- However, producers will respond to this stimulus by expanding the quantity supplied, perhaps by running down their stocks.

- This expansion in supply to Q_2 reduces some of the shortage, bringing price down to P_2, a new equilibrium position, which is above the old equilibrium P.

Note that if we had drawn the diagram with steeper supply (and demand) curves, then the price fluctuations would have been greater. The more inelastic the demand and supply of a good, the greater the price volatility when either demand or supply shifts.

The longer-term effects of these changes in the market depend upon the reactions of the consumers and producers. The consumers may adjust their preferences and producers may reconsider their production plans. The impact of the latter on supply depends upon the length of the production period. Generally, the longer the production period, and the more inelastic the supply is, the more unstable price will be.

Overall:

- Price acts as a signal to sellers on what to produce.

- Price rises, with all other market conditions unchanged, will act as a stimulus for extra supply.

- Equilibrium price is where the plans of both buyers and sellers are satisfied.

BUSINESS AWARENESS

 Test your understanding 4

Much of the world's coffee is grown in South America.

What would happen to the equilibrium price and quantity of the market for coffee if bad storms in South America damaged much of the coffee crop?

5 Competition

Healthy competition in a market benefits consumers. If competition is strong, with suppliers vying for the attention of customers, product/service quality will tend to rise and prices will be reasonable.

If competition is reduced, consumers may lose out. Suppliers can charge higher prices for lower quality goods.

In this section, we look at various factors that determine the levels of competition for microeconomic markets.

5.1 Product features

Competition will be higher among products that are undifferentiated from their competitors' products. Those that are differentiated will have something about them that stands out and attracts customers that other products do not.

Differentiation can be achieved on a cost basis – aiming to sell at the low-cost end of the market. Companies such as Ryanair and Aldi do this.

But differentiation is often thought of in relation to products that have different features to those of their competitors. Examples of such products are:

- Apple iPhone – differentiated by ease of use, quality of associated apps, brand reputation.
- Tesla cars – differentiated by innovation, environmentally friendly credentials, fun features, online updates.
- Cadbury – differentiated by taste.

The more unique a product is, the more differentiated it will be and the fewer direct competitors it will have.

5.2 Number of sellers and buyers

The fewer suppliers there are in a market, the more dominant they will be. There are a number of different competitive states that reflect a different number of suppliers in the market:

Monopoly

Monopolies occur when one company controls all or nearly all of the market for a particular product or service and has no major competitors. The key features include:

- Only one major supplier in the market
- No close substitutes are available for this supplier's products
- The supplier is free to set prices due to the lack of competition.

This situation is often caused by high barriers to entry for the market, or by government legislation.

Example: Monopolies

Many pharmaceutical companies enjoy monopolies in the provision of certain medicines. This is due to the high costs of research, development and testing which create barriers to other companies developing similar drugs.

In addition, as new medicines are usually protected by patents, it may be impossible for competitors to provide legal versions of the same drugs.

This allows pharmaceutical companies to charge relatively high prices for their products.

Monopolistic competition

This type of market occurs when a business has many different competitors, but each offers a somewhat differentiated product. For example, restaurants exist in such a market. Each restaurant is trying to attract the same customers, but each one offers different menu options cooked in a different way.

Monopolistic competition typically has the following features:

- each business makes independent decisions about the products it offers and the price it charges
- there are no major barriers to entering or leaving the market

- products are differentiated between each business, meaning that each business can charge more or less than its competitors – customers will be willing to spend more if they feel that one business has a product that is 'better' than those sold by its rivals
- due to the large amount of competition in the market, there is typically significant advertising expenditure by all the businesses in the market.

Oligopolies

Oligopolies are another form of imperfect market where the market is controlled by a small number of organisations. While there is no precise number, typically the market must be dominated by between two and six different firms for it to be classed as an oligopoly.

If only two firms dominate the market, this is referred to as a duopoly.

The dominant position of the businesses in an oligopoly will tend to:

- make it difficult for new firms to enter the market; and
- give them significant influence over the prices of the goods and services that they sell.

Example: Oligopolies

In the UK, the major supermarkets can be thought of as forming an oligopoly. As at May 2021, the top six supermarkets by market share (Tesco, Sainsbury's, Asda, Morrisons, Aldi and the Co-Op) held 81% of the market.

The market power they wield between them makes it very difficult for small, independent grocers to remain competitive. They are able to negotiate much lower supplier prices than the small grocers. As a result many stores have been replaced by small branches of the major supermarkets, such as Tesco Express and Sainsbury's Local.

5.3 Barriers to entry

New entrants into a market will bring extra capacity and intensify competition. The threat from new entrants will depend upon the strength of the barriers to entry and the likely response of existing competitors to a new entrant.

Definition

Barriers to entry are factors that make it difficult for a new entrant to gain an initial foothold in a market.

The microeconomic environment: Chapter 8

There are many possible sources of barriers to entry:

- Economies of scale, where the industry is one in which unit costs decline significantly as volume increases, such that a new entrant will be unable to start on a comparable cost basis.

- Product differentiation, where established firms have good brand image and customer loyalty. The costs of overcoming this can be prohibitive.

- Capital requirements, where the industry requires a heavy initial investment (e.g. steel industry, rail transport).

- Switching costs, i.e. one-off costs in moving from one supplier to another (e.g. a garage chain switching car dealership).

- Access to distribution channels may be restricted (e.g. for some major toiletry brands 90% of sales go through 12 buying points), i.e. chemist multiples and major retailers. Therefore it is difficult for a new product or manufacturer to gain shelf space.

- Cost advantages independent of scale, e.g. patents, special knowledge, favourable access to suppliers, government subsidies.

- Expertise, it may be difficult for new entrants to compete with an established firm that has developed their expertise in the industry over a number of years.

- Licences, patents or restrictions due to the regulatory environment, may prevent new firms from entering the market as they are not legally allowed to do so.

Test your understanding 5

Which of the following definitions best describes a barrier to entry?

A   Anything that protects a firm from the arrival of new competitors

B   A government regulation that bars a monopoly from earning an economic profit

C   Something that establishes a barrier to expanding output

D   Firms already in the market incurring economic losses so that no new firm wants to enter the market

5.4 Location

The location of customers, buyers and raw materials has an influence on both the location of an organisation and the level of competition it faces.

Although technology and transportation developments in the modern world have enabled many businesses to have a global customer and supplier base, there are still businesses for whom location is crucial:

- Supermarkets must be based close to customers.
- Farmers must be based where they are able to grow their crops.
- Wind farms must be based where the wind is strong enough on a consistent basis to make efficient use of the turbines.
- Tech companies may find it easier to recruit staff in a location where suitably trained staff live. For example, the concentration of tech companies (for example Apple, Google, Facebook) in Silicon Valley means that there is an abundance of appropriately skilled staff in that area.

5.5 Availability of information

A number of features define a 'perfect market'. There are a large number of customers and suppliers, none of whom dominate the market. The products sold are very similar to each other and there are low barriers to entry and exit from the market.

One of the features that leads to this high level of competition is 'perfect information'.

Definition

Perfect information. All customers and suppliers have complete information on the prices that goods and services are being sold at elsewhere in the market.

In theory, a local fruit and vegetable market would act as a perfect market. The products sold by different traders will be very similar to each other – in fact they may even have come from the same farmer. It is relatively easy to rent a pitch and set up as a trader, or to leave the market. Crucially, it is very easy for customers and traders to see the prices and examine the quality of the other goods being sold. Competition is high and with little product differentiation, traders may attempt to lure in customers using the force of their personality instead.

6 Summary

Having an understanding of the microeconomic environment that your organisation operates in can give insight that will help such decisions as product pricing and marketing, where to set up new operations and how to be more competitive.

In conjunction with an understanding of the macroeconomic environment and the use of PESTLE analysis, decision makers within the organisation can gain an understanding of their current position in the markets they operate in, as well as being able to make appropriate strategic decisions for the future success of the organisation.

BUSINESS AWARENESS

Test your understanding answers

Test your understanding 1

The correct answer is D

Correct answer is D since a change in exchange rates effectively changes the price of foreign holidays and leads to a movement along the demand curve, not a shift in the curve itself.

An advertising campaign should stimulate demand at the existing price and lead to the curve shifting to the right (A). A fall in disposable income would reduce demand at the existing price point and should lead to a shift of the curve to the left (B). A rise in the price for domestic holidays could cause consumers to switch to foreign holidays, increasing demand for foreign holidays even though their price hasn't changed, and leading to a rightward shift of the curve (C).

Test your understanding 2

The correct answers are A and D

Decreases in supply (leftwards or upwards shifts in the supply curve) are caused by increases in the costs of making and/or selling the product. This means that, even if the selling price stays constant, the profitability of the product will fall, meaning that suppliers like L will not wish to produce as many units of the product as they are less profitable.

In order to avoid raising prices and deterring customers, suppliers may absorb the change in VAT, leading to lower sales revenues for the product. This will make the product less profitable. This leads to a decrease in supply (A).

There is a similar effect for option (D); costs rise, making the product less profitable.

Test your understanding 3

The correct answer is C

When the price of a good is held above the equilibrium price suppliers will be willing to supply more at this higher price. However, consumers will demand less. The combined effect of this is to create a surplus of supply of the goods.

 Test your understanding 4

In the short-term, the equilibrium price would rise and the equilibrium quantity would fall.

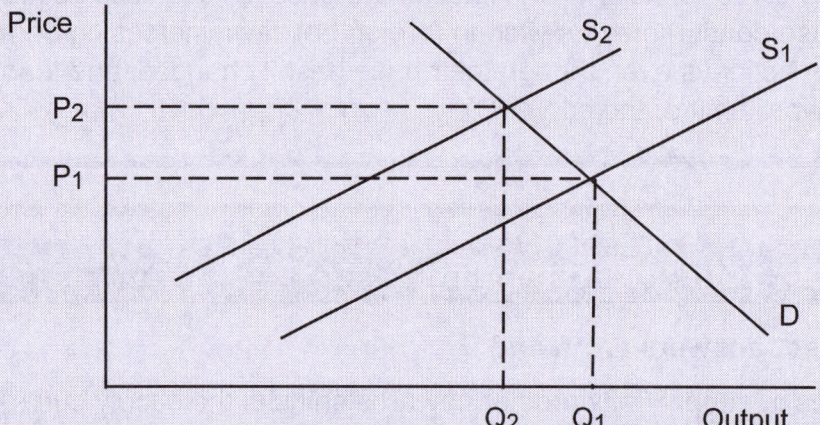

The poor harvest will shift the supply curve to the left (a decrease in supply) but the demand curve is unlikely to move (consumers are probably unaware of the supply issues and even if they are, it won't affect their desire for coffee).

The equilibrium point will move from P1, Q1 to P2, Q2, giving a price rise.

The demand curve, as mentioned, hasn't shifted, but demand will contract due to the higher price.

Over the longer-term, harvests may improve or other suppliers may be drawn to the market due to the higher prices now being achieved.

> **Test your understanding 5**
>
> **The correct answer is A**
>
> Barrier to entry = Anything that protects a firm from the arrival of new competitors.
>
> Note that some firms, for example, Tesla, are happy to make losses, as mentioned in (D), to establish themselves as market leaders and make it difficult for others to enter the market, but this definition is too narrow and (A) is better.

BUSINESS AWARENESS

Sustainability

Introduction

Sustainability means that organisations should use resources in such a way that they do not compromise the needs of future generations. Businesses should seek social and environmental sustainability in addition to economic sustainability.

For example, a paper manufacturer may consider planting a tree for everyone it fells. This will ensure that future generations will have enough timber to meet their needs.

Taking this approach will benefit a range of stakeholders.

ASSESSMENT CRITERIA	CONTENTS
The importance of sustainability (2.3)	1 Sustainability 2 Triple Bottom Line (TBL) reporting 3 The role and responsibilities of the finance professional

Sustainability: **Chapter 9**

1 Sustainability

1.1 The meaning of sustainability

> **Definitions – Sustainability**
>
> There are a number of different definitions of sustainability:
>
> - Sustainable development is development that meets the needs of the **present** without compromising the ability of **future** generations to meet their own needs.
>
>   (The UN's Bruntland Report)
>
> - A sustainable business is a business that offers products and services that fulfil society's needs while placing an equal emphasis on people, planet and profits.
>
>   (The Sustainable Business Network)
>
> - Sustainable trading is a trading system that does not harm the environment or deteriorate social conditions while promoting economic growth.
>
>   (European Union (EU) website)

Sustainability can thus be thought of as an attempt to provide the best outcomes for the human and natural environments, both now and into the indefinite future.

One aspect of this is the ability of the business to continue to exist and conduct operations with no effects on the environment that cannot be offset or made good in some other way.

Importantly, it refers to both the inputs and outputs of any organisational process.

- Inputs (resources) must only be consumed at a rate at which they can be reproduced, offset or in some other way not irreplaceably depleted.

- Outputs (such as waste and products) must not pollute the environment at a rate greater than can be cleared or offset.

Firms should use strategies to neutralise these impacts by engaging in environmental practices that will replenish the used resources and eliminate harmful effects of pollution.

BUSINESS AWARENESS

Example: Firms acting sustainably

- IKEA source more than half of their wood and cotton from sustainable sources.
- For over 35 years Patagonia has pledged 1% of their sales to the conservation of the natural environment.
- Pela produce compostable phone cases produced using renewable resources.

1.2 Three aspects of sustainable performance

It is important to note that sustainability is more than just looking at environmental concerns:

- environmental,
- social, and
- economic aspects of human society.

Example: Unsustainable practices

Environmental

- deforestation
- the use of non-renewable resources including oil, gas and coal
- long-term damage from carbon dioxide and other greenhouse gases.

Social

- anything contributing to social injustice
- rich consuming countries and poorer manufacturing countries
- rich companies exploiting third world labour as cheap manufacturing.

Economic

- strategies for short term gain (e.g. cutting staff costs to increase reported profits) at the expense of the long term
- paying bribes (also unethical and often illegal)
- underpayment of taxes.

Test your understanding 1

Why do you think the under-payment of taxes (by large businesses in particular) is considered to be an unsustainable practice?

Test your understanding 2

Explain whether ongoing growth in air travel is sustainable in terms of the economic, environmental and social aspects of sustainability.

1.3 Benefits of acting sustainably

Business sustainability is about ensuring that organisations implement strategies that contribute to long–term success.

Organisations that act in a sustainable manner not only help to maintain the well–being of the planet and people, they also create businesses that will survive and thrive in the long run.

In addition, it may be in the firm's **financial** interest to act sustainably.

Directors have a duty to try to increase the wealth of their shareholders and some would see sustainability as conflicting with this objective.

However, many would argue that sustainability should result in better business performance in the long run.

The benefits of acting in a more sustainable fashion are evidenced by the large number of businesses adopting sustainable policies. Stakeholder benefits can be listed as follows:

- **Workers/local community**: reduced waste and pollution will lead to a more pleasant, healthier environment. Guarantee of an appropriate minimum wage will lead to a better standard of living. Better workplace conditions will attract a higher calibre of workers and reduce accidents/injuries.

- **Customers**: many customers prefer dealing with businesses that follow sustainable policies such as looking after the environment or providing good working conditions and opportunities for workers, as they are seen as being more ethical.

- **Supply chain**: integrating sustainability into the supply chain will help suppliers achieve their own sustainability goals.

- **Shareholders**: Shareholders look for an economically sound investment. Reduction of waste and increased efficiency can improve business profits. This could lead to higher long-term returns for investors.
- **Public**: Businesses that are economically sound provide a stable job market for workers. Reduced emissions or a lower carbon footprint can lead to fewer environmental problems, such as acid rain and soil erosion.

As well as the ethical arguments above, organisations may want to consider acting sustainably for other reasons such as the positive impact it can have on organisational profits.

Example: How sustainability can boost profits

- Sustainability may help directly **increase sales** of products and services in the short-term by making products more attractive to buyers.

    For example, some customers may buy your product because a label on it says it has been manufactured using extra-safe working conditions for the labour force, or because it is Fairtrade.

- It may result in **cost savings**.

    For example, lower energy usage may reduce costs and increase profit.

- It may create **positive PR** and thus contribute to the business in the long run.

    While sustainability may not enhance product sales right away, it can enhance the image of a company, which in turn contributes to better business in the long term.

- Avoiding **fines** for pollution.

    The Deepwater Horizon oil spill in 2006 resulted in BP being fined $4.5 billion by the US Department of Justice. However, it is estimated that the total cost to date is in excess of $42 billion in terms of criminal and civil settlements and payments to a trust fund.

Better practices and standards are also likely to lead to better risk management. This may allow an organisation to pre-empt risks from changes in regulations and avoid the disruption that this might cause to the business when regulations are introduced. For example, in the UK some retailers took a decision to switch from using plastic bags for customers to instead using recycled paper bags. The UK government subsequently introduced charges for the use of the plastic bags. Those organisations that had already made the change avoided any costs and disruption caused by this change in regulations.

 Test your understanding 3

ACZ is a supermarket company which is considering improving its environmental image.

Which of the following would NOT help ACZ to limit the damage it is doing to the environment?

A   Charging customers for using plastic carrier bags

B   Improving sales forecasting to reduce wastage of inventory

C   Improving accessibility for less able customers

D   Reducing packaging of fresh food

 Example: Holcim (Lanka) Ltd

Holcim (Lanka) Ltd, one of the leading suppliers of cement and aggregates in Sri Lanka, worked with local communities, focusing on communication and education, in combination with introducing more efficient waste management options.

As a result it has managed to:

- create more profit ('profit')
- increase employment ('people') and
- reduce carbon emissions ('planet').

BUSINESS AWARENESS

Sustainability affects every level of life, from the local neighbourhood to the entire planet. The main argument in favour of acting in a sustainable manner is that we have an ethical duty to do so. It is ethically wrong for this generation to benefit at the expense of future generations.

This means that organisations must look at sustainability from a **long-term** viewpoint.

More specific examples of the problems of not acting ethically can be classified using the headings of economic, social and environmental risks.

Example: The risks of not acting sustainably

Environmental

- Deterioration of the environment and loss of some resources.
- Climate change – one of the greatest threats facing mankind.

Social

- Social sustainability encompasses human rights, labour rights, social justice and supporting the capacity of current and future generations to create healthy and liveable communities.
- Failure results in social injustice, infringement of human rights and a widening gap between the world's richest and poorest countries.

Economic

- There are limits to economic growth as the earth is a finite system.
- Only through sustainable development can a firm ensure long-term growth.

1.4 Sustainability and Corporate Social Responsibility (CSR)

Corporate Social Responsibility (CSR) refers to the idea that a company should be sensitive to the needs and wants of all its stakeholders, rather than just the shareholders.

It refers to an organisation's obligation to maximise its positive impacts upon stakeholders while minimising the negative effects.

A formal definition of CSR has been proposed by the World Business Council for Sustainable Development (WBCSD):

> **Definition – CSR**
>
> 'CSR is the continuing commitment by businesses to behave ethically and contribute to economic development while improving the quality of life of the workforce and their families as well as of the local community and society at large.'
>
> (WBCSD meeting in The Netherlands, 1998)

Sustainability is one aspect of Corporate Social Responsibility (CSR) and the two concepts are closely linked.

This is significant because many companies already have a commitment to CSR, setting targets and producing reports, for example. Calls to improve sustainability can be seen in the context of developing a firm's existing CSR policies and responsibilities, rather than creating something different and new.

2 Triple Bottom Line (TBL) reporting

2.1 Introduction

A well-known saying in the world of business is 'what gets measured gets done'. If we want firms to change their behaviour with respect to sustainability, then there need to be systems in place that measure the economic, social and environmental impact of the firm's activities. Once these areas can be quantified in some way, then managers will take steps to improve their performance and incorporate such issues into future decisions.

A number of reporting frameworks have been developed to help in accounting for sustainability, including the notion of triple bottom line (TBL) reporting.

TBL reporting expands the traditional company reporting framework to take into account environmental and social performance in addition to financial (economic) performance.

TBL attempts to show the full cost of any plans or development.

BUSINESS AWARENESS

A key aspect of TBL is that it relates to both performance measurement and decision making. Once targets are set for these aspects and performance is measured, then firms will incorporate the effects into decision making.

The concept is often explained using the triple 'P' headings of 'Planet, People and Profit'. This is similar to the environmental, social and economic aspects discussed above.

 Example: Triple Bottom Line Reporting

Planet

- A TBL company will try to reduce its 'ecological footprint' by managing resource consumption and energy usage and limiting environmental damage.

  For example, production processes will be efficient in terms of resource use and environmentally-damaging outputs such as toxic waste eliminated.

- The drive for environmental sustainability also means that TBL companies will not be involved in resource depletion.

  For example, fish stocks are maintained at sustainable levels and timber use is balanced by replanting to retain the resource into the future.

People

- A TBL business will ensure workers' rights are respected.

  For example, it will pay its workers fair wages, maintain a safe working environment and not use child labour.

- Similarly, the company would promote its surrounding community, for example by providing educational opportunities or a safe community to live in.

  For example, the Bourneville estate established by Cadbury, a chocolate maker in England.

Profit

- A TBL company will try to balance the profit objective with the other two elements of the TBL.

2.2 Problems with TBL

The first problem with TBL is that it can be difficult to measure the three factors concerned.

Example: Measuring performance using TBL

Typical measures include the following:

Planet

- Electricity consumption
- Fossil fuel consumption
- Water usage
- Amount of greenhouse gases and other pollutants produced
- Percentage of resources recycled compared with dumped as landfill.

People

- Jobs created/unemployment rates
- Average pay levels
- Health and safety measures, such as accident rates
- Equality measures such as the diversity of employees.

Profit

- Profitability of individual businesses/divisions
- Taxes paid.

Test your understanding 4

A UK company is looking at building a new factory in a developing country where there is currently high unemployment. Employees will work long hours with hazardous materials and the factory will produce levels of pollution that are legal in the country concerned but not in the UK. The company plans to build houses, schools and a health centre near the factory to look after employees.

Comment on the plan from a TBL perspective.

BUSINESS AWARENESS

 Test your understanding 5

The C Company manufactures a wide range of construction machinery such as diggers, tractors and large lorries. Each type of equipment is manufactured by one of seven different divisions, and each division is located in a major city, meaning that there are hundreds of kilometres between each division.

C also has an administration headquarters. This has been moved recently from an urban location to a new purpose built office building on an out-of-town site. The move has enabled C to provide extensive employee facilities including a sports complex and restaurant. Flexible working hours have also been introduced to allow employees to stagger their journey times; there is no public transport so all employees must travel in their own private cars.

The board of C are currently considering proposals for the use of the 'old' administration office site. The plan favoured by the finance director is the building of a waste disposal site as this has the highest return on investment. There is some disagreement over this move as the site is in a residential area, although the local council has indicated agreement in principle to the proposal.

The finance director has also amended creditor payment terms from 30 to 60 days in order to improve C's cash flow situation. This move was part of a package of measures to improve cash flow. However, proposals to hold divisional meetings by video conference rather than visiting each site, and carrying out an energy audit were vetoed by the board.

Discuss the sustainability performance of C Company by reference to the TBL headings of 'People, Planet and Profit'.

The second problem is that there are limits to how far firms allow sustainability to impact decision making across the organisation.

> **Example: TBL in the banking industry**
>
> - Many banks claim to be committed to sustainability:
>
> **Planet**
>
> - They may have very energy-efficient buildings.
>
> **People**
>
> - Some banks give staff free days when they are paid to go out and engage in community assistance programmes.
> - Others run 'managing your money' programmes, in which staff assist struggling families with financial planning and budgeting.
> - Other activities include support programmes for hospitals, the Red Cross and schools.
>
> **Profit**
>
> - However, CIMA's research on the banking industry in New Zealand found **no evidence** that banks turn away profitable but less sustainable business in favour of sustainable but potentially less profitable business.

3 The role and responsibilities of the finance professional

Professional accountants have a responsibility to act in the public interest. This includes supporting sustainability and sustainable development and considering the risks to society as a whole of not acting sustainably.

3.1 Creating an ethics-based culture

Culture refers to the sum total of all the beliefs, attitudes, norms and customs that prevail within an organisation – 'the way we do things around here'. Ideally we want a culture that supports sustainability.

Finance professionals can help in creating and promoting an ethics-based culture that discourages unethical or illegal practices, including money laundering, terrorist financing, fraud, theft, bribery, non-compliance with applicable regulations, bullying and short-term decision-making.

3.2 Championing sustainability

Rather than taking a reactive, passive approach to sustainability, finance professionals should take the initiative in raising awareness of social responsibility and the need to consider the impact of decisions and actions on sustainability. However, they need to remain objective while doing this.

This will involve promoting sustainable practices through the organisation in relation to the following:

Products and services

- Does making the product use inputs/materials/ingredients from renewable sources only?
- Does the firm source raw materials in ways that support their replenishment, safeguard natural habitats and ensure good animal welfare standards?
- What is the expected life of the product?
- How much of the product (including packaging) can be recycled?
- Is the level of packaging excessive?
- Can the product/service be made more inclusive? E.g. the introduction into the Mattel Barbie range of dolls with different skin tones, hair types and body types and dolls with disabilities.

Customers

- Does the firm have a recycling programme?
- What incentives are given to customers to encourage them to recycle?
- Does the firm encourage/help customers reduce their carbon footprint?

The supply chain

- Does the firm incorporate environmental considerations when selecting suppliers? For example, would it use a supplier with a poor record on pollution?
- Does the firm use suppliers who are geographically close to reduce the impact of transportation in terms of fuel used and exhaust emissions?
- Does the firm pay fair prices to suppliers or does it use its buying powers to drive prices down to very low levels?
- Does the firm encourage/help suppliers reduce their carbon footprint?
- Does the firm help suppliers reduce waste sent to landfill?

The workplace

- Does the firm have measurable targets for energy/water usage?
- Is the building energy efficient?
- Is the workplace a safe, comfortable, pleasant environment to work in?

Employees

- Does the firm look after its employees in terms of working conditions, employment rights, job security, etc. or are staff 'hired and fired' when necessary?
- Does the firm contribute to community projects?
- Does the firm ensure equitable treatment to all employees?

Other business functions and processes

- Does the firm take into account environmental impacts of activities when making decisions?
- Does the firm measure the impact of social initiatives?

3.3 Risk management

Many finance professionals are involved in risk management as it is a key aspect of good corporate governance. For many firms this includes assessing risks such as the actions of competitors, the risk of machine breakdown, bad publicity, terrorist attacks etc.

However, this needs to be extended to include evaluating and quantifying reputational and other ethical risks.

In particular accountants can help highlight the risks of not acting sustainably.

3.4 Performance management

Performance management and decision making are areas that traditionally involve accountants and other finance professionals. As discussed above, accountants could encourage the firm to switch to 'triple bottom line reporting'.

Example: Marks and Spencer

Marks and Spencer's 'Plan A' approach to sustainability and CSR is seen by many as an example of best practice in the retail industry and the company has received many industry and independent awards in this area.

Marks and Spencer has objectives in the following categories:

Climate change

- Help customers reduce carbon footprint
- Reduce operational greenhouse emissions
- Improve energy efficiency
- Help suppliers reduce their carbon footprint.

Waste

- Help customers reuse or recycle all products and packaging
- Reduce level of operational and construction waste sent to landfill
- Help suppliers reduce waste sent to landfill.

Natural resources

- Ensure efficient use of natural resources
- Source raw materials in ways that support their replenishment, safeguard natural habitats and ensure good animal welfare.

Being a fair partner

- Pay fair prices to suppliers
- Support local communities
- Ensure good working conditions for everyone involved in the supply chains.

Health and wellbeing

- Improve health and nutritional benefits of products sold
- Influence diet and lifestyle choices, through clear nutritional labelling and information
- Encourage customers and employees to become more active.

Note: These are broken down into over 180 sub-objectives.

Test your understanding 6

Jadie works as a management accountant for a company that makes fish pies, fish fingers and breaded scampi for a major supermarket chain. The company's marketing includes a statement that all fish is obtained from renewable sources.

Recently Jadie came across a supplier's invoice for monkfish, a species identified by Greenpeace as being under particular pressure from fishing.

Comment on the situation, firstly from a sustainability perspective and secondly from an ethical perspective. What should Jadie do?

4 Summary

A key to understanding sustainability is to consider the UN Bruntland Report definition – we (the present generation) must not compromise future generations in the pursuit of our own objectives and plans.

In particular we need to incorporate social, economic and environmental considerations (also known as people, profit and planet) into performance management and decision making. One way of doing this is via Triple Bottom Line Reporting.

The finance professional can contribute towards this by creating an ethics-based culture, championing sustainability, incorporating it into risk management and by ensuring sustainability features in performance management and decision making.

BUSINESS AWARENESS

Test your understanding answers

Test your understanding 1

Underpayment of tax is considered to be unsustainable as the organisations concerned are not contributing to maintaining the country's infrastructure (schools, roads, etc.).

Test your understanding 2

Economic sustainability

- In the short term, airline companies are stable due to demand for air travel, although during the COVID19 pandemic, this sustainability was compromised.

- In the long term, airline companies may not be sustainable as air travel in its current form cannot be provided indefinitely.

- There are limits to growth as air travel currently depends on the use of non-renewable resources (primarily oil).

Environmental sustainability

- Air travel does not appear to be sustainable due to damage to the environment (carbon dioxide emissions).

- As noted above, air travel also uses non-renewable resources.

- Damage to the environment may continue, as long-term effects, such as global warming, take longer to be noticed.

Social sustainability

- It could be argued that air travel has a positive social benefit because it can change communities by providing cheap and quick methods of moving people around the world.

- Individual communities find it more difficult to be 'isolated' or unchanged by other social systems.

- However, while appearing 'cheap', air travel is still expensive for poorer communities. In social terms it accentuates the difference between richer countries (where 'cheap' air travel is affordable) and poorer countries (where air travel is still 'expensive').

Test your understanding 3

The correct answer is C

While C would be an ethical activity for ACZ to undertake, it would not directly reduce ACZ's impact on the environment.

Test your understanding 4

Planet

- The level of pollution is worrying. Of particular concern is the fact that this would not be legal in the UK indicating that even if the pollution is legal in the country concerned the level is ethically wrong.

- Furthermore, there is no evidence that the firm is planning any clean up or off-setting activities.

People

- Working conditions would be considered unethical and unsustainable.

- However, in defence of the firm they are contributing to the local community via wages, job creation, housing, schools and a health centre.

Profit

- Despite the social initiatives described above, it is difficult not to conclude that the firm is building the factory in the country concerned primarily to save costs and avoid UK legislation regarding employment and environmental standards.

Test your understanding 5

People

The C Company appears to be meeting this objective for its own staff. The provision of flexible working hours, staff restaurant and sports facilities all indicate a caring, sustainable attitude towards staff.

However, the ability of C Company to take into account other stakeholder interests is unclear. Specific areas of concern include the following.

- Delaying payment for raw materials will adversely affect the cash flow of C's suppliers. This could compromise their (i.e. the suppliers') long-term survival.

- Moving the administration headquarters 'out of town' does not necessarily help the community. For example, there will be increased pollution as C's employees drive out to the administration building (note that there is no public transport).

- While flexible working time is allowed, this may mean travel time has increased. This may place pressure on workers regarding collection of children on 'school runs' and mean more cars on the road, increasing the risk of accidents. Provision of company buses out to the new headquarters would help decrease pollution but would not necessarily assist with the working hours issue.

- The proposal for the redevelopment of the old administration headquarters into a waste disposal centre is unlikely to benefit the community. There will be additional heavy lorries travelling through residential areas while the burning of rubbish provides the risk of fumes and smoke blowing over residential properties. Finding an alternative use, even if this was less profitable, would benefit the community overall.

Planet

Areas of concern include the following.

- Lack of an energy audit. A review of energy consumption could identify areas for energy saving, even if this was only the use of low wattage light bulbs.

- The relocation of the administration office to an out-of-town area may enhance working conditions for staff, but it also means that public transport cannot be used to reach the offices. This increases fuel use as employees must use their own transport.

- The insistence of the chairman in holding all divisional review meetings in person rather than using newer technology such as video conferencing means increased use of air travel and therefore carbon dioxide emissions.

Profit

At present, the C Company appears to be placing a lot of importance on the profit motive. Two specific decisions to increase profits are:

- delaying payment to creditors to provide additional cash within C and therefore decreasing the need for bank overdrafts, which in turn decreases interest payments.
- the proposal for the redevelopment of the old administration headquarters into a waste disposal site, which appears to be focused entirely on the amount of profit that can be made.

Test your understanding 6

- From a sustainability perspective the use of monkfish should be discouraged as (1) overfishing could result in it no longer being a feasible food source – i.e. the fishing is unsustainable – and (2) overfishing could result in the species becoming extinct.

- In addition, from an ethical perspective, it is wrong for the company to mislead customers with its claims that all fish are from renewable sources if, in fact, that is not the case.

- In the first instance Jadie should try to gather more information. It may be that this particular monkfish is sourced from a fish farm and hence is sustainable, or that the invoice was wrong or the supplier sent the wrong fish and the company wouldn't knowingly use it or that the Greenpeace advice is not considered authoritative or some other reasonable explanation.

- If there is still a concern, then this should be discussed with Jadie's manager and/or the head of purchasing.

BUSINESS AWARENESS

Professional ethics in accounting and business

Introduction

In this chapter we look at the fundamental ethical principles of integrity, objectivity, professional and technical competence, due care, confidentiality and professional behaviour.

These principles underpin the whole syllabus so it is vital that you know, understand and can apply them.

The Business Awareness syllabus does **not** require you to have a detailed knowledge of the AAT Code of Ethics and other AAT regulations. However, you are expected to know the key aspects of the underpinning IFAC Code of Ethics for Professional Accountants:

- The purpose of the code.
- The fundamental principles and the conceptual framework.

ASSESSMENT CRITERIA	CONTENTS
The relevance of the ethical code for professional accountants (3.1)	1 Introduction to business ethics
Ethical conflicts and reporting unethical behaviour (3.2)	2 Fundamental principles
	3 Threats and safeguards
	4 Dealing with ethical conflicts

KAPLAN PUBLISHING

Professional ethics in accounting and business: **Chapter 10**

1 Introduction to business ethics

1.1 What do we mean by 'ethics'?

Definition – Ethics

Ethics can be defined as the "moral principles that govern a person's behaviour or the conducting of an activity".

The Oxford English Dictionary

Ethics is concerned with how one should act in a certain situation, about 'doing the right thing' and ultimately about morality – the difference between right and wrong.

Example: Ethical choices

Consider the following ethical dilemmas:

- You buy something in a shop and later discover that they have under-charged you for an item. Do you go back and tell them?

- You want a new designer label t-shirt but think it is too expensive. Would you buy a cheap fake copy if you saw one for sale while on holiday?

- Have you ever told your employer that you were sick when the truth was you simply wanted a day off?

- Would you stop buying a particular product if you found out that the working conditions in the factories where it was made were far below UK standards (e.g. concerning hours worked, pay rates, sickness policy, discrimination, use of child labour, etc.)?

- Have you ever 'exaggerated' an expense claim?

Does the fact that you are a (student) member of a professional body affect your answers?

1.2 Business ethics

Business ethics is the application of ethical principles to the problems typically encountered in a business setting.

There is no separate 'business ethic' that puts it beyond the range of normal moral judgements.

> **Example: Typical issues in business ethics**
>
> Some typical issues addressed in business ethics include:
>
> - 'creative accounting' to misrepresent financial performance
> - misleading advertising
> - aggressive personal selling (e.g. insurance or double glazing)
> - unfair terms in contracts (e.g. cancelling a gym membership)
> - data protection and privacy
> - the difference between corporate hospitality and bribery
> - the difference between business intelligence and industrial espionage
> - political contributions to gain influence
> - corporate governance
> - corporate crime, including insider trading and price fixing
> - employee issues, such as discrimination or unfair dismissal
> - whistleblowing
> - environmental issues and related social concerns
> - marketing, sales and negotiation techniques
> - product issues such as patent and copyright infringement, planned obsolescence, product liability and product defects
> - using legal loopholes to avoid paying tax.

When ethical values get distorted or compromised, the impact can be enormous. Ethics and ethical standards have consequently become the focus of greater attention by organisations, especially in the area of reputation management. More emphasis is now placed on accountability, ethics, codes of conduct and monitoring and reporting of violations.

1.3 Ethical influences

Each of us has our own set of values and beliefs that we have evolved over the course of our lives through our education, experiences and upbringing. We all have our own ideas of what is right and what is wrong and these ideas can vary between individuals and cultures.

There are a number of factors that affect ethical obligations.

(i) **The law**

For example, deceptive advertising is illegal and violators of this law are liable for large fines, court action and/or loss of goodwill.

Legislation hopefully makes it very clear what is acceptable as a minimum standard. However, ethics is more than just obeying the law.

For example, using legal loopholes to minimise a global firm's tax bill may not be illegal but is increasingly viewed as unethical.

(ii) **Government regulations**

For example, regulations set standards on issues such as unfair competition, unsafe products, etc. Failure to comply with these regulations could lead to criminal charges, or fines.

Unfortunately, some firms will still find ways to get round such regulations.

Example: Artificial sweeteners

In 1970 cyclamates (a type of artificial sweetener) were banned in the USA following evidence that they were carcinogenic.

Following the ban a major US food manufacturer still sold 300,000 cases of cyclamate sweetened food overseas instead.

(iii) **Ethical codes**

Many organisations have codes that clearly state the ethical standards and principles an employee or member should follow.

For example, as an AAT student you are expected to follow the AAT Code of Professional Ethics.

Generally, written codes clarify the ethical issues and principles but leave the resolution to the individual's conscience.

Ethical codes are usually followed if written down and enforced – say by disciplinary procedures. However, many companies have 'unwritten' codes of practice and/or have no method of enforcement.

(iv) **Social pressure**

Many people draw their values from what they see other people doing, whether on the news or people they know. However, social pressure can change, just as society changes.

For example, many politicians comment on a decline in family values in the UK.

Many protest groups and activists hope to change public values with the long-term hope that new values become reflected in law. A good example of this is the change in discrimination legislation over the last hundred years.

(v) **Corporate culture**

 Definition – Corporate culture

Corporate culture is defined as "the sum total of all the beliefs, attitudes, norms and customs that prevail within an organisation" or "the way we do things around here".

Ideally we want a culture that supports and encourages ethical behaviour.

For example, if everyone else is exaggerating expense claims or covering up mistakes, then this can quickly become a norm of behaviour that new employees soon adopt.

Of particular importance is the example set by senior management – sometimes referred to as the 'tone at the top'.

It is important to note that there can often be tension between personal standards and the goals of the organisation.

Suppose you work for a company selling banned substances overseas. It is not illegal, but it may be against your personal values to sell these products to unsuspecting overseas clients. What would you do if this action were a direct order from a superior? Does this take away your responsibility?

1.4 The costs and benefits of business ethics

It can be argued that the primary purpose of a business is to try and earn a profit. In a company, for instance, the directors have been employed in order to earn the owners of the business a return on their investment.

Some have concluded from this that going beyond the **legal** minimum standard of behaviour is contrary to the directors' duty to make money and that behaving ethically increases costs and reduces profits.

For example:

- Increased cost of sourcing materials from ethical sources (e.g. Fairtrade products or free range eggs).
- Having to turn away business from customers considered to be unethical (e.g. an 'ethical' bank may choose not to invest in a company that manufactures weapons).
- The management time that can be taken up with the planning and implementation of ethical practices.

However, as well as the moral argument to act ethically, there can be commercial benefits to firms from acting ethically:

- Having good ethics can attract customers.

  Good ethics tend to enhance a company's reputation and therefore its brand. Given the choice, many customers will prefer to trade with a company they feel is ethical.

- Good ethics can result in a more effective workforce.

  A reputation for good business ethics is likely to involve good working conditions for employees, allowing the business to attract a higher calibre of staff.

  Avoiding discrimination against workers is likely to give the company access to a wider human resource base.

- Ethics programmes can cultivate strong teamwork and improve productivity.

- Ethics can give cost savings.

  Avoiding pollution will tend to save companies in the long run – many governments are now fining or increasing taxes of more polluting businesses.

- Ethics can reduce risk.

  Many firms have failed due to unethical practices within them.

Example: Enron

Enron, a major US energy company, filed for bankruptcy in 2001. Among the many reasons for its failure were dubious accounting practices (for example, in how they recognised revenue), poor corporate governance and failure by their external auditors, Arthur Andersen.

There were even attempts to hide the problems, with workers being told to destroy all audit material, except for the most basic work papers.

1.5 The Institute of Business Ethics – Simple test

According to the Institute of Business Ethics, a simple ethical test for a business decision could be taken by assessing the following criteria:

Criteria	Explanation
Transparency	Do I mind others knowing what I have decided?
Effect	Does my decision affect or hurt anyone?
Fairness	Would my decision be considered fair by those affected?

2 Fundamental principles

2.1 The Code of Ethics for Professional Accountants

The Code of Ethics for Professional Accountants, published by The International Federation of Accountants (IFAC), forms the basis for the ethical codes of many accountancy bodies, including the AAT, ICAEW, ACCA and CIMA.

The code adopts a principles-based approach. Unlike a rules-based approach, it does not attempt to cover every situation where a member may encounter professional ethical issues, prescribing the way in which they should respond. Instead, it adopts a value system, focusing on fundamental professional and ethical principles which are at the heart of proper professional behaviour.

The main advantages of a principles-based approach over a rules-based approach are that a principles-based approach is applicable to all situations, and gives individuals less chance of finding loopholes.

The five key principles are as follows:

(a) **Integrity**

(b) **Objectivity**

(c) **Professional competence and due care**

(d) **Confidentiality**

(e) **Professional behaviour**

These are discussed in more detail below.

2.2 A conceptual framework

Professional accountants may face a range of specific threats to compliance with the fundamental principles.

It is impossible to define every situation that creates such threats and specify the appropriate action. In addition, the nature of engagements and work assignments may differ and consequently different threats may exist, requiring the application of different safeguards.

A conceptual framework requires a member to identify, evaluate and address threats to compliance with the fundamental principles, rather than merely comply with a set of specific rules which may be arbitrary.

It also requires that if identified threats are not clearly insignificant, a member shall, where appropriate, apply adequate safeguards to eliminate the threats or reduce them to an acceptable level, so that compliance with the fundamental principles is not compromised.

2.3 Compliance with ethical codes

A professional accountant's responsibility is not just to satisfy the needs of an individual client or employer. It should also be to act in the public interest.

In acting in the public interest a professional accountant should observe and comply with the fundamental ethical requirements shown in the IFAC Code.

AAT members should note that disciplinary action may be taken for non-compliance with the AAT code where the member's conduct is considered to prejudice their status as a member or to reflect adversely on the reputation of the AAT. For the purposes of this paper, you do not need to be concerned with the differences between the IFAC code and the AAT code.

Where professional accountants are members of more than one professional body, there may be differences in some areas between the professional and ethical conduct requirements of the different bodies. Where there are differences, members should follow the more stringent provision.

Unethical and dishonest behaviour (and its legal consequences) creates powerful negative public relations within the profession, the wider community and the organisation itself.

2.4 Integrity

Definition – Integrity

Integrity means that a member must be straightforward and honest in all professional and business relationships. Integrity also implies fair dealing and truthfulness.

Accountants are expected to present financial information fully, honestly and professionally and so that it will be understood in its context.

Example: Integrity

A professional accountant should not be associated with reports where the information:

- contains a materially false or misleading statement
- contains statements or information furnished recklessly
- has omissions that make it misleading.

Accountants should abide by relevant law and regulations and remember that, as well as legal documents, letters and verbal agreements may constitute a binding arrangement.

Accountants should strive to be fair and socially responsible and respect cultural differences when dealing with overseas colleagues or contacts. Promises may not be legally binding but repeatedly going back on them can destroy trust, break relationships and lose co-operation.

To maintain integrity, members have the following responsibilities:

2.5 Objectivity

Definition – Objectivity

Objectivity means that a member must not allow bias, conflict of interest or undue influence of others to override professional or business judgements.

Example: Objectivity

Suppose you are part of the audit team at a major client:

- If you also own shares in the client company, then this could be viewed as a conflict of interest.

- If you receive excessive hospitality and discounts from the client then this could be seen as an attempt to influence (bribe?) you and compromise your objectivity.

Objectivity can also be defined as 'the state of mind which has regard to all considerations relevant to the task in hand but no other.' It is closely linked to the concept of independence:

- **Independence of mind** is the state of mind that permits the provision of an opinion without being affected by influences that compromise professional judgement, allowing an individual to act with integrity and exercise objectivity and professional scepticism.

- **Independence of appearance** is the avoidance of facts and circumstances that are so significant that a reasonable and informed third party, having knowledge of all relevant information, would reasonably conclude that a firm's or a member's integrity, objectivity or professional scepticism had been compromised.

Whatever capacity members serve in, they should demonstrate their objectivity in varying circumstances.

Objectivity is a distinguishing feature of the profession. Members have a responsibility to:

- Communicate information fairly and objectively.

- Disclose fully all relevant information that could reasonably be expected to influence an intended user's understanding of the reports, comments, and recommendations presented.

2.6 Professional competence and due care

Definition – Professional competence

Professional competence means that a member has a continuing duty to maintain professional knowledge and skill at the level required to ensure that a client or employer receives competent professional service based on current developments in practice, legislation and techniques.

Definition – Due care

Due care means a member must act diligently and in accordance with applicable technical and professional standards when providing professional services.

In agreeing to provide professional services, a professional accountant implies that there is a level of competence necessary to perform those services and that their knowledge, skill and experience will be applied with reasonable care and diligence.

Example: Professional competence

Suppose you are an accountant in practice. A new client asks you to perform their tax computations but it would involve aspects of inheritance tax that you have not looked at for many years.

Unless you have other people with the required tax expertise in the practice, you should decline the tax work as you are not competent to do it.

Professional accountants must therefore refrain from performing any services that they are not competent to carry out unless appropriate advice and assistance is obtained to ensure that the services are performed satisfactorily.

Professional competence may be divided into two separate phases:

1. Gaining professional competence – for example, by training to gain the AAT qualification.

2. Maintaining professional competence – accountants need to keep up to date with developments in the accountancy profession including relevant national and international pronouncements on accounting, auditing and other relevant regulations and statutory requirements.

Members have a responsibility to:

- Maintain an appropriate level of professional competence by ongoing development of their knowledge and skills.
- Maintain technical and ethical standards in areas relevant to their work through continuing professional development.
- Perform their professional duties in accordance with relevant laws, regulations, and technical standards.
- Prepare complete and clear reports and recommendations after appropriate analysis of relevant and reliable information.

Members should adopt review procedures that will ensure the quality of their professional work is consistent with national and international pronouncements that are issued from time to time.

Due professional care applies to the exercise of professional judgement in the conduct of work performed and implies that the professional approaches matters requiring professional judgement with proper diligence.

Keeping knowledge up to date is covered in more detail in Chapter 2.

2.7 Confidentiality

 Definition – Confidentiality

A member must, in accordance with the law, respect the confidentiality of information acquired as a result of professional and business relationships and not disclose any such information to third parties without proper and specific authority unless there is a legal or professional right or duty to disclose.

Confidential information acquired as a result of professional and business relationships must not be used for the personal advantage of the member or third parties.

Note that confidentiality is not only a matter of disclosure of information – it also concerns using information for personal advantage or for the advantage of a third party.

Example: Confidentiality

Suppose you are an accountant in practice and you discover that the client has just won a major contract. This has yet to be publicised but when a press release is made, then the share price will go up significantly.

If you then buy the (undervalued) shares, then you have breached the principle of confidentiality – not because you told someone but because you used confidential information with the expectation of making a personal gain.

Members should:

- be prudent in the use and protection of information acquired in the course of their duties. (Please note that the duty of confidentiality continues even after the end of the relationship between the member and the employer or client.)

- not use information for any personal gain or in any manner that would be contrary to the law or detrimental to the legitimate and ethical objectives of the organisation.

- inform subordinates as appropriate regarding the confidentiality of information acquired in the course of their work and monitor their activities to assure the maintenance of that confidentiality.

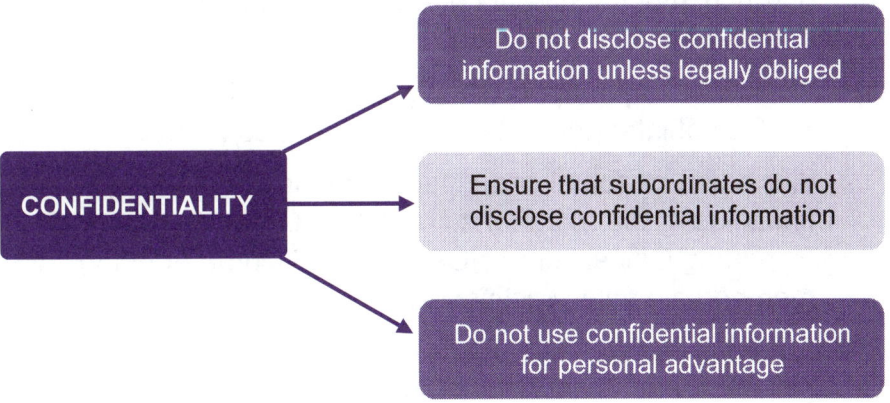

A member must take care to maintain confidentiality even in a social environment. The member should be alert to the possibility of inadvertent disclosure, particularly in circumstances involving close or personal relations, associates and long established business relationships.

Professional ethics in accounting and business: Chapter 10

> **Test your understanding 1**
>
> You visit a client who is a dealer in sports cars. They sell one of their cars to a customer for £16,000; however they later tell you that the car has a faulty braking system.
>
> **What should you do?**
>
> - Nothing.
> - Tell the customer.
> - Tell the client you believe they acted unethically, but that you are bound by confidentiality therefore cannot tell anyone.
> - Report your client to the authorities.

The problem with confidentiality is that there are times when disclosure may be permitted or even mandatory.

The following are circumstances where members are or may be required to disclose confidential information or when such disclosure may be appropriate:

(a) where disclosure is permitted by law and is authorised by the client or the employer

(b) where disclosure is required by law, for example:

   (i) production of documents or other provision of evidence in the course of legal proceedings or

   (ii) disclosure to the appropriate public authorities (for example, HMRC) of infringements of the law that come to light or

   (iii) disclosure of actual or suspected money laundering or terrorist financing to the member's firm's MLRO (Money Laundering Reporting Officer) or to NCA (National Crime Agency) if the member is a sole practitioner, or

(c) where there is a professional duty or right to disclose, which is in the public interest, and is not prohibited by law. Examples may include:

   (i) to comply with the quality review of an IFAC member body or other relevant professional body

   (ii) to respond to an inquiry or investigation by the AAT or a relevant regulatory or professional body

   (iii) where it is necessary to protect the member's professional interests in legal proceedings or

   (iv) to comply with technical standards and ethics requirements.

In deciding whether to disclose confidential information, members should consider the following points:

- whether the interests of all parties, including third parties, could be harmed even though the client or employer (or other person to whom there is a duty of confidentiality) consents to the disclosure of information by the member

- whether all the relevant information is known and substantiated, to the extent that this is practicable. When the situation involves unsubstantiated facts, incomplete information or unsubstantiated conclusions, professional judgement should be used in determining the type of disclosure to be made, if any

- the type of communication or disclosure that may be made and by whom it is to be received; in particular, members should be satisfied that the parties to whom the communication is addressed are appropriate recipients.

2.8 Professional behaviour

Definition – Professional behaviour

A professional accountant should comply with relevant laws and regulations and should avoid any action that discredits the profession.

A profession is distinguished by certain characteristics including:

- mastery of a particular intellectual skill, acquired by training and education

- adherence by its members to a common code of values and conduct established by its administrating body, including maintaining an outlook which is essentially objective; and

- acceptance of a duty to society as a whole (usually in return for restrictions in use of a title or in the granting of a qualification).

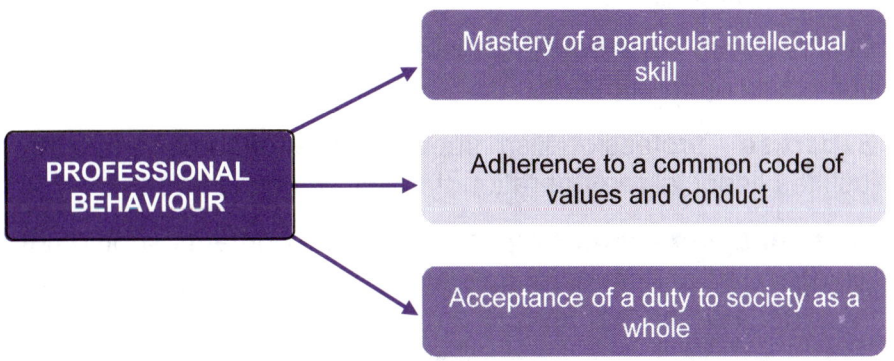

Professional ethics in accounting and business: Chapter 10

The objectives of the accountancy profession are to work to the highest standards of professionalism, to attain the highest levels of performance and generally to meet the public interest requirement. These objectives require four basic needs to be met:

(i) **Credibility** – there is a need for credibility in information and information systems.

(ii) **Professionalism** – there is a need to be clearly identified by employers, clients and other interested parties as a professional person in the accountancy field.

(iii) **Quality of services** – assurance is needed that all services obtained from a professional accountant are carried out to the highest standards of performance.

(iv) **Confidence** – users of the services of professional accountants should be able to feel confident that there is a framework of professional ethics to govern the provision of services.

The most important privilege conferred on professionals is the right to a 'professional opinion'. Professionals can be distinguished from others in society by their right to form an opinion and to base their services and/or products on this opinion. Misuse of this privilege can result in serious harm, thus it is only granted to those who are able to show by education and experience the ability to properly exercise this right.

What is understood by the term 'professionalism' will depend on the context and culture of the organisation.

It should include:

- **Professional/client relationship:**
    - the client presumes their needs will be met without having to direct the process
    - the professional decides which services are actually needed and provides them
    - the professional is trusted not to exploit their authority for unreasonable profit or gain.

- **Professional courtesy** – this is a bare minimum requirement of all business communication.

- **Expertise** – professionalism implies a level of competence that justifies financial remuneration. Incompetence is bad PR.

- **Marketing and promoting services** – accountants should not make exaggerated or defamatory claims in their marketing. This is covered in more detail in Chapter 5.

BUSINESS AWARENESS

 Test your understanding 2

When it comes to ethical principles, discussions often reveal that many employees think it is:

- acceptable to borrow money from the petty cash system if they have access (or their friends have access) and they are short of cash
- fine to browse the Internet or use the work telephone for unlimited numbers of personal calls
- quite appropriate to take a 'sickie' if they need a day off
- fun to invent a good story for being late or going early, and
- use work materials and tools for personal use.

Which of the fundamental principles is being flouted in these examples?

3 Threats and safeguards

3.1 Threats

Threats to compliance with the fundamental principles can be general in nature or relate to the specific circumstances of an appointment.

General categories of threats to the principles include the following:

- **The self-interest threat** – a threat to a member's integrity or objectivity may stem from a financial or other self-interest conflict.

  This could arise, for example, from a direct or indirect interest in a client or from fear of losing an engagement or having their employment terminated or as a consequence of undue commercial pressure from within or outside the firm.

- **The self-review threat** – there will be a threat to objectivity if any product or judgement of the member or the firm needs to be challenged or re-evaluated by them subsequently.

- **The advocacy threat** – there is a threat to a member's objectivity if they become an advocate for or against the position taken by the client or employer in any adversarial proceedings or situation. The degree to which this presents a threat to objectivity will depend on the individual circumstances. The presentation of only one side of the case may be compatible with objectivity provided that it is accurate and truthful.

- **The familiarity or trust threat** – is a threat that the member may become influenced by his/her/their:
    - knowledge of the issue
    - relationship with the client or employer
    - judgement of the qualities of the client or employer to the extent that he/she/they becomes too trusting.

- **The intimidation threat** – the possibility that the member may become intimidated by threat, by a dominating personality, or by other pressures, actual or feared, applied by the client or employer or by another.

Each of the categories of threat may arise in relation to the member's own person or in relation to a connected person e.g. a family member or partner or person who is close for some other reason, for instance by reason of a past or present association, obligation or indebtedness.

Where members decide to accept or continue an engagement in a situation where any significant threat to objectivity has been identified, they should be able to demonstrate that they have considered the availability and effectiveness of safeguards and have reasonably concluded that those safeguards will adequately preserve their objectivity.

Test your understanding 3

Consider each of the following threats to independence and label them according the classification given above.

- Accountancy firm does both management accounting services and auditing for the same client.
- Having audited the client firm for many years, the audit partner has become close friends with the Directors.
- Auditor owns shares in the client company.
- Directors threaten to change auditors if they do not get an unqualified audit report.
- Auditor promotes an audit client's position or opinion in an article.

3.2 Safeguards

> **Definition**
>
> Safeguards may eliminate or reduce such threats to an acceptable level.
>
> They fall into two broad categories:
>
> (i) safeguards created by the profession, legislation or regulation and
>
> (ii) safeguards in the work environment.

Safeguards created by the profession, legislation or regulation include (but are not restricted to):

(i) educational, training and experience requirements for entry into the profession

(ii) continuing professional development requirements

(iii) corporate governance regulations

(iv) professional standards

(v) professional or regulatory monitoring and disciplinary procedures

(vi) external review of the reports, returns, communications or information produced by a member and carried out by a legally empowered third party.

Safeguards in the work environment include (but are not restricted to):

(i) the employing organisation's systems of corporate oversight or other oversight structures

(ii) the employing organisation's ethics and conduct programmes

(iii) recruitment procedures in the employing organisation emphasising the importance of employing high calibre competent staff

(iv) strong internal controls

(v) appropriate disciplinary processes

(vi) leadership that stresses the importance of ethical behaviour and the expectation that employees will act in an ethical manner

(vii) policies and procedures to implement and monitor the quality of employee performance

(viii) timely communication of the employing organisation's policies and procedures, including any changes to them, to all employees and appropriate training and education on such policies and procedures

(ix) policies and procedures to empower and encourage employees to communicate to senior levels within the employing organisation any ethical issues that concern them without fear of retribution

(x) consultation with another appropriate professional.

The nature of the safeguards to be applied will vary depending on the circumstances. In exercising professional judgement, a member should consider what a reasonable and informed third party, having knowledge of all relevant information, including the significance of the threat and the safeguards applied, would conclude to be unacceptable.

Test your understanding 4

From time to time, you may receive or give gifts that are meant to show friendship, appreciation or thanks from or to people who do business with your company. You know you should never accept or offer gifts or entertainment when doing so may improperly influence or appear to influence your or the recipient's business decisions. If you are involved in any stage of a decision to do business with another company or person, you also know that you must refrain from accepting or giving any gift or entertainment that may influence or appear to influence the decision to do business.

Jot down some work-based safeguards that colleagues would find helpful in deciding whether to accept or reject a gift.

4 Dealing with ethical conflicts

Given the above principles, threats and safeguards, a process of resolving ethical conflicts can be given as follows:

Step 1: Gather information

Rumour and hearsay are insufficient evidence upon which to base a decision. The accountant should seek to gather further information to clarify the situation.

Step 2: Analysis

In analysing the scenario, the accountant should first consider the legal perspective – have any laws been broken?

Next they can look at each of the fundamental principles to see which apply and whether there is an ethical issue to resolve.

BUSINESS AWARENESS

Step 3: Action

If it is clear that there is a problem to resolve, the accountant should weigh up the different courses of action:

- Is behaviour dictated by law?
- Who are the affected parties?
- Internal escalation – is there someone within the organisation who could/should be approached to discuss the matter further – for example, the Board of Directors or Audit Committee?
- If the matter is still unresolved, then they should seek professional advice without breaching confidentiality.
- External escalation – should the accountant report the matter externally?
- Ultimately the accountant should consider resigning from the assignment.

Test your understanding 5

You are an accountant of a large multinational organisation and have gained information about a takeover bid to acquire a rival firm.

By coincidence, a family friend is considering selling shares in this rival organisation and has asked you, as an expert in the industry, for advice on this matter.

What would you do? Which principles are affected and how?

Test your understanding 6

You are the newly appointed accountant of a struggling manufacturing company. You have just discovered that tax benefits were wrongly claimed in previous years, reducing the tax bill and boosting profit.

You have told the Finance Director about the error but they are unwilling to disclose the misleading tax bill as by telling the tax authorities (as required by law) the organisation may go bust and 300 employees could lose their jobs.

What would you do? Which principles are affected and how?

Test your understanding 7

You are a trainee accountant in your second year of training within a small practice. A more senior trainee has been on sick leave, and you are due to go on study leave.

You have been told by your manager that, before you go on leave, you must complete a complicated task that the senior trainee was supposed to have done. The deadline suggested appears unrealistic, given the complexity of the work.

You feel that you are not sufficiently experienced to complete the work alone but your manager appears unable to offer the necessary support. You feel slightly intimidated by your manager, and also feel under pressure to be a 'team player' and help out.

However, if you try to complete the work to the required quality but fail, you could face repercussions on your return from study leave.

Required:

Analyse the scenario with particular reference to the following:

(a) Which fundamental principles are involved?

(b) Recommended action.

5 Summary

This chapter has introduced the concept of ethics in the business environment and has outlined the fundamental ethical principles that should be adhered to.

Also covered have been the independence threats and safeguards.

All three, the fundamental Principles, the independence threats and the safeguards to help prevent unethical behaviour are highly examinable and underpin the whole syllabus.

It is critical that you know and can apply the different principles.

Test your understanding answers

Test your understanding 1

Report your client to the authorities

An example of a point that should be considered in determining the extent to which confidential information may be disclosed is:

When the law specifically requires disclosure, it could lead to a member producing documents or giving evidence in the course of legal proceedings and disclosing to the appropriate public authorities infringements of the law.

Test your understanding 2

In all of these examples, the employees are not being honest or straightforward – they are therefore operating against the principle of **Integrity**.

Test your understanding 3

- Self-review
- Familiarity
- Self interest
- Intimidation
- Advocacy

Test your understanding 4

Possible safeguards when considering whether to accept a gift:

- Set up clear policies and guidance for staff stating the following:
  - Cash gifts should never be accepted.
  - Do not accept a gift if it could cause you to feel an obligation.
  - Do not accept a gift from a vendor if it may give the vendor, other suppliers or subcontractors the impression that they have to provide similar gifts or favours in order to obtain company business.
  - Do not justify accepting a gift by arguing, 'Everybody else does it,' 'I deserve a break today,' or 'No one will ever find out'.
- Establish a code of ethics in the workplace that bans gifts.
- Ensure senior management are not seen accepting gifts.

 Test your understanding 5

The basic issue here is that you know that it is a bad time to sell, as the price will most likely rise when the bid is announced. However, should you tell a family friend?

(a) **Integrity** – This situation has a clear impact on your integrity as it impacts on fair dealing and truthfulness.

(b) **Objectivity** – Your objectivity would be at risk if you allow a personal relationship to influence the ethical and legal responsibilities you have to your employer.

(c) **Confidentiality** – You have an obligation to refrain from disclosure of information outside the firm or employing organisation.

(d) **Professional behaviour** – You cannot compromise your professional judgement as a result of a personal relationship.

In this case, the main issue is confidentiality. In advising your family friend, you would not only risk losing your job, but are also compromising your professional judgement, integrity and future career.

You should decline to discuss the issue.

Test your understanding 6

The basic issue here is whether to cover up the tax problem to save the jobs of 300 employees.

(a) **Integrity** – By not declaring the unlawful tax benefits your integrity is clearly compromised.

(b) **Objectivity** – Firstly, you need to ascertain the facts. Your objectivity is threatened by the perceived threat of job losses. The short-term and unlawful actions to increase profit will not help the business model in the long term.

(c) **Professional competence and due care** – By not declaring you are undermining your professional competence as well as not acting with due care and diligence as a professional accountant.

(d) **Confidentiality** – In this case there is a legal and professional right and duty to disclose. The issue will not go away and you will be seen as complicit.

(e) **Professional behaviour** – There is a need to comply with the relevant law and regulations on this matter. By failing to declare your actions discredit the profession and put you in disrepute.

Firstly you must be clear that there is an issue and find out the facts. Should you find that tax benefits have been unlawfully declared you should take action.

In this situation, you have to think about the long-term effects of your actions.

By not declaring the misleading tax bill the organisation might keep afloat for the moment – but it will not make the issue go away, and it will not necessarily save the jobs at risk in the long run. Doing this would severely damage your integrity and professional competence, and risk your reputation and future career.

You are legally required to disclose all information. This is clearly a tough decision to make, as jobs are at risk, but by refraining from reporting you will only worsen the situation. In addition, by self-declaring there may be ways to negotiate a reduced tax bill with the authorities.

The issue needs to be discussed further with the Finance Director and then with the Board of Directors.

Test your understanding 7

(a) **Key fundamental principles affected**

(i) **Integrity**: Can you be open and honest about the situation?

(ii) **Professional competence and due care**: Would it be right to attempt to complete work that is technically beyond your abilities, without proper supervision? Is it possible to complete the work within the time available and still act diligently to achieve the required quality of output?

(iii) **Professional behaviour**: Can you refuse to perform the work without damaging your reputation within the practice? Alternatively, could the reputation of the practice suffer if you attempt the work?

(iv) **Objectivity**: Pressure from your manager, combined with the fear of repercussions, gives rise to an intimidation threat to objectivity.

(b) **Possible course of action**

You should explain to your manager that you do not have sufficient time and experience to complete the work to a satisfactory standard.

However, you should demonstrate a constructive attitude, and suggest how the problem may be resolved. (Your professional body is available to advise you in this respect.) For example, you might suggest the use of a subcontract bookkeeper.

Explore the possibility of assigning another member of staff to supervise your work.

If you feel that your manager is unsympathetic or fails to understand the issue, you should consider how best to raise the matter with the person within the practice responsible for training. It would be diplomatic to suggest to your manager that you raise the matter together, and present your respective views.

It would be unethical to attempt to complete the work if you doubt your competence.

However, simply refusing to, or resigning from your employment, would cause significant problems for both you and the practice. You could consult your professional body. If you seek advice from outside the practice (for example legal advice), then you should be mindful of the need for confidentiality as appropriate.

You should document, in detail, the steps that you take in resolving your dilemma, in case your ethical judgement is challenged in the future.

BUSINESS AWARENESS

Money laundering

Introduction

As well as being influenced by ethical principles and professional considerations, the professional accountant must ensure compliance with relevant legislation, thus reducing firms' risk exposure.

This chapter focuses primarily on the issues of money laundering and whistleblowing.

ASSESSMENT CRITERIA
Money laundering (3.3)

CONTENTS
1 What is money laundering and terrorist financing?
2 Procedure for reporting money laundering
3 Tipping off
4 Customer Due Diligence
5 Whistleblowing

Money laundering: **Chapter 11**

1 What is money laundering and terrorist financing?

1.1 Money laundering

 Definitions

Money laundering is the process by which criminally obtained money or other assets (criminal property) are exchanged for 'clean' money or other assets with no obvious link to their criminal origins. It also covers money, however come by, which is used to fund terrorism.

Criminal property is property which was obtained as a result of criminal conduct and the person knows or suspects that it was obtained from such conduct. It may take any form, including money or money's worth, securities, tangible property and intangible property.

In simple terms:

- Criminals make money through illegal actions.
- This money can be traced by the police, so criminals will try to stop this by buying and selling valuable items.
- The proceeds are continually re-invested and it becomes very difficult to trace the money.
- 'Dirty cash' becomes a nice clean cheque.

There are three acknowledged phases to money laundering:

- **Placement**

  Cash generated from crime is placed in the financial system, for example paid into a bank account. This is the point when proceeds of crime are most apparent and at risk of detection.

- **Layering**

  Once proceeds of crime are in the financial system, layering obscures their origins by passing the money through complex transactions. These often involve different entities like companies and trusts and can take place in multiple jurisdictions.

- **Integration**

  Once the origin of the funds has been obscured, the criminal is able to make the funds reappear as legitimate funds or assets. They will invest funds in legitimate businesses or other forms of investment such as property.

BUSINESS AWARENESS

Activities related to money laundering include:

- Acquiring, using or possessing criminal property.
- Handling the proceeds of crimes such as theft, fraud and tax evasion.
- Being knowingly involved in any way with criminal or terrorist property.
- Entering into arrangements to facilitate laundering criminal or terrorist property.
- Investing the proceeds of crimes in other financial products.
- Investing the proceeds of crimes through the acquisition of property/assets.
- Transferring criminal property.

1.2 Terrorist financing

 Definitions

Terrorism is the use or threat of action designed to influence government, or to intimidate any section of the public, or to advance a political, religious or ideological cause where the action would involve violence, threats to health and safety, damage to property or disruption of electronic systems.

Terrorist financing is fund raising, possessing or dealing with property or facilitating someone else to do so, when intending, knowing or suspecting, or having reasonable cause to suspect, that it is intended for the purposes of terrorism.

Terrorist property is money or property likely to be used for terrorist purposes or the proceeds of commissioning or carrying out terrorist acts.

The definition of 'terrorist property' means that all dealings with funds or property which are likely to be used for the purposes of terrorism, even if the funds are 'clean' in origin, is a terrorist financing offence.

Money laundering involves the proceeds of crime while terrorist financing may involve both legitimate property and the proceeds of crime.

1.3 UK anti-money laundering legislation (AMLL)

The AMLL consists of:

- The Proceeds of Crime Act 2002 as amended (POCA)
- The Money Laundering Regulations 2017 (MLR)
- The Terrorism Act 2000 as amended (TA)

The UK legislation on money laundering and terrorist financing applies to the proceeds of conduct that are a criminal offence in the UK and most conduct occurring elsewhere that would have been an offence if it had taken place in the UK.

1.4 To whom does the AMLL apply?

Anyone can commit a money laundering offence.

However, the Proceeds of Crime Act (POCA) and the Terrorism Act (TA) include additional offences which can be committed by **individuals working in the regulated sector,** that is by people providing specified professional services such as accountancy.

This means that an **accountant** (i.e. an AAT member in practice) will be personally liable for breaching POCA and/or TA if he/she/they acts as an accountancy service provider while turning a 'blind eye' to a client's suspect dealings.

The Money Laundering Regulation (MLR) imposes duties on 'relevant persons' (sole traders and firms (not employees) operating within the regulated sector) to establish and maintain practice, policies and procedures to detect and deter activities relating to money laundering and terrorist financing. It is the sole trader or firm which will be liable therefore for any breach of the MLR.

The practice, policies and procedures required by the MLR of accountancy service providers include:

- Customer Due Diligence on clients
- reporting money laundering/terrorist financing
- record keeping.

Materiality or **de minimis** exceptions are not available in relation to either money laundering or terrorist financing offences – meaning no amount is too small not to bother about.

BUSINESS AWARENESS

 Definition

'de minimis' means **'considered trivial'**.

In this context it means that all potential offences must be reported as no amount is too small to be of consequence.

1.5 What are the specific money laundering and terrorist financing offences?

Under the POCA, the three money laundering offences are

- Concealing, disguising, converting, transferring or removing criminal property.
- Taking part in an arrangement to facilitate the acquisition, use or control of criminal property.
- Acquiring, using or possessing criminal property.

Conviction of any of these offences is punishable by up to 14 years imprisonment and/or an unlimited fine.

Under MLR 2017 any individual who recklessly makes a statement in the context of money laundering which is false or misleading commits an offence punishable by a fine and/or up to two years' imprisonment.

2 Procedure for reporting money laundering

2.1 Summary of key points

- **Suspicious activity reports (SARs)** submitted by the regulated sector are an important source of information used by the **NCA** in meeting its harm reduction agenda, and by law enforcement more generally.

- Businesses are required to have procedures which provide for the nomination of a person, called a **Money Laundering Reporting Officer (MRLO),** to receive disclosures (internal reports) and requires that everyone in the business complies with the Proceeds of Crime Act (POCA) in terms of reporting knowledge, suspicion or reasonable grounds for knowledge or suspicion of money laundering.

- Without the presence within an organisation of an MLRO an individual MUST report directly to the National Crime Agency (NCA). **Note:** The NCA was previously known as the Serious Organised Crime Agency (SOCA).

- An individual other than the MLRO fulfils his/her/their reporting obligations by making an internal report to his/her/their MLRO.

- The MLRO is responsible for assessing internal reports, making further inquiries if need be (either within the business or using public domain information), and, if appropriate, filing SARs with the NCA.

- When reports are properly made they are 'protected' under POCA in that nothing in them shall be taken to breach confidentiality.

- A person who considers he/she/they may have engaged or is about to engage in money laundering, should make an 'authorised' disclosure. Such a disclosure, provided it is made before the act is carried out, or is made as soon as possible on the initiative of that person after the act is done and with good reason being shown for the delay, may provide a defence against charges of money laundering. When properly made such reports shall not be taken to breach confidentiality.

2.2 An accountant's duty to report

POCA and TA impose an obligation on accountants (individuals within the regulated sector, including those involved in providing accountancy services to clients i.e. AAT members in practice), to submit in defined circumstances:

- An internal report to a Money Laundering Reporting Officer (MLRO), by those employed in a group practice.

- A Suspicious Activity Report (SAR) to the National Crime Agency (NCA), by sole practitioners and MLROs.

There are two circumstances when a required disclosure in an internal report or a SAR, collectively referred to below as a report, must be made by an accountant:

1   When the accountant wishes to provide services in relation to property which it is actually known or suspected relates to money laundering or terrorist financing. In such circumstances, the reporter must indicate in the report that consent is required to provide such services, and must refrain from doing so until consent is received.

2   When the accountant actually knows or suspects, or there are reasonable (objective) grounds for knowing or suspecting, that another person is engaged in money laundering or terrorist financing, whether or not he/she/they wishes to act for such person. The person in question could be a client, a colleague or a third party.

2.3 Required disclosure

The required disclosure which must be included in a suspicious activity report (SAR) is as follows:

- The identity of the suspect (if known).
- The information or other matter on which the knowledge or suspicion of money laundering (or reasonable grounds for such) is based.
- The whereabouts of the laundered property (if known) is passed as soon as is practicable to the MLRO.
- Additional information held by the individual that identifies other parties involved in or connected to the matter should also be given to the MLRO.

2.4 Failure to disclose

An offence is committed if an individual fails to make a report comprising the required disclosure as soon as is practicable either in the form of an:

- Internal report to his/her/their MLRO or
- A SAR to a person authorised by the National Crime Agency (NCA) to receive disclosures.
- The obligation to make the required disclosure arises when: a person knows or suspects, or has reasonable grounds for knowing or suspecting that another person is engaged in money laundering.

An MLRO is obliged to report to the NCA if he/she/they is satisfied that the information received in an internal report is serious in nature.

An MLRO may commit an offence if he/she/they fails to pass on reportable information in internal reports that he/she/they has received, as soon as is practicable, to NCA.

The maximum penalty for failure to disclose is five years imprisonment and/or an unlimited fine.

2.5 Exceptions to the duty to report

The obligation of an accountant to report does NOT apply if:

1. The information which forms the basis of knowledge or suspicion or the reasonable grounds to know or suspect was obtained other than in the course of the accountant's business, for example, on a social occasion

2. The information came about in privileged circumstances, For example, when the accountant is providing legal advice, such as explaining a client's tax liability (except when it is judged that the advice has been sought to enable the client to commit a criminal offence or avoid detection) or expert opinion or services in relation to actual or contemplated legal proceedings

3. There is a reasonable excuse for not reporting, in which case the report must be made as soon as reasonable in the circumstances.

2.6 Protected and Authorised disclosures

Reports made under POCA are either protected disclosures or authorised disclosures.

Protected disclosure

Any report providing the required disclosure which is made by any person, not just an accountant, forming a money laundering suspicion, at work or when carrying out professional activities (whether or not providing accountancy services to clients), is a protected disclosure.

This means the person is protected against allegations of breach of confidentiality, however the restriction on disclosure of information was imposed.

Note: Any individual, business or organisation may make a voluntary protected disclosure; it is only in the regulated sector that such reports are compulsory.

Authorised disclosure

Any person who realises they may have engaged in or be about to engage in money laundering should make what is known as an authorised disclosure to the appropriate authority.

This may provide a defence against charges of money laundering provided it is made before the act is carried out (and the NCA's consent to the act is obtained), or it is made as soon as possible on the initiative of that person after the act is done and with good reason being shown for the delay.

For example, the person did not realise that criminal property was involved and made the report on their own initiative as soon as this was suspected/known).

BUSINESS AWARENESS

If the NCA's consent is refused within seven working days, law enforcement has a further 31 calendar days (the 'moratorium period') to further the investigation into the reported matter and take further action e.g. restrain or seize funds.

If consent, or a refusal, is not received by the member within 7 working days, starting on the first working day after the consent request was made, consent is deemed to have been received.

If a refusal is received within that 7 working days, then the member may continue with the client relationship or transaction after a further 31 days has elapsed, starting with the day on which the member received notice of the refusal, unless a restraining order is obtained to prohibit this.

There is no deemed consent in relation to suspicions of terrorist financing.

Test your understanding 1

Is the MLRO an internal or external person?

Is the NCA is an internal or external body?

Test your understanding 2

Sam is an accountant working for McIntosh Ltd.

Recently Meg plc, a customer of McIntosh Ltd, sent in a cheque for £100,000 in payment of an invoice for £20,000. When Sam queried this, the client said it was a mistake and asked for a cheque for the difference of £80,000 to be written to Omnivac plc, a sister company of Meg plc.

Advise Sam.

Test your understanding 3

Emma is an accountant in practice working on the audit of Ghest Ltd.

During the audit Emma discovered that some customers of Ghest Ltd have overpaid their invoices and some have paid twice. On further investigation Emma discovers that Ghest Ltd has a policy of retaining all overpayments by customers and crediting them to the profit and loss account if they are not claimed within a year.

Advise Emma.

Money laundering: **Chapter 11**

 Test your understanding 4

Chris works as a trainee accountant within a firm of accountants. They are preparing a personal tax return for a client.

To prepare the personal tax return Chris requires information about the client's capital gains so they have been looking at the various share purchases and sales that the client has made through the tax year.

Chris has become suspicious as they have noticed that the client only buys shares in small amounts of less than £100 at a time, but does several of these transactions a day and uses a number of different brokers to buy the shares.

Discuss whether or not the client has committed any offences and advise Chris.

3 Tipping off

3.1 The offence of tipping off for accountants

 Definition

Tipping off is a legal term meaning:

- to tell the potential offender of money laundering that the necessary authorities have been informed, or
- to disclose anything that might prejudice an investigation.

Once an accountant has made a report, or has become aware that a report has been made, a criminal offence is committed if information is disclosed that is likely to prejudice any actual or contemplated investigation following the report.

The person making the disclosure does not have to intend to prejudice an investigation for this offence to apply.

Note: The report does not have to have been made by the person making the tip-off; that person merely needs to know or suspect that one has been made to a MLRO, the NCA, HMRC or the police.

The maximum penalty for tipping off is two years imprisonment or an unlimited fine.

BUSINESS AWARENESS

Tipping off is a serious criminal offence. You commit the offence if you make any disclosure likely to prejudice an investigation. An example might be if you tell the client that a SAR has been or is about to be filed in respect of them. You don't have to speak to commit the offence. You can even tip off by failing to respond where an answer is expected.

There are exceptions that apply in certain circumstances, including those where a person does not know or suspect that the disclosure would prejudice a money laundering investigation, and where the disclosure is made in a valid attempt to persuade a client not to commit a money laundering offence.

Considerable care is required in carrying out any communications with clients or third parties following a report. Before any disclosure is made relating to matters referred to in an internal report or SAR, it is important to consider carefully whether or not it is likely to constitute the offences of tipping off or prejudicing an investigation.

It is suggested that businesses keep records of these deliberations and the conclusions reached.

However, individuals and businesses in the regulated sector will frequently need to continue to deliver their professional services and a way needs to be found to achieve this without falling foul of the tipping off offence.

3.2 Prejudicing an investigation

An offence may be committed where **any** person (not just an accountant):

- knows or suspects that a money laundering investigation is being conducted or is about to be conducted; and
- makes a disclosure which is likely to prejudice the investigation; or
- falsifies, conceals or destroys documents relevant to the investigation, or causes that to happen.

The person making the disclosure does not have to intend to prejudice an investigation for this offence to apply.

However, there is a defence available if the person making the disclosure did not know or suspect the disclosure would be prejudicial, did not know or suspect the documents were relevant, or did not intend to conceal any facts from the person carrying out the investigation.

3.3 Record keeping

Under the MLR, records should be maintained to assist any future law enforcement investigation relating to clients, and to demonstrate that the accountant has complied with statutory obligations. Such records should include:

- copies of or reference to the Customer Due Diligence identification evidence (see below). These records must be kept for five years starting with the date on which the accountant's relationship with the client ends

- copies or originals of documents relating to transactions that have been subject to Customer Due Diligence measures or ongoing monitoring. These must be kept for five years starting with the date on which the accountant completed the client's instructions.

4 Customer Due Diligence

4.1 AAT ethics guidelines

When considering **any** new client engagement, the AAT member should assess the likelihood of money laundering.

4.2 When to apply Customer Due Diligence? (CDD)

CDD must be applied by accountants in practice to all clients **before** services are provided to them.

The one exception to this is where to do so would interrupt the normal conduct of business and there is little risk of money laundering or terrorist financing, in which case the accountant must always:

- find out who the client claims to be before commencing the client's instructions and

- complete CDD as soon as reasonably possible afterwards.

BUSINESS AWARENESS

Money laundering regulations state that CDD must be applied in the following situations:

- When establishing a business relationship.
- When carrying out an occasional transaction (i.e. involving £8,361, or the equivalent in Euros, or more).
- Where there is a suspicion of money laundering or terrorist financing.
- Where there are doubts about previously obtained customer identification information.

If an organisation has a turnover of less than £100,000 (or the equivalent in Euros) they may be exempt as there is little risk of money laundering activity and to comply with the regulations would be an unnecessary burden.

4.3 Elements of Customer Due Diligence for new clients

There are three elements to CDD for new clients:

1. Find out who the client claims to be – name, address, and date of birth – and obtain evidence to check that the client is as claimed.
2. Obtain evidence so the accountant is satisfied that he/she/they knows who any beneficial owners are. Beneficial owners must be considered on an individual basis. Generally, a beneficial owner is an individual who owns 25% or more of the client or the transaction property.
3. Obtain information on the purpose and intended nature of the transaction.

The evidence obtained can be documentary, data or information from a reliable and independent source, or a mix of all of these.

If CDD cannot be completed, **the accountant must not act for the client** and should consider whether to submit an Internal Report or Suspicious Activity Report, as appropriate.

4.4 Ongoing monitoring of existing clients

Ongoing monitoring must be applied to existing clients. This means that an accountant must:

- Carry out appropriate and risk-sensitive CDD measures to any transaction which appears to be inconsistent with knowledge of the client or the client's business or risk profile.

  For example, if a client suddenly has an injection of significant funds, check the source of funds. If a beneficial owner is revealed, obtain evidence of the beneficial owner's identity and the nature and purpose of the injection of funds.

- Keep CDD documents, data and information up-to-date.

  For example, if a client company has a change to its directorship, update records accordingly.

Test your understanding 5

A prospective new client comes to see you and asks you to invest £20,000 in cash into a business opportunity. However, they do not want to tell you their name or address.

Do you continue with the transaction?

5 Whistleblowing

5.1 The ethics of whistleblowing

Thousands of workers witness wrongdoing at work. Most remain silent. They decide that it is not their concern; that nothing they can do would improve things, or they cannot afford problems at work.

Other workers choose to speak out. They 'blow the whistle' on unethical and illegal conduct in the workplace.

Definition

Whistleblowing means disclosing information that a worker believes is evidence of illegality, gross waste, gross mismanagement, abuse of power, or substantial and specific danger to public health and safety.

Whistleblower actions may save lives, money, or the environment. However, instead of praise for the public service of 'committing the truth' whistleblowers are often targeted for retaliation, harassment, intimidation, demotion, dismissal and blacklisting.

Example: Whistleblowing

Jamie, a civil engineer, believes that a certain building practice is unsafe and reports this to their employer. The employer does not act on the report so Jamie takes it to their professional body. This body also does not act to Jamie's satisfaction, so they then decide to take the report to the media. The employer dismisses Jamie for gross misconduct in breaching confidentiality.

The ethics of whistleblowing highlights the matters that you should consider before you blow the whistle. It takes a realistic look at the effectiveness of the protection provided by the Public Interest Disclosure Act 1998.

BUSINESS AWARENESS

5.2 Public Interest Disclosure Act (PIDA) 1998

Generally, as an employee, you owe a duty of loyalty to your employer as well as to the accountancy profession. However, there may be times where there is a conflict between the two.

For example, your manager may ask you to 'cook the books' to reduce the company's VAT liability. Although this is clearly wrong and you should not be involved in doing this, how do you resolve such a problem?

In this particular scenario, you would need to speak to your manager and advise him or her that you have concerns about doing this and cannot be involved in such an activity. If there is still a disagreement about a significant ethical issue with your manager, you should then raise the matter with higher levels of management or non-executive directors. Finally, if there is a material issue and you have exhausted all other avenues, you may wish to consider resigning – however, it is strongly recommended that you obtain legal advice before doing so.

In addition, you may decide to take the bolder step of external whistle blowing.

Note: The syllabus for EFTA includes both internal **and** external aspects of whistleblowing.

If you blow the whistle but decide not to resign, in certain circumstances you may be protected from dismissal by the Public Interest Disclosure Act 1998 (PIDA) where you disclose otherwise confidential information. The Act (which has also been referred to as 'the Whistleblowers' Charter') gives protection where you have made a 'qualifying disclosure' (i.e. disclosure of information which you reasonably believe shows that a criminal offence, breach of a legal obligation, miscarriage of justice, breach of health and safety legislation or environmental damage has occurred, is occurring or is likely to occur).

You need to show that you made the disclosure in good faith, reasonably believed that the information disclosed was true and that you would otherwise be victimised or the evidence concealed or destroyed; or that the concern has already been raised with the employer/external prescribed regulator (i.e. a body prescribed under PIDA such as Customs and Excise).

Test your understanding 6

Sam, an accountant working in industry, discovered that the company they worked for was involved in illegal pollution and decided to leak this information anonymously to the press.

A month later Sam's department was closed down and Sam was made redundant. Sam is now claiming that they have been victimised because they were a whistleblower and is seeking protection under PIDA.

Comment on Sam's case.

6 Summary

This chapter has introduced you to some important concepts around the problem of money laundering.

It is vital that you are able to both recite and apply the money laundering regulation in order to progress through this assessment.

Make sure you know what the definitions are! To start with, the three phases of money laundering (placement/layering/integration) need to be learnt well. Layering, for example, was examined in the AAT's practice assessment.

It is also important for accountants to be aware of the consequences of failing to act appropriately in response to money laundering, including the potential to commit the offences of 'tipping off', 'failure to disclose' and 'prejudicing an investigation'. Reporting suspected money laundering in accordance with regulations is essential.

Test your understanding answers

Test your understanding 1

The MLRO is an **internal** person.

The NCA is an **external** body.

Test your understanding 2

The overpayment and request to pay a third party are grounds for suspicion of money laundering (see note below).

Any overpayment by a customer should be thoroughly investigated by a senior member of finance function staff and only repaid to the customer once it has been established that it is right/legal to do so.

Similarly the request to pay a third party should be scrutinised before any payment is agreed to. Without further information the transaction does not make commercial sense.

Unless investigations satisfy any concerns raised, then

- Sam should report the matter to the firm's MRLO.
- McIntosh Ltd should refuse the payment.
- The MRLO should fill in a Suspicious Activity Report (SAR) to be sent to the NCA.

Tutorial note: It seems highly unlikely a customer would overpay by £80,000 by accident! Also, why doesn't the client, Meg plc, simply want McIntosh Ltd to repay them and then it is up to them whether they want to pay anything to Omnivac plc? Is it to make funds difficult to trace, so 'dirty' cash becomes a nice 'clean' cheque from a reputable accounting firm?

Test your understanding 3

Emma should consider whether the retention of the overpayments might amount to theft by Ghest Ltd from its customers. If so, the client will be in possession of the proceeds of its crime, a money laundering offence.

In the case of minor irregularities where there is nothing to suggest dishonest behaviour, (for example where Ghest Ltd attempted to return the overpayments to its customers, or if the overpayments were mistakenly overlooked), Emma may be satisfied that no criminal property is involved and therefore a report is not required.

If there are no such indications that Ghest Ltd has acted honestly, Emma should conclude that Ghest Ltd may have acted dishonestly.

Emma must therefore make a report to her firm's MLRO.

 Test your understanding 4

In this example it is probably the case that the client is a harmless eccentric who chooses to buy shares in small amounts or is indecisive, so often buys some shares only to buy more soon after.

On the other hand it may be that the client buys shares in small amounts and then sells them to disguise the source of their funds and make the proceeds from the sale of shares appear to be more legitimate. In that case they would have hidden the original source of the money. The use of different brokers to carry out the same activities could indicate that they do not wish to cause suspicion by making one large transaction.

As Chris works for a firm of accountants, they are required to make a disclosure to their firm's nominated money laundering reporting officer if they suspect money laundering. It is up to the MLRO to decide whether Chris has been 'over-enthusiastic' and that the situation is harmless or if there are genuine grounds for taking the matter further.

BUSINESS AWARENESS

 Test your understanding 5

You would be unable to complete a due diligence report on this potential customer, therefore you should not continue with the transaction.

Also the way in which you have been approached could be grounds for suspicious activity. It would be appropriate to report the dealings to the MLRO if possible, if not to the NCA.

 Test your understanding 6

To gain protection from PIDA, Sam would have to demonstrate that they were made redundant because they were a whistleblower.

In this case that would be very difficult as they made their disclosure anonymously.

BUSINESS AWARENESS

Technology affecting business and finance

Introduction

In the previous chapters, we looked at the different roles of the finance function and the activities that finance professionals perform to fulfil these roles. We also discussed the importance of ethics, CSR and corporate governance for an organisation and its people and, more specifically, for the finance function.

In this chapter we are going to continue to learn about the finance function, with a focus on how technology can transform its nature, affecting the costs of running the function and the work that its staff undertake.

Technologies such as **cloud computing**, **big data**, **data analytics**, **process automation**, **artificial intelligence**, **data visualisation**, and **blockchain** are some of the more commonly known developments predicted to drive this transformation.

ASSESSMENT CRITERIA
Technology (4.1)

CONTENTS
1 The impact of emerging and developing technologies on accounting systems
2 Offshoring and outsourcing
3 Cloud accounting

Technology affecting business and finance: **Chapter 12**

1 The impact of emerging and developing technologies on accounting systems

The basic activities of the finance function are still relevant in today's organisations but there has been a shift in emphasis regarding the importance of each of the activities.

Historically, the overall mandate of the finance function was to focus on organisational efficiencies and to reduce operational costs. This focus has resulted in organisations achieving optimum operational efficiency.

Technology has, to a large extent, replaced one of the historical mandates of the finance function, as machines have become capable of monitoring operational costs and patterns of organisational efficiency.

1.1 Automation of processes

Advances in technology are providing opportunities to automate many of the activities of the finance function. Technology has enabled the automation of many complex business processes. It is often aimed at improving consistency, quality and speed whilst delivering cost savings.

The introduction of process automation was one that had a machine carrying out a simple repetitive task, replacing a job that would have been done by hand or in a semi-automated fashion. This type of automation is everywhere and has driven industrialisation through its ability to produce ever higher volumes of products, with fewer problems and at less cost.

For example, robotic process automation (RPA) is providing opportunities to automate many routine, clerical 'assembly' activities. RPA is a software-based approach that replicates user actions to reduce or eliminate human intervention in mundane, repetitive and manually intensive processes.

RPA started off in manufacturing (for example, with robotic vehicle assembly lines) but is now used across other functions such as finance. Rapid strides in the development of this technology mean machines are now encroaching on activities previously assumed to require human judgement and expense, such as data entry, automated formatting, reconciliations and foreign exchange transactions. This allows finance staff to re-focus on higher value, customer-focused activities.

BUSINESS AWARENESS

 Example: Process automation

Customer contact centres are an area that many businesses are keen to automate. It is a business function deemed to be relatively low skilled in comparison to other business processes, but is an area that customers value so must be handled with care.

This was evidenced by the wave of contact centres being moved overseas to countries with lower labour costs in the 1990s/2000s, driven by the aim of achieving cost savings. Customers were, however, often dissatisfied with the level of service received resulting in a large number of companies bringing their contact centres back to the home country.

British Telecom is an example of a UK business that did exactly this. Having moved its call centres to India and the Philippines, a process that started in 1995, it announced in 2018 that it would return the centres to the UK and Ireland and this was completed in 2020. Their reasoning behind 'onshoring' the centres back home was to 'deliver personal and local customer service'.

Companies are still keen to realise cost savings in this area but require a new approach to doing so. Developments in technology have led to significant improvements in process automation. Contact centres are now typically heavily automated, using the technology in conjunction with humans. The use of automation allows workers to use their time more efficiently, by redesigning and streamlining processes as well as fully automating simple tasks and processes.

Developments in voice recognition technology and the ability of artificial intelligence allows contact centre calls to be answered robotically. The automated system will typically ask the nature of the call, analyse the customer's voice response and then direct the call appropriately. Many calls can be handled fully autonomously. For instance, making payments or tracing orders can be achieved without involving a call centre worker. Callers who do require a contact centre operative will then begin the security process. This will interrogate the system to bring the customer and case information up on the operative's screen before they even speak.

Data capture and analytics are also used to monitor and understand call types, monitoring for new or emerging trends and suspicious or potentially fraudulent activity. This enables workers to be more prepared and trained specifically to deal with high risk call types.

All of these improvements have led to cost savings and service improvements through more targeted and efficient use of contact centre workers time, focused on activities where value can be added.

Finance professionals should not view automation as a threat but as an opportunity. The core accounting role will still be an essential foundation of the finance function; but, enabled by new technologies, the function can now be a more influential player in the organisation.

Technology allows the contemporary finance function to refocus its energy on revenue and value creation.

The finance function will no longer work largely in isolation but will work with others from across the organisation to drive business transformation that creates shareholder value through automation. This will involve a reallocation of resources.

Test your understanding 1

Read the following statements and decide if each one is true or false.

A   Because of advancements in technology, the basic activities of the finance function are no longer relevant.

B   Technology allows the contemporary finance function to refocus its energy on value creation.

C   Technology enabled a large amount of the assembly and analysis activities to be automated.

D   Technology enabled a large amount of the advising and applying activities to be automated.

1.2   AI and machine learning

Artificial Intelligence (AI) is an area of computer science that emphasises the creation of intelligent machines that work and react like human beings.

Definition

Artificial Intelligence is a "system's ability to correctly interpret external data, to learn from such data, and to use those learnings to achieve specific goals and tasks through flexible adaptation". (Kaplan and Haenlein). This is often considered in the context of human-type robotics but reaches much further than this, and is set to transform the way we live and work.

BUSINESS AWARENESS

Some of the more advanced activities and skills artificial intelligence can now master, presenting huge opportunities for developers and companies alike, include:

- Voice recognition
- Planning
- Learning
- Problem solving

Example: Artificial intelligence

Companies such as Apple and Amazon have developed and marketed voice recognition systems, either to be built into an existing product (such as Apple with its Siri system) or into newly-developed products whose main function is voice recognition (such as Amazon and 'Alexa').

Chat GPT is one of the companies developing incredibly powerful AI, and many companies are considering the impact of these developments on their ability to become more efficient in their day to day processes.

Machine learning is a subset of AI, where effectively AI computer code is built to mimic how the human brain works. It essentially uses probability based on past experiences through data, events and connections between events. The computer then applies this learning to a given situation to give a fact driven plausible outcome. If the conclusion the computer reaches turns out to be incorrect this will act to add more experience and enhance its understanding further, so in future the same mistake will not be repeated.

Essentially, machine learning algorithms detect patterns and learn how to make predictions and recommendations, rather than following explicit programming instruction. The algorithms themselves then adapt to new data and experiences to improve their function over time.

As part of a finance function, AI and machine learning could, for example, be used to identify 'unusual' transactions or patterns, allowing it to spot errors or potential overruns on costs. It could also be used to generate forecasts and budgets.

> **Example: Artificial intelligence 'Move 37'**
>
> Go is a highly complex strategy game, believed to originate in China over 2,500 years ago. It is considered to be more complicated and advanced than Chess, with a larger board and more elements meaning each move has many more alternatives to be considered.
>
> In 2016 Google DeepMind (GDM), an AI technology, played a challenge match against Go world champion Lee Sedol. The match was won by GDM in what many considered to be a significant milestone in AI research and development.
>
> Essentially the program had been built from uploading thousands of previous Go games, which allowed the software to learn moves, patterns and responses to moves, to become a Go expert.
>
> One moment in the match, referred to as Move 37, is considered to be a particularly seminal moment in AI development. GDM played its 37th move which to all commentators and indeed Lee Sedol himself, appeared to be completely abstract and in effect a 'bad' move. It turned out to be an innovative new move never seen before. The significance of the move wasn't felt until much later in the game but it turned out to be the pivotal moment, which enabled GDM to win the match.
>
> The fact that the computer software, whose 'knowledge' was built upon past games of Go and the moves and permutations encountered, was then able to take this learning and build upon it, doing something completely new, was a demonstration of the power of AI and machine learning.
>
> Interestingly Lee Sedol was later able to beat GDM by effectively identifying limitations in its coding. He made moves that were outside of GDM's understanding and the system therefore struggled to respond appropriately. This is a useful illustration of why AI and human thinking will need to be used in a mutual and collaborative way to help achieve innovations.

BUSINESS AWARENESS

Test your understanding 2

Dollar Co is a chain of banks. It collects data from customers who visit the banks in person, and also from online transactions. For the online banking system, customers need to log in via the website using their login and password. Recently, Dollar Co invested in a system that promoted certain products to customers when they were online, based on past transactions and banking history.

What is this is an example of?

A   Traditional process automation

B   Data visualisation

C   Artificial intelligence

D   Virtual reality

1.3 Blockchain

Definition

A blockchain is a decentralised, distributed and public digital ledger that is used to record transactions across many computers. This means the record cannot be altered retroactively without the alteration of all subsequent blocks and the consensus of the network.

Alternatively, 'blockchain' is defined by the Bank of England as' a technology that allows people who do not know each other to trust a shared record of events'.

Benefit of a blockchain

The main benefit of blockchain is security. In the digital era, cyber security is a key risk associated with the use of IT systems and the internet. This is because traditional systems have been 'closed', and so modifications to data have been carried out by just one party. If the system is hacked, there is little control over such modification to prevent it from happening.

Technology affecting business and finance: **Chapter 12**

 Example: Risks of a closed system

A simple illustration is the relationship that individuals have with their banks or credit card companies. If a credit card transaction is carried out, there is only one party that records the payment side of the transaction, the credit card company. How is that company to know that the transaction is valid? If the details appear reasonable, the transactions will be authorised. This allows those who carry out credit card fraud to make their (illegal) gains.

A blockchain provides an effective control mechanism aimed at addressing such cyber security risks. It is a record keeping mechanism that is 'open' or public, as it utilises a distributed ledger; it has been described as a form of collective bookkeeping.

Key features of a blockchain

- In a blockchain system, transactions are recorded by a number of participants using a network which operates via the internet. The same records are maintained by a number of different parties; as a transaction is entered, it is recorded by not just two parties, but instead by all of the parties that make up the overall chain. This can happen because all of the records in the blockchain are publicly available and distributed across everyone that is part of that network.

- When a transaction takes place (for example, between a buyer and a seller) the details of that deal are recorded by everyone – the value, the time, the date and the details of those parties involved. All of the ledgers that make up the blockchain are updated in the same way, and it takes the **agreement of all participants** in the chain to update their ledgers for the transaction to be accepted.

- The process of verifying the transaction is carried out by computers; it is effectively the computers making up the network that audit the transaction. If all of the computers review the transaction and verify the details are correct, the systems of all participants in the blockchain have updated records. The computers work together to ensure that each transaction is valid before it is added to the blockchain. This decentralised network of computers ensures that a single system cannot add new blocks to the chain.

- When a new block is added to a blockchain, it is linked to the previous block using a cryptographic hash (this turns data into a format that can only be read by authorised users) generated from the contents of the previous block. This ensures that the chain is never broken and that each block is permanently recorded. It is intentionally difficult to alter past transactions in the blockchain because all of the subsequent blocks must be altered first.

It is this control aspect of blockchain technology which addresses the main concern of cyber security. If anyone should attempt to interfere with a transaction, it will be rejected by those network parties making up the blockchain whose role it is to verify the transaction. If just one party disagrees, the transaction will not be recorded.

Test your understanding 3

Which TWO of the following are advantages of blockchain technology?

A   Anything of value can be transferred

B   Everybody understands it

C   Easy for management to override

D   No need for an intermediary

Typical stages in a blockchain transaction

1. A transaction is requested

2. A block is created as a digital representation of the transaction

3. The block is sent to every node in the network (distributed ledger)

4. The nodes validate the authenticity of the transaction

5. The nodes receive a reward for the proof of work i.e. some Bitcoin

6. The completed authorised block is added to the chain

BUSINESS AWARENESS

 Example: Cryptocurrency

Bitcoin is a digital currency that was introduced in 2009 (Other cryptocurrencies exist, such as Ethereum and Litecoin).

There is no physical version of Bitcoin; all Bitcoin transactions take place over the internet. Unlike traditional currencies, Bitcoin is decentralised: this means it is not controlled by a single bank or government. Instead, Bitcoin uses a peer-to-peer (P2P) payment network made up of users with Bitcoin accounts.

Bitcoins can be acquired in two different ways: (1) exchanging other currencies for bitcoins, and (2) bitcoin mining.

The first method is by far the most common, and can be done using a Bitcoin exchange such as Mt.Gox or CampBX. These exchanges allow users to exchange sterling, dollars etc. for bitcoins.

Bitcoin mining involves setting up a computer system to solve maths problems generated by the Bitcoin network. As a bitcoin miner solves these complex problems, bitcoins are credited to the miner. The network is designed to generate increasingly complex math problems. This ensures that new bitcoins are generated at a consistent rate. When a user obtains bitcoins, the balance is stored in a secure 'wallet' that is encrypted using password protection. When a bitcoin transaction takes place, the ownership of the bitcoins is updated in the network on all ledgers, using blockchain technology, and the balance in the relevant wallets updated accordingly. There is no need for a central bank to authorise transactions, since they are verified by those computers that make up the system. This therefore has the advantages of speed, reduced cost (transaction fees are small, typically $0.01 per transaction), and increased security. Additionally, there are no pre-requisites for creating a Bitcoin account, and no transaction limits. Bitcoins can be used around the world, but the currency is only good for purchasing items from vendors that accept Bitcoin.

Blockchains and accounting

Ultimately, blockchain provides an unalterable, transparent record of all accountancy-related data.

Examples of how blockchain can benefit the accounting profession include:

- Reducing the cost of maintaining and reconciling ledgers.

Technology affecting business and finance: **Chapter 12**

- Providing absolute certainty over the ownership and history of assets, the existence of obligations and the measurement of amounts owed to a business and owed by a business.
- Freeing up time to allow staff to concentrate on other responsibilities such as planning, valuation, reporting etc., rather than record-keeping.

1.4 Electronic filing of documents

An electronic file management system is a good option for a variety of businesses across a number of different industries. Government agencies, medical practices, insurance companies, legal firms, finance functions and highly technical industries may all benefit from an electronic file management system.

Documentation previously stored on paper (or some physical format), becomes more valuable and easier to use when translated into an electronic format. Although each business has its own way of accessing information, an electronic file management system can be tailored to precisely fit how users search and retrieve data from an electronic index.

The amount of physical space made available by converting hard copies to electronic files is just one benefit of an electronic file management system.

Other benefits include:

- Reliable backup assistance and disaster recovery methods
- Accurate, organised electronic databases
- Instant, 24/7 access, no matter where the user is located
- Increased workplace productivity
- Enhanced customer service.

Disadvantages include:

- A sizeable initial set up cost for the system
- The need to keep hardware and software up to date
- Data security and the risk of data breaches.

1.5 Electronic signing of documents

Electronic signatures deliver a way to sign documents in the online world, much like one signs a document with a pen in the offline world.

Businesses and individuals involved in commercial transactions or messaging activities need to have confidence in, and be trusting of, any communication that is sent in relation to that activity. This helps to ensure that documents sent electronically have not been altered in any way, that the sender can be easily recognised, and that the document has the necessary security.

Trust between business partners can be enhanced by the use of electronic signatures. Electronic signatures can prove the origin of the communication or document, show whether a message has been altered and ensure messages remain confidential.

Electronic signatures come in many forms, including:

- Typewritten
- Scanned
- An electronic representation of a handwritten signature
- A unique representation of characters
- A digital representation of characteristics, for example, fingerprint or retina scan
- A signature created by cryptographic means

Electronic signatures can be divided into three groups:

- Simple electronic signatures – these include scanned signatures and tickbox plus declarations.
- Advanced electronic signatures – these are uniquely linked to the signatory, are capable of identifying the signatory, and are linked to data within the signature that can detect any changes made.
- Qualified electronic signatures – an advanced electronic signature that is created by a qualified electronic signature creation device, and which is based on a qualified certificate for electronic signatures.

Electronic signatures are only as secure as the business processes and technology used to create them. High value transactions need better quality electronic signatures – signatures used for these transactions need to be more securely linked to the owner in order to provide the level of assurance needed and to ensure trust in the underlying system.

Better quality electronic signatures can offer:

- Authentication – linking the signatory to the information
- Integrity – allowing any changes to the information provided to be detected more easily
- Non-repudiation – ensuring satisfaction (in a legal sense) about where the electronic signature has come from.

1.6 Data analytics

Understanding the potential value of data and its significance to an organisation presents a real opportunity to gain unique insight. This can be used to improve competitive position and potentially gain competitive advantage over rivals.

> **Definition**
>
> **Data analytics** is the process of collecting, organising and analysing large sets of data (big data) to discover patterns and other information which an organisation can use to inform future decisions.

Collection of data
Organisations have access to greater quantities of data available from a number of internal and external sources

Organisation of data
Once the data has been captured it needs to be organised and stored for future use, using data warehousing facilities

Analysis of data
Data mining software uses statistical algorithms to discover correlations and patterns to create useful information

BUSINESS AWARENESS

Business consultants Mckinsey summarised the following benefits an organisation can realise from effective data analytics:

- **Fresh insight and understanding** – Seeing underlying patterns through the intelligent use of data can reveal patterns and insight into how a business operates, revealing issues that they may not have known existed

- **Performance improvement** – Data, processed and sorted into relevant management information in real time, can lead to significant operational gains and improved decision making and resource utilisation

- **Market segmentation and customisation** – Refining customer groups into ever more specific segments and understanding the wants and needs of those groups can lead to increased personalisation and customisation of products and services

- **Decision making** – Real time information that is relevant can lead to faster decisions and decisive advantage over competitors

- **Innovation** – Existing products can be improved by understanding the features and elements that customers enjoy and use. This can also lead to the development of new products

- **Risk management** – Risk management and control are vital in the effective running of any organisation. The use of data can enhance all stages of the risk management process.

2 Offshoring and outsourcing

Contemporary developments in technology (such as improved communications, cloud storage and enhanced digital security measures) and in the role and activities of the finance function, have for some organisations meant a structural reconfiguration, with solutions based on greater or less centralisation, offshoring, shared service provision, business partnerships and outsourcing.

Technology affecting business and finance: **Chapter 12**

2.1 Offshoring

 Definition

Offshoring refers to the process of outsourcing or relocating some of an organisation's functions from one country to another, usually in an effort to reduce costs.

For example, many companies in the UK have moved their customer call centres to other countries, such as India and the Philippines. These countries have significantly lower wage rates than the UK, making the call centres cheaper for the offshoring company to operate.

This would not have been possible without the improvements in technology that allowed seamless communication between customers and business functions in locations across the world.

Setting up an operation in a different country can also allow a business to gain access to different markets.

While the cost savings can be significant, offshoring can create additional problems for the organisation, including problems with cultural differences and language barriers.

2.2 Outsourcing

 Definition

Outsourcing means contracting out aspects of the work of the organisation previously done in-house, to specialist providers.

The outsourcing of many aspects of business activity is one strategy that has been suggested as a source of adding value and streamlining activities to maintain competitiveness.

It has become **increasingly common over the past two decades**.

In theory, any of the operations that a business performs can be outsourced. However, an organisation will **often outsource its non-core services** to a third party, allowing them to focus on the core competencies which are integral to the organisation's ability to create and to add value.

Non-core activities may include:

- facilities management
- human resource management
- cleaning services
- catering services and
- legal services.

The organisation's core competencies are activities and skills that drive competitive advantage and which are very difficult for a competitor to emulate. It **may be unwise for an organisation to outsource activities in which they have a core competence** as this could erode competitive advantage.

For example, in clothing retail, most firms may have outsourced production to manufacturers in a foreign country in order to achieve lower production costs. This outsourcing may be essential just to operate in the market. However, the clothing retailers may still retain aspects of the work in which they have a core competence in-house. For example, a particular clothing retailer may have core competencies relating to design and brand management and may retain these activities within the organisation.

Test your understanding 4

Canterell is a bank based in country Z. It is considering outsourcing its IT function. Its current IT systems are considered excellent, which is important, as the banking industry in country Z is highly competitive and innovative.

Which of the following statements regarding this proposal is correct?

A   Canterell will definitely be able to improve its in house IT expertise as a result

B   Outsourcing could cause Canterell a loss of competitive advantage

C   It will be easy for Canterell to bring IT back in-house if they are not satisfied with the outsource supplier

D   It is not possible to outsource IT

Advantages of outsourcing

- Staff are freed up to focus on value-adding activities to gain competitive advantage.
- The cost structure of the business will change, allowing cost savings to be achieved.
- Improved productivity as the outsourced work is now being done by experts who may also use automation.
- Supplier expertise can also lead to improved accuracy and adherence to regulations.

> **Example: Cost structure changes**
>
> The advantages of outsourcing include cost advantages – outsourcing is cheaper. The cost structures of the business involved will change. For instance, capital costs previously incurred may become operational costs.
>
> Cost savings can come from a number of sources:
>
> - A large supplier may benefit from economies of scale in production.
> - The firm concerned will benefit from reduced capital expenditure as this is now incurred by the supplier.
> - Reduced headcount will lead to lower payroll costs.
> - Research and development expenditure and staff training costs may also be saved.

Disadvantages of outsourcing

- Cost issues – the supplier will want to make a profit margin, suggesting it may be cheaper to do the work in house. In addition, if dealing with a major supplier the organisation may be vulnerable to future price rises.
- Loss of core competence – the service may represent a core competence for the organisation and therefore outsourcing may lead to a loss of competitive advantage.
- Transaction costs – arise from the effort put into specifying what is required, co-ordinating delivery and monitoring quality.
- Finality of decision – once a service has been contracted out it may be difficult to take back in-house at a later date, for example due to a loss of in-house expertise.

- Risk of loss of confidential information. For instance, accounting information can be highly sensitive and valuable to competitors.
- Risk of continuity of supply if the supplier has problems.
- Difficulty agreeing/enforcing contract terms.
- Damage to employee morale if redundancies occur or if organisational culture is eroded.

2.3 Outsourcing/offshoring the activities of the finance function

Outsourcing/offshoring of the finance function's activities has become increasingly common in organisations in recent times. The **emphasis has been on reducing costs** but outsourcing has also **enabled the retained finance function to focus on strategic change** by working more closely with the business (sometimes referred to as business partnering) to provide help to improve decision making.

A key consideration is which finance activities should be outsourced:

- Transactional processes (such as accounts payable/receivable, travel and entertainment and cash management) tend to be very popular to outsource.
- However, improvements in provider capabilities have resulted in outsourcing of services such as statutory and regulatory accounting, financial reporting and tax, management accounting, budgeting and forecasting.

Test your understanding 5

Which THREE of the following are drawbacks of outsourcing the non-core activities of the finance function?

A   Loss of control

B   Risk of data breaches

C   Erosion of internal knowledge

D   Increased costs

E   Loss of competitive advantage

F   Major set up costs

Technology affecting business and finance: **Chapter 12**

3 Cloud accounting

3.1 Cloud computing

Definition

Cloud computing is the delivery of different services through the internet, allowing data to be stored, managed, and processed using remote servers. As files are stored on remote servers rather than locally, they can be accessed through electronic devices with access to the internet, regardless of location. As a result, cloud computing allows on-demand access to real-time data.

The basic idea and application of cloud computing sees users log in to an account in order to access, manage and process files and software via remote servers hosted on the internet. This replaces the traditional method of owning and running software locally on a computer or networked server.

There are two main types of cloud setups:

- **Public cloud** hosted by a third-party company. Specialist companies sell their cloud computing services to anyone over the public internet who wishes to purchase them

- **Private cloud** sees IT services provided over a private infrastructure, typically for the use of a single organisation. They are usually managed internally also.

Example: Amazon, cloud and computing services

Amazon's market value briefly broke the $1 trillion mark in 2018. A large contributor to this was the continued growth of Amazon Web Services (AWS). They are the market leader in cloud computing, controlling a third of the market in an industry expected to be worth $145bn by 2020. Their customers range from individuals to government agencies.

Significantly their AWS business supports operations of other core areas of Amazon's business including e-commerce, Amazon prime video and music and the Amazon home assistant. This is a gateway to the 'internet of things', another marketplace projected to grow significantly in the coming years.

BUSINESS AWARENESS

Features of cloud computing

Advantages	Disadvantages
Flexibility and scalability – Cloud computing allows simple and frequent upgrades allowing access to the latest systems developments. A company doesn't become laden with expensive hardware and software that quickly becomes obsolete. This allows organisations to evolve and change, to adapt to new opportunities and working practices.	**Organisational change** – Working methods and roles need to be modified to incorporate a move to cloud computing. It may also lead to job losses, primarily in IT support and maintenance roles.
Cost efficient – Limited IT maintenance costs and reduced costs of IT hardware sees capital expenses and fixed costs become operating expenses. Cloud technology also allows pay as you go computing, with charges based on what a company actually needs.	**Contract management** – The cloud provider will immediately become a very significant supplier. Managing this relationship, monitoring performance and ensuring contractual obligations will introduce new challenges and costs.
Security – Cloud service providers, like any outsource provider, are specialists. The security and integrity of their systems is fundamental to their business model and will be a strategic priority. Disaster recovery and backups are built in.	**Security, privacy and compliance** – Whilst cloud providers will be specialists, they are bigger targets for malicious agents. This can threaten the security of sensitive information. Additionally, compliance with data regulations is put largely in the hands of a third party.
Flexible working – The increase in remote and home working is supported by cloud computing and the ability to access your 'desktop' from any location.	**Reliance** – More so than with a standard outsource arrangement, the reliability of the cloud service provider is essential. Often the entire provision of information systems fundamental to the operation of a business is passed to this third party.
Environment – Less waste from disposal of obsolete technology. More efficient use of scarce resources.	

3.2 Cloud accounting

Problems with traditional accounting software are numerous: the data in the system is not always up-to-date, it only works on one computer or one private network and data gets moved from place to place, for example, on a USB drive which is not secure or reliable.

Users may have to be in a particular physical location to access the system. Hardware and software must be kept up-to-date at a cost to the business. IT staff must be employed to ensure the integrity and security of the system. System backups (if they're done at all) can be costly and complicated.

Traditional accounting software can also be expensive, difficult and time consuming to upgrade. Cloud accounting aims to remedy these issues. Any system where data is accessed remotely, instead of onsite, is a type of 'cloud' system.

Definition

Cloud accounting is a system whereby users subscribe to an online accounting software solution and move their books to the cloud. Cloud accounting software holds accounts data remotely on secure servers (not onsite on the company's computers).

Benefits of cloud accounting software

- **Real-time** financial performance and position can be checked any time. Many providers offer add ins that allow you to customise the reports produced by the software.

- Multi-user access enables online **collaboration** with colleagues.

- Online software means there's nothing to install or update, and **data is backed up automatically**. The business doesn't have to maintain servers to hold the data or employ specialist IT personnel to maintain the software and hardware.

- The level of access for different users can be controlled – this is much **more secure** than the old-fashioned way of emailing files or sending out a USB stick.

- Cloud-based software companies ensure that the **security and privacy of data** about the business is always airtight.

- Users can **access the software from any location** with an internet connection and via laptops, home computers, computer tablets and smartphones. Tablets and phones may have dedicated apps to allow access.
- **Software updates** can be developed and delivered faster and more easily in the cloud.

Disadvantages of cloud accounting software

- Users' ability to connect to the software will **depend on their internet connection**.
- The suppliers' ability to adhere to **data protection regulations** will be crucial.
- It may become very **difficult to switch** to a different accounting system.

4 Summary

Technological developments in areas such as process automation, AI, machine learning, data security, etc. have allowed business areas, including finance departments, to change the way they operate.

Many of the 'traditional' tasks associated with running a finance department, such as data entry, reconciliations and repetitive decision making, can either be outsourced, offshored or automated.

This means that staff in the accounting function can focus on more of the core competencies and value adding activities that will allow the business to flourish.

Businesses that do not take advantage of these developing technologies may end up with increased costs, lower flexibility and a reduced ability to adapt in comparison to their competitors.

Technology affecting business and finance: **Chapter 12**

Test your understanding answers

Test your understanding 1

Answer A: Because of advancements in technology the basic activities of the finance function are no longer relevant – FALSE they are still relevant, but there has been a shift in emphasis on the importance of each of the activities.

Answer B: Technology allows the contemporary finance function to refocus its energy on value creation – TRUE.

Answer C: Technology enables a large amount of the assembly and analysis activities to be automated – TRUE. Many of these activities will be repetitive and straightforward and thus suitable for automation.

Answer D: Technology enables a large amount of the advising and applying activities to be automated – FALSE, although some of these activities can be automated the finance function will need to reallocate its resources to these activities as they are more subjective and still require a human point of view.

Test your understanding 2

The correct answer is C

Artificial intelligence has algorithms that processes data and can use it to make recommendations. Traditional process automation is carrying out a simple repetitive task, which this is not. Data visualisation allows complex data to be viewed in a visually appealing way. Virtual reality is a computer generated experience in a simulated environment.

BUSINESS AWARENESS

Test your understanding 3

The correct answers are A and D

Anything of value can be transferred, and it removes the need for an intermediary. Not everybody understands blockchain, and there may be some resistance to it. Blockchain technology makes it more difficult to interfere with transactions.

Test your understanding 4

Answer B is the correct answer – outsourcing is likely to cause a loss of competitive advantage as IT is a core competence within this highly competitive and innovative industry. In addition, Canterell will have no way to create its own unique systems. Outsourcing IT would be likely to mean the closure of their own IT department, which will mean the loss of skilled staff. This will make it difficult to bring IT back in-house in the future (answer C) and will result in a loss of IT expertise (answer A). It is possible to outsource the IT function (answer D) although this decision may not be in the best interest of the company.

Test your understanding 5

The correct answers are A, B and C – The organisation will become reliant on the external provider and will not have as much control over the function being outsourced (answer A). This leads to the erosion of internal knowledge (answer C) and could increase the risk of data breaches (answer B).

Outsourcing should be a cheaper option thereby reducing costs (answer D). Outsourcing the non-core activities means the remaining activities retained within finance can focus on business partnering, consequently enhancing competitive advantage (answer E). Set up costs would be incurred by the supplier rather than the outsourcing business (answer F).

BUSINESS AWARENESS

Data protection, information security and cybersecurity

Introduction

As discussed in Chapter 5, data is a central aspect of the technology developments driving the 4th industrial revolution.

The amount of personal data available to and used by organisations means that the privacy, sensitivity and security of this data are significant considerations in modern business.

A business must ensure it is compliant with all legislation but there are also ethical and social responsibilities to consider.

ASSESSMENT CRITERIA
Data protection, information security and cybersecurity (4.2)

CONTENTS
1 General Data Protection Regulation (GDPR)
2 Information Security
3 Cybersecurity

1 General Data Protection Regulation (GDPR)

1.1 Data Protection principles

General Data Protection Regulation (GDPR) was introduced throughout the EU in 2018. It is legislation which details the principles of data protection:

- **Used fairly, lawfully and transparently:** If a business is using personal data, it should have a good reason for doing so, and should be open and honest about the reasons.

- **Purpose limitation:** the data should only be used for the specified, explicit purposes for which the data was originally provided.

- **Data minimisation:** Used in a way that is adequate, relevant and limited to only what is necessary.

- **Accuracy:** Data collected should be accurate and, where required, kept up-to-date.

- **Storage limitation:** The data should be kept for no longer than is necessary.

- **Integrity and confidentiality (security):** Handled in a way that ensures appropriate security. Including protection against unlawful or unauthorised processing, access, loss, destruction or damage.

- **Accountability:** The business should be able to prove that the regulations are being complied with. This includes regular training for staff and evaluation of data handling processes.

Data controllers within organisations have to ensure adequate safeguards and controls are in place to implement these data principles.

There is strong legal protection for sensitive information, such as:

- race, ethnic background, religious beliefs
- political opinions
- trade union memberships
- genetics, biometrics (where used for identification), health
- sex life or orientation.

The need for consent underpins the principles. Individuals must opt-in whenever data is collected and there must be clear privacy notices. Those notices must be concise and transparent and consent must be able to be withdrawn at any time.

BUSINESS AWARENESS

Background to GDPR

This new legislation was designed to overhaul the previous Data Protection Act from 1995. This was written at a time when the internet was in its infancy, smartphones didn't exist and some of the largest and most influential companies in the world such as Facebook, Google and Amazon were barely even conceived.

The way data would be used in 2018 and beyond required new laws that were fit for purpose, designed with the modern landscape in mind and able to safeguard the privacy and rights of individuals today.

Example: Facebook and Cambridge Analytica scandal

Facebook received a £500,000 fine for its role in the Cambridge Analytica scandal. The fine was the maximum available under the data protection legislation in place at the time (prior to the introduction of GDPR legislation).

Facebook was found to have breached data protection legislation by allowing third party app developers access to users' data without sufficiently clear and informed consent. They also failed to make suitable checks on apps and developers using the platform.

What was the Cambridge Analytica scandal?

A third party app designed as a personality quiz collected the data of 87 million Facebook users without their knowledge or explicit content. This data was then sold on to third parties, one of whom was Cambridge Analytica.

They then used this data to profile voters in the US election based on personality and psychology before targeting advertising which took advantage of this information.

Around one million UK users' data was obtained in the scandal.

Data protection, information security and cybersecurity: **Chapter 13**

 Test your understanding 1

GDPR legislation in the EU attempts to ensure that organisations follow the principles about data.

Which of the following are contained in those principles? Select all that apply.

A   Data is kept up-to-date

B   Data is kept for longer than is necessary

C   Data is used for implicit purposes

D   Data is protected against unlawful access

E   Data should always be in hard copy format

Quite apart from the adherence to regulations, businesses should aim to protect data for ethical and corporate social responsibility reasons.

Showing that you are compliant with data protection regulations gives confidence to stakeholders and improves your brand.

1.2   Data Protection breaches

As the business world becomes more complex, organisations are holding increasing amounts of data about individuals.

 Definition

Data protection is concerned with protecting individuals against the misuse of personal information.

If an organisation fails to comply with the GDPR, it can be fined. Brexit has led to the separation of the regulations in the UK and the EU.

- The maximum fine that can be levied in the EU (which applies to the processing of EU residents' personal data) is the higher of €20 million or 4% of annual global turnover, enforceable against an organisation for non-compliance.

- In the UK, the maximum fine levels relating to the processing of UK residents' personal data is £17.5 million or 4% of annual global turnover.

- The amount of the fine actually raised will depend on the severity of the breach.

BUSINESS AWARENESS

 Example: Fines levied for breaches of GDPR

In 2019, Doorstep Dispensaree Ltd, a London-based pharmacy, was fined £275,000 for failing to ensure the security of special category data.

Approximately 500,000 documents containing names, addresses, dates of birth, NHS numbers and other medical information were left in unlocked containers at the back of its premises. A director of The Information Commissioner's Office (ICO), who carried out the investigation into the breach, described the company's behaviour as 'careless' and 'falls short of what the law expects and it falls short of what people expect'.

In 2021, a Spanish airline, Air Europa, was fined €600,000 for failing to have appropriate data security measures in place and for delaying the notification of a personal data breach.

Organisations that discover a breach of GDPR must report the it to the relevant supervisory authority within **72 hours** of becoming aware of the breach, where feasible.

If the breach has a high risk of adversely affecting individuals' rights and freedoms, the organisation must inform those individuals without undue delay.

Organisations should ensure that they have robust breach detection, investigation and internal reporting procedures in place, in order to facilitate decision-making about whether or not there is a need to notify the relevant supervisory authority or the affected individuals, or both.

Records must be kept of any personal data breaches, regardless of whether notification to the authorities or the individuals concerned is required.

Data subjects have the right to find out what information the government and other organisations store about them.

 Definition

Data subject refers to the identified or identifiable living individual to whom personal data relates.

This includes the right to:

- be informed about how their data is being used
- access personal data
- have incorrect data updated
- have data erased

- stop or restrict the processing of their data
- data portability (allowing them to get and reuse their data for different services)
- object to how their data is processed in certain circumstances.

Data subjects can raise concerns with an organisation if they feel that organisation has mishandled their data. If they are not satisfied with the organisation's response, they can raise their concern with the relevant authority. In the UK, they may raise their concern with the Information Commissioner's Office (ICO), who will investigate the issue.

2 Information Security

2.1 Data security

Data security is concerned with keeping data safe from various hazards that could destroy or compromise it.

These include:

- **Physical risks** – impact on the physical environment in which the system exists (e.g. fire or flood).
- **Human risks** – access is gained to the system by an unauthorised user, either physically or remotely (e.g. hacking, virus infection or fraud).

Example: Data security

In April 2011, hackers gained access to over 77 million PlayStation user accounts held by Sony. These accounts included personal information and credit card details for many customers.

This security failure led to significant loss of reputation and sales for Sony, who estimated the cost of the breach to be around £109m, excluding the costs of compensating customers whose details were stolen.

Test your understanding 2

Leslie has found that a utility supplier has sold information about them to a market research company.

Is this an issue of data protection or data security?

BUSINESS AWARENESS

The main risks to computer systems and the data they contain include the following:

Potential threats	Counter measures
Physical damage, due to: • fire • flooding • terrorist acts • power failures • other environmental factors such as heat, cold, humidity, dust.	• Well-documented fire procedures. • Staff training. • Provide fire extinguishers and smoke/heat detectors, fire-doors. • Computer equipment might be located in a segregated area in which air conditioning and dust controls operate effectively. • Back-up generators. • Off-site facilities to cater for the possibility of total destruction of the in-house computer equipment. • Off-site back-up copies of data files.
Human Damage caused by human interference, such as unauthorised access resulting in theft, piracy, vandalism.	• Restricted access to the computer room (e.g. PIN codes). • CCTV and security guards. • Hardware can be physically or electronically tagged to sound an alarm if it is removed from the building. • Hardware can be locked down.
Operational problems, such as program bugs and user operational errors.	• Thorough testing of new programs. • Strict operating procedures. • Adequate training of all staff members.
Data corruption, e.g. viruses, hackers.	• Anti-virus and firewall software. • Passwords and user number limits. • Off-site back-up copies of data files.
Data theft, e.g. fraud, industrial espionage, loss of confidentiality.	• Data encryption techniques. • Passwords and user numbers. • Physical access controls. • Accounting system access levels.

Data protection, information security and cybersecurity: Chapter 13

 Test your understanding 3

Ragu Ltd holds data about many of its customers. It has recently set up an off-site back-up of this data to improve its data security.

Which potential data security threat will this measure most likely reduce?

A   Hacking

B   Data theft

C   Viruses

D   Fire or flood

3 Cybersecurity

3.1 What is cyber security?

 Definition

Cyber security is the protection of internet-connected systems, including hardware, software and data, from cyber attacks.

A cyber attack is a malicious and deliberate attempt by an individual or organisation to breach the information system of another individual or organisation. Usually, the attacker seeks some type of benefit from disrupting the victim's network.

In a computing context, security comprises cyber security and physical security – both are used by organisations to protect against unauthorised access to data and systems.

3.2 Key risks of cyber attacks

If the data on an organisation's computer system is accessed without authorisation or damaged, lost or stolen, it can lead to disaster.

A number of different technical methods are deployed by cybercriminals. There are always new methods proliferating, and some of these categories overlap, but these are the terms that you are most likely to hear discussed:

- **Malware** – short for malicious software. It is software designed to cause damage to a single computer, server or computer network. Worms, viruses and trojans are all varieties of malware, distinguished from one another by the means by which they reproduce and spread. These attacks may render a computer or network inoperable, or grant the attacker access so that they can control the system remotely.

- **Phishing** – a technique by which cybercriminals craft emails to fool a target into taking some harmful action. The recipient might be tricked into downloading malware that is disguised as an important document, for example, or urged to click on a link that takes them to a fake website where they will be asked for sensitive information like usernames and password.

- **Denial of service attacks** – a brute force method to try to stop an online service from working properly. For example, attackers might send so much traffic to a website or so many requests to a database that it overwhelms the system's ability to function, making it unavailable to anybody.

- **Man in the middle attacks** – a method by which attackers manage to interpose themselves secretly between the user and a web service that they are trying to access. For example, an attacker might set up a Wi-Fi network with a login screen designed to mimic a hotel network; once a user logs in, the attacker can harvest any information that user sends, including their password.

The use of cyber security measures such as firewalls, anti-virus software, password protection, data encryption and adequate staff training on cyber security awareness will help to prevent such attacks occurring.

Example: Cyber attack on Marriott International

What happened?

On 30 November 2018, Marriott International announced that the records of up to 500 million customers had been compromised in what may be one of the largest data breaches in history.

The global chain revealed that hackers accessed the guest reservation database at Marriott-owned Starwood hotels as early as 2014.

The company said it received an alert on 8 September that warned of an attempt by an 'unauthorised party' to access the Starwood guest reservation database in the US. That discovery prompted further investigation, which uncovered the long-term unauthorised access across the Starwood network.

The hacker copied and secured the data with encryption, making it more difficult for authorities to determine the contents. The Marriott group lists the categories of data exposed in the leak as:

Name, Mailing address, Phone number, Email address, Passport number, Starwood Preferred Guest account information, Date of birth, Gender, Arrival and departure information, Reservation date, Communication preferences.

Test your understanding 4

Which of the following is a common example of a 'phishing' attack?

A   You receive an email from an acquaintance who you are rarely in contact with that contains only a web link.

B   You receive an email that appears to be from your bank asking you to enter your account number and password, but the web address looks unfamiliar.

C   You receive a text message claiming that you won a contest and asking you to click on the link.

D   All of the above.

BUSINESS AWARENESS

4 Summary

This chapter has introduced you to the principles of General Data Protection Regulation (GDPR) and why it is important, not least because of the penalties that may be levied against organisations that breach it.

They aim to ensure that in this ever-changing world of advancing technology, including new means of storing and transmitting data, the rights of individuals are maintained.

In this context, security of data and information is paramount. Businesses should take appropriate steps to ensure that data is secure, whether from physical risk, system bugs, human errors or directed cyber attacks.

Test your understanding answers

Test your understanding 1

The correct answers are A and D

Data should NOT be kept for longer than is necessary. Data should only be kept for explicit rather than implicit purposes. Data can be kept in hard or soft copy format as long as there is sufficient security in place.

Test your understanding 2

Data protection – there is no indication of the market research firm obtaining the information through hacking or other underhand means.

Test your understanding 3

The correct answer is D

Off-site backups will not help prevent the theft of data.

Test your understanding 4

The correct answer is D

BUSINESS AWARENESS

Information and Big Data

Introduction

Organisations hold and receive massive amounts of data every day. In order to be useful to the organisation this data must be converted into good quality information.

This chapter helps explain what makes good information and how different types of information will be required at different levels of the organisation.

The increased use of technology has led to the rise in what is called Big Data. This is data that is so large that it is difficult for an organisation to process. This chapter examines how Big Data might be converted into useful information and how this data might be analysed in order to help an organisation in its future planning and decision making.

ASSESSMENT CRITERIA	CONTENTS
Information requirements in a business organisation (5.1)	1 The attributes of good quality information 2 Information at different levels in the organisation 3 Big Data 4 Data Analytics

Information and Big Data: **Chapter 14**

1 The attributes of good quality information

1.1 Data versus information

Data are facts or figures in a raw, unprocessed format. Data consists of numbers, letters, symbols, raw facts, events and transactions, which have been recorded but not yet processed into a form that is suitable for making decisions.

To become useful to a decision maker, data must be transformed into information. Information is data that has been processed in such a way that it has a meaning to the person who receives it. This person may then use this information to improve the quality of decision-making.

1.2 Information requirements

Information is a vital requirement within any business and is required both internally and externally. Management requires information:

- To provide records, both current and historical
- To analyse what is happening within the business
- To provide the basis of decision making in the short term and long term
- To monitor the performance of the business by comparing actual results with plans and forecasts.

Various third parties require information about the business, including:

- The owners, e.g. shareholders
- Customers and suppliers
- The employees
- Government agencies such as tax authorities.

 Test your understanding 1

A working definition of information would be:

A   facts you can work with
B   facts
C   facts useful to the production manager
D   facts useful to the decision maker

1.3 Characteristics of good information

The information produced by a system should have the following characteristics (identified by the acronym ACCURATE):

Accurate – sufficiently accurate to be relied upon.

Complete – managers should be given all the information they need, but information should not be excessive.

Cost effective – the value of information should exceed the cost of producing it.

Understandable – information needs to be clearly presented and displayed in an understandable form.

Relevant – the information should be relevant to its purpose.

Accessible or **A**uthoritative – information should be trusted and provided from reliable sources, and easily available to users, so that the users can have confidence in their decision making.

Timely – information should be provided in sufficient time for decisions to be made based upon that information.

Easy to use – the information should be clear and easy to use.

Data processing is the conversion of data into information, perhaps by classifying, sorting or producing total figures. The conversion process may be manual or automated. In general, data may be transformed into information by:

- bringing related pieces of data together
- summarising data
- basic processing of data
- tabulation and diagrammatic techniques
- statistical analysis
- financial analysis.

Information and Big Data: **Chapter 14**

 Test your understanding 2 – Information

Consider the following statements:

(i)   Good information must be obtained cheaply

(ii) Information consists of raw facts and figures which have been recorded but not yet processed into a useful form.

Which of the above statements is/are correct?

A   (i) only

B   (ii) only

C   Both

D   Neither

2 Information at different levels in the organisation

There are three levels of planning and control within an organisation:

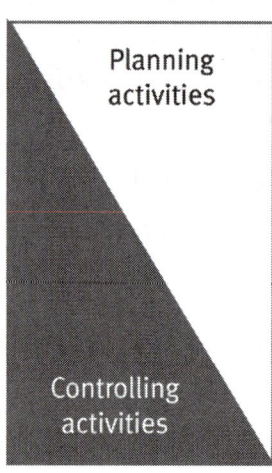

BUSINESS AWARENESS

Level of control	Key characteristics	Example of accounting Information requirements
Strategic planning	• Takes place at the top of the organisation. • Concerned with setting a future course of action for the organisation.	• Long-term forecasts
Management control	• Concerned with the effective use of resources to achieve targets set at strategic planning.	• Budgetary measures • Productivity measures • Labour statistics, e.g. hours, turnover • Capacity utilisation
Operational control	• Concerned with the day-to-day implementation of the plans of the organisation.	• Detailed, short-term transactional data

 Example: Organisational levels

At the operational level, sales ledger staff will be posting into the sales ledger accounts, sending out statements and dealing with accounts queries. Credit approval for new orders are also given at this level.

At the managerial level, credit control managers will want to follow up slow paying customers. This is to ensure that bad debts are minimised and that cash flow remains healthy.

At the strategic level, the board might decide that more working capital funding is needed to support receivables and that factoring debts or invoice discounting might offer useful ways of raising cash balances.

Decisions at each of these levels will require different types of information, with different characteristics.

2.1 Types of information systems

As we have just seen, there are three levels of management – **strategic**, **tactical** and **operational**.

Each level creates different types of strategy within the organisation and therefore needs different types of information, as outlined by the following chart:

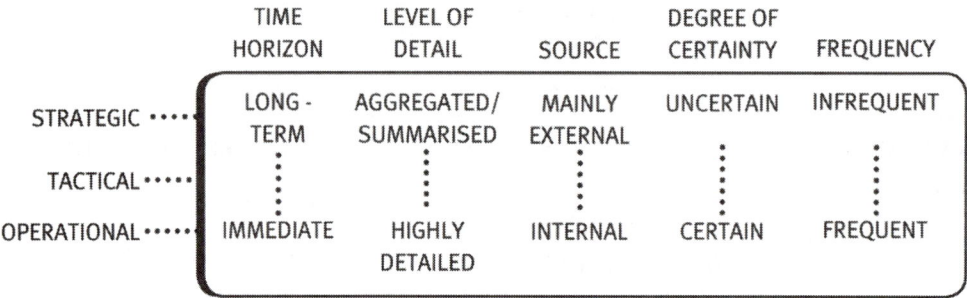

- The **strategic** level of management requires information from internal and external sources in order to plan the long-term strategies of the organisation. Internal information – both quantitative and qualitative – is usually supplied in a summarised form, often on an ad-hoc basis. **Strategic information** would relate to the longer-term strategy on the company's market share, which in turn informs the production plan. This plan would be used to predetermine the level of investment required in capital equipment, in the longer term. This process would also lead to investigating new methods and technology.

- The **tactical** level of management requires information and instructions from the strategic level of management, together with routine and regular quantitative information from the operational level of management. The information would be in a summarised form, but detailed enough to allow tactical planning of resources and manpower. **Tactical information** could include, for example, the short-term budget for 12 months and would show the budgeted machine use in terms of machine hours for each item of plant. The total machine hours being predetermined from the production budget for the period.

- The **operational** level of management requires information and instructions from the tactical level of management. The operational level is primarily concerned with the day-to-day performance of tasks and most of the information is obtained from internal sources. The information must be detailed and precise. For example, operational information would include a current week's report for a cost centre on the percentage capacity of the plant used in the period.

2.2 Information systems at different business levels

A modern organisation needs a wide range of systems to process, analyse and hold information. The different management decision-making levels within an organisation need different types of information:

Executive information system
(EIS): gives senior executives access to internal and external information. Information is provided in a summarised form with the option to 'drill down' to a greater level of activity

Decision support system
DSS: an aid to making decisions. The system predicts the consequences of a number of possible scenarios and the manager then uses their judgement to make the final decision

Transaction processing system
TPS: a system for processing routine business transactions, often in large volumes, e.g sales and purchase information

As a basic idea, the systems towards the top of the pyramid will support the strategic decisions and they will use data from systems in the levels below.

 Example

Decision-making is an important aspect of any organisation.

Three levels of decision-making are normally identified; strategic, tactical and operational. Each level has different information requirements.

Strategic decisions are long-term, complex decisions made by senior management. For example, a UK-based supermarket chain may put a strategic plan in place outlining its aim to be the market leader. This is a long-term plan and the achievement of this aim will have far reaching implications for the whole organisation.

Tactical decisions are medium-term, less complex decisions made by middle management. They follow on from strategic decisions. For example, in order to become the market leader the supermarket chain may have to launch new products/services or open new branches.

Operational decisions are day-to-day decisions made by junior managers, e.g. the ordering of supplies to ensure the new product lines are stocked.

As decisions at each level are different, the information required at each level will be different.

Strategic information is mainly used by directors and senior managers to choose between alternative courses of action, to plan the organisation's overall objectives and strategy and to measure whether these are being achieved. For example:

- profitability of main business segments
- prospects for present and potential markets.

Tactical information is used by managers at all levels, but mainly at the middle level for tactical planning and management control activities, such as pricing, purchasing, distribution and stocking. For example:

- sales analysis
- stock levels
- productivity measures.

Operational information is used mainly by managers on the operational level such as foremen and section heads who have to ensure that routine tasks are properly planned and controlled. For example:

- listings of debtors and creditors
- payroll details
- raw materials requirements and usage.

3 Big Data

3.1 Big Data: definitions

Definition

Big Data is a term for a collection of data which is so large it becomes difficult to store and process using traditional databases and data processing applications.

BUSINESS AWARENESS

Although Big Data does not refer to any specific quantity, the term is often used when speaking about petabytes and exabytes of data.

The definition can be extended to incorporate the types of data involved. Big Data will often include much more than simply financial information and can involve other organisational data which is operational in nature along with other internal and external data which is often unstructured in form.

One of the key challenges of dealing with Big Data is to identify repeatable business patterns in this unstructured data, significant quantities of which is in text format. Managing such data can lead to significant business benefits such as greater competitive advantage, improved productivity and increased levels of innovation.

3.2 Sources of Big Data

Big Data can come from anywhere. Data generated by the company itself is known as internal data. Data generated elsewhere is known as external data.

Examples of such sources are:

Internal

- accounting systems
- website tracking data
- call centre logs

External

- national data (e.g. Office for National Statistics)
- industry data (e.g. from trade organisations)
- social media

and many more.

3.3 Big Data characteristics

The following, known as the 'five Vs', represent the defining characteristics of Big Data:

Velocity

Data is now streaming from sources such as social media sites at a virtually constant rate. Current processing servers are often unable to cope with this flow or to generate meaningful real-time analysis.

Volume

More sources of data, together with an increase in data generation in the digital age, combine to increase the volume of data to a potentially unmanageable level.

Variety

Traditionally, data was structured and in similar and consistent formats such as Excel spreadsheets, or standard databases. Data can now be generated and collected in a huge range of formats including rich text, audio, images and GPS data, video files, etc.

It is estimated that 80% of the data in the world today is unstructured and at first glance does not show any indication of relationships. Big Data algorithms sort data files in a structured manner and examine them for relationships.

Veracity

Because there are so many different sources of data, there is an increased risk of inaccuracies. Data quality is less controllable: for instance, Twitter data includes colloquial speech, hashtags, abbreviations, and spelling mistakes or typos. It often comes from biased sources.

But analytics technology now allows us to work with data that may lack accuracy/veracity. The volumes of data involved often make up for the lack of quality or accuracy caused by occasional outliers.

Value

All the volumes of fast-moving data of different variety and veracity have to be turned into value for business users.

Embarking on 'big data' projects without a clear understanding of the business value it will bring is dangerous. Value denotes the added value for companies. Many companies have recently established their own data platforms, filled their data pools and invested a lot of money in infrastructure. It is now a question of generating business value from their investments.

Test your understanding 3

The definition of Big Data is most commonly based on the '5 Vs' model.

Which TWO of the following statements are true?

1. 'Variety' refers to the huge amount of data produced. The amount of data is so large that it can no longer be saved or analysed using conventional servers and data processing methods.

2. 'Velocity' refers to the speed at which the data is generated, analysed and reprocessed.

3. 'Veracity' refers to the authenticity and credibility of the data. Big Data involves working with all degrees of quality. This is because of the enormous amount of data available, which is usually paired with a shortage of quality.

3.4 Big Data: Benefits

Why is Big Data so important?

Several major business benefits arise from the ability to manage Big Data successfully:

- Driving **innovation** by reducing time taken to answer key business questions and therefore make decisions
- Gaining **competitive advantage**
- Improving **productivity**.

Example: Big Data benefits – UPS

Delivery company UPS equips its delivery vehicles with sensors which monitor data on speed, direction, braking performance and other mechanical aspects of the vehicle.

Using this data to optimise performance and routes has led to significant improvements, including:

(i) Over 15 million minutes of idling time eliminated in one year, saving 103,000 gallons of fuel.

(ii) 1.7 million miles of driving eliminated in the same year, saving a further 183,000 gallons of fuel.

3.5 Big Data: Risks

There are risks and limitations associated with Big Data:

- **Availability of skills** to use Big Data systems, which is compounded by the fact that many of the systems are rapidly developing and support is not always easily and readily available. There is also an increasing need to combine data analysis skills with a deep understanding of the industry being analysed and this need is not always recognised.

- **Security of data** is a major concern in the majority of organisations and if the organisation lacks the resources to manage data then there is likely to be a greater risk of leaks and losses.

- **Data Protection** issues as organisations collect a greater range of data from increasingly personal sources (e.g. Facebook).

It is important to recognise that just because something CAN be measured, this does not necessarily mean it should be. There is a risk that valuable time is spent measuring relationships that have no organisational value.

Just because data has been collected does not mean that it is reliable or helpful for decision-making. **Professional scepticism** should always be applied when making decisions based on Big Data, especially when the decisions are being made on the basis of data that is largely from external (and therefore potentially less trustworthy) sources or when the decisions themselves could change the strategic direction of the organisation.

For example, people have a tendency when online to complain more than praise. Conclusions could be drawn about a product being poor quality when that may not be true for most customers.

Example: Big Data risks – Walmart

It is widely reported that Walmart tracks data on over 60% of adults in the US, including online and in-store purchasing patterns, Twitter interaction and trends, weather reports and major events. The company argues that this gives them the ability to provide a highly personalised customer experience.

Walmart detractors criticise the company's data collection as a breach of human rights and believe the company uses the data to make judgements on personal information such as political view, sexual orientation and even intelligence levels.

BUSINESS AWARENESS

 Test your understanding 4

Which of the following statements is/are true?

1   Big Data analytics enables businesses to gain a more detailed understanding of customer behaviour.
2   Big Data requires analysis by a skilled data analyst.

 Test your understanding 5

Andy has recently started looking at ways of gathering Big Data for their business. They are concerned that some of the sources of data they have chosen are unreliable and may therefore lead to inaccurate conclusions.

Which features may be missing from the Big Data they collect?

A   Variety
B   Velocity
C   Veracity
D   Volume

4 Data Analytics

4.1 Big Data analytics

Big Data analytics is the process of scrutinising Big Data to identify patterns, correlations, relationships and other insights. This information can inform decision-making and have a wide-reaching effect on the organisation's competitive strategy and marketing campaigns. It can therefore have a direct impact on future profitability.

Information and Big Data: Chapter 14

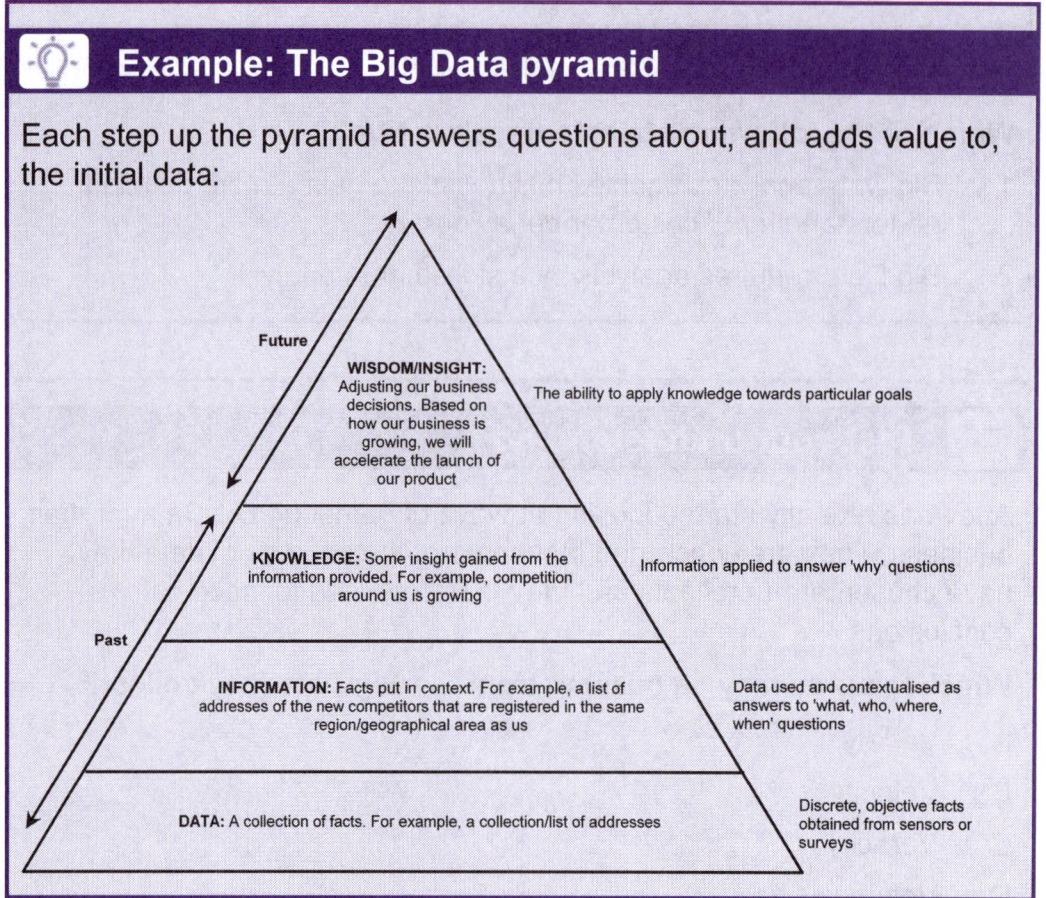

Example: The Big Data pyramid

Each step up the pyramid answers questions about, and adds value to, the initial data:

4.2 Ability to undertake Big Data analytics

Due to the characteristics of Big Data discussed in section 3.3 above, it may not be possible for an organisation, particularly a small one with limited resources, to fully undertake data analytics and gain insight from the data it collects. The organisation may consider that the time and investment needed to undertake such an analysis is not cost effective or feasible.

It may instead choose to outsource the analysis to a professional analytics company. In this way it gains the expertise of a business whose core competencies are focused on analysing such data. It will not have to employ analytics specialists itself, or invest in computer systems capable of processing the data.

However, it must be willing to compromise on the security of sensitive information to allow the analytics company to undertake the work. Additionally, it will be reliant on the insights of the analytics company into products/markets, regardless of whether or not the analytics company has sufficient experience or expertise in these areas.

BUSINESS AWARENESS

5 Summary

Information is crucial to effective decision-making within an organisation. But if information is not of an adequate quality, the integrity of the decisions will be compromised. Poor quality information can lead to poor quality decisions. In addition, if the users of the information do not perceive it to be of the correct quality, it may be ignored altogether.

Information needs to be tailored to its user. For instance, board members at the strategic level of the organisation will not need information at the same level of detail, or as frequently, as operational supervisors in a credit control team. Different information systems should be used, as appropriate, to provide the right type of information to the right people.

Big Data can be very useful to organisations to help them gain insights that their competitors may miss. However, caution should be taken when drawing conclusions from such data, especially when it may be from less reliable or potentially biased sources.

The analysis of data does not necessarily have to be done in-house. Recently, companies that specialise in data analytics have offered their expertise for this purpose.

Test your understanding answers

Test your understanding 1

The correct answer is D

Facts useful to the decision maker. Answers A and B are too wide-ranging and answer C is too specific.

Test your understanding 2

The correct answer is D

While information should not cost more to obtain than the benefit derived from it, this does not mean it will always be cheap to obtain.
The definition in (ii) is of data – not information.

Test your understanding 3

Statements (2) and (3) are correct.

Statement (1) is not correct: it refers to the 'volume' characteristic, not the 'variety'. 'Variety' refers to the diversity of data types and data sources.

BUSINESS AWARENESS

 Test your understanding 4

Both statements are true. Sources of Big Data (such as customers' conversations in social media about different products or services) can provide businesses with a better understanding of customer behaviour and customer expectations. In turn, this can help businesses to develop products and services which meet customers' needs more effectively.

Also, one of the current problems with Big Data is that there is a shortage of digital skills, for example skilled data analysts, in the labour market.

 Test your understanding 5

The correct answer is C

Veracity refers to the accuracy and truthfulness of the data. If this is missing, it can lead to inaccurate conclusions being drawn.

BUSINESS AWARENESS

Visualising information

15

Introduction

This chapter starts with the various principles and rules concerned with presenting information. It focuses on the advantages of charts and graphs as visual aids, and draws attention to the use of IT packages in presenting information to management. It then goes on to cover how management information is communicated and how confidential information should be handled.

ASSESSMENT CRITERIA

Visualising information (5.2)

Communicating information (5.3)

CONTENTS

1. Methods of communicating
2. Presentation of data
3. Tables
4. Using images to visualise information
5. Using technology in data visualisation
6. Communicating information

Visualising information: **Chapter 15**

1 Methods of communicating

1.1 Introduction

Accountants are used to dealing with figures, but they must also learn to express themselves clearly using words and possibly images. Accountants will be expected to use a wide range of communication methods that are suited to different audiences and different types of data.

1.2 The characteristics of professional communication

An accountant should communicate in a professional manner. There are a number of factors to consider in achieving professional communications:

Conciseness

The information presented should be concise, avoiding unnecessary length and detail. Recipients have a limited amount of time to take in communications and therefore they would prefer these to be as short as possible.

For communications which require a lot of detail (such as a report) the detailed statements and tables should form appendices to the main report rather than being included in the main body of the report. If such statements are numerous they should be clearly numbered in appendices for ease of reference. The main conclusions and recommendations, if any, should be summarised and highlighted separately in the report.

Structure

Longer communications should be broken down into logical sections with a heading for each section. These should be numbered for easy reference, particularly if the communication is quite lengthy.

Style

Short sentences expressed in simple, clear and professional language are preferable to long and elaborate sentences. The aim is to communicate quickly and unambiguously, not to entertain. Opinion must be clearly separated from facts. Slang terms should be avoided in order to keep the language professional.

Presentation

Information should be easy to follow and it should be clear who the communication is aimed at and what the objectives are. The communication should have a descriptive title. If the message does not cover some content or is not intended for some audiences this should be made clear at the beginning.

Visualising information

Modern software packages make it easy to create graphs, charts, diagrams and other images from numerical data. These can enhance the appearance of communications as well as improving clarity and impact. For example, a report discussing sales trends over the last few accounting periods could be illustrated by any or all of the following visual aids:

- a table
- a bar chart analysing sales by product category
- a line graph showing the ups and downs of sales levels over the period
- a pie chart analysing sales by geographical destination.

1.3 Methods of communication

A report

Reports may be prepared routinely, as a part of the regular reporting system within the company. These routine reports will contain standard information that is often produced at set times.

An ad hoc report is prepared only once or occasionally. It will not have a set content and the content will vary according to the requirements of the recipient. An ad hoc report may be prepared, for example, if a manager is making a one-off decision that requires more detail on a particular aspect of the business than is available from the routine reporting system.

A report is a good way to communicate in a business setting. The following guidelines for report writing should be observed:

(a) Reporting objectives

Reports will be created for specific objectives. The objective might be to explain some data, provide information or to resolve problems. If, for example, it is the last of these then the report should define the problem, explain and evaluate the alternative courses of action to resolve the problem and make a reasoned recommendation for a specific alternative.

(b) Recipient

The writer should consider the position of the recipient and design the report accordingly. Some recipients will require detailed calculations; others will have little time to study a lengthy report and should therefore be given one of minimum length with the required information.

Some recipients will have some accounting knowledge whereas others may have little. The report will therefore have to be adjusted accordingly. If a report is going to be read by more than one recipient then both elements will have to be accounted for. A common way to do this is to have more complex and detailed information in an appendix to the report whilst the main body of the report focuses on the key issues which are explained in less technical language.

If it is necessary to use technical terms, these should be fully explained, as should any techniques with which the recipient may be unfamiliar e.g. marginal costing, flexible budgets, etc.

(c) Heading

Each report should be headed to show who it is from and who it is being sent to, the subject and the date.

(d) Paragraph point system

Each paragraph should make a point; each point should have a paragraph. This simple rule should always be observed. Important points may be underlined.

These paragraphs are likely to focus on the interpretation and analysis of data rather than repeating the data itself. Key visualisations may help communicate the data in a way that is easily understood. Detailed data should be presented in an appendix.

(e) Conclusion

A report should always reach a conclusion. This should be clearly stated at the end of the report, and justified. It is not enough simply to state all the alternatives and then to recommend one of them without supportive reasoning.

(f) Figures and data

All detailed figures, data and calculations should be relegated to appendices, only the main results should appear in the body of the report. Remember that comparative figures will often be useful.

A note

There is no set format for a note. Notes typically are short and don't contain a lot of data. They are also unlikely to have many visualisations of data.

In most cases the information that you are reporting on will be important management information and therefore it is unlikely that a note would be the most appropriate format.

A letter

A more formal method of communicating information is in the form of a letter. A letter is most likely to be used when communicating with someone outside the organisation. It would be quite unusual to communicate with another person in the same organisation in this way, although a letter may be appropriate if the recipient works in a separate location.

A memorandum

Definition

A **memorandum** (or memo) is a written communication between two persons within an organisation. The plural of memorandum is memoranda.

A memorandum serves a similar purpose to a letter. However, the main difference is that letters are usually sent to persons outside the organisation, whereas memoranda or memos are for communication within the organisation itself. Memos can range from brief handwritten notes, to typed sets of instructions to a junior, to a more formal report to a superior. In general a memo can be used for any purpose where written communication is necessary within the organisation, provided this is according to the rules of the organisation.

If a memo is to be sent to a superior in the organisation, either showing information requested or making recommendations, then both the tone and the content might be slightly more formal.

If a manager is writing to junior personnel in the department the style may be more formal than if the manager were writing to another manager within the organisation.

Informal business report

An informal business report sits somewhere between a memorandum and a formal business report. It is likely to have more structure than a memorandum but use less formal language and tone than a formal business report. It may have an introduction, explanation of the circumstances, recommendations and conclusions. But, it would normally have less scene-setting information, use bullet points and lists, use personalised language and have few appendices.

These reports are often internal in nature and are used for areas such as reporting variances, making initial business proposals and exception reporting.

Visualising information: **Chapter 15**

Internally-produced information can be provided to managers:

- in as much or as little detail as management require
- relating to whatever items management need information about
- in whatever format is preferred (for example, there are no regulations about how management accounting statements should be formatted and presented)
- as frequently or infrequently as management require.

 Test your understanding 1

Which of the following is not true of internal reports?

A   They should be concise and avoid unnecessary information

B   They should include visual information that makes the report easier to understand

C   They should avoid complex terms that only those inside the business will understand

D   They should not be made available to people outside the organisation without prior approval

An email

Most organisations are now fully computerised and most individuals within an organisation can communicate with each other via electronic mail or email. In terms of the format, an email's content has no rules other than any organisational procedures that should be followed. Emails are a way to quickly communicate data and are flexible enough to take the form of a note, a letter or a memorandum; they can therefore be used as a replacement for any of these. However, emails bring extra risks in ensuring that they are sent to and read by the correct recipient.

BUSINESS AWARENESS

2 Presentation of data

2.1 Introduction

The two main methods of presenting data are in the form of a table or as an image/diagram.

The choice as to whether a table or an image is the most appropriate method to illustrate data will depend upon three main factors:

- the nature and complexity of the data itself
- the audience that the data is designed for
- the method of delivery of the data.

2.2 Nature of the data

An image or diagram is often most suitable if only a few specific points about a set of data are to be made. A diagram can make these points or relationships very clear. However if a large number of relationships or points are to be made by a set of data, then a table is more appropriate.

For example, if the breakdown of sales into the four products that an organisation produces is required then this might well be shown clearly in a diagram. However if the purpose of the data was to indicate the detailed makeup of the profit or loss on each of the four types of product then a table would probably be more useful.

2.3 Nature of the audience

When determining the method of presenting data it is important to consider exactly who the data is being prepared for. For example in some circumstances the data might be prepared for the board of a company or alternatively to inform the workforce of the company as a whole.

Some individuals might find images more easy to understand than tabulated data. However, the level of detail of data required at board level might be higher than that required to inform the workforce of the relevant information. Therefore, tables may be more relevant and useful at that level.

2.4 The method of delivery

The method of eventual delivery of the data will often affect the choice of the most appropriate form of presentation.

For example, if the data is to be presented in the form of a written report to management which the management team will have time to study and digest, then tabulated data might be most appropriate. However if the data is to be presented as part of an oral presentation then a diagram or image might be most useful in order to highlight the key points quickly and clearly.

Test your understanding 2

Which of the following would not be considered to be a visualisation of data?

A   Attachments
B   Charts
C   Graphs
D   Tables

3 Tables

3.1 Data tables

Very often raw data is in a form that is not easy to understand or form a clear opinion on. The purpose of writing any type of report is to present the necessary information clearly. Tabulation is a common method of achieving this aim of clarity.

In order to do this, the layout that is chosen for the table is important. A table typically consists of an ordered arrangement of rows and columns.

BUSINESS AWARENESS

💡 Example

	20X4	20X3	20X2
	£k	£k	£k
Revenue	1,803	1,085	923
Costs	1,032	618	479
Gross profit	771	467	444
Gross profit %	**42.8%**	**43.0%**	**48.1%**

Advantages

- Tables can cope with presenting large quantities of data together. When data is presented as a narrative it is often spread across various parts of a report and can distract from the key messages. A table will pull the information together into one location and can be as large as necessary.

- When designed properly, tables are easy to navigate and figures can be easily located. Column and row headings should allow report users to quickly navigate to the data that they need. For example, in the above table a user could quickly identify that Gross profit in 20X3 was $467,000.

- Comparisons can be made. On a row-by-row basis or column-by-column basis a manager can see changes in data in different categories. For example, in the table above a manager could easily compare sales over each year.

- Patterns can be highlighted. So a manager using the above table, for example, could easily see that revenue is increasing each year.

- Tables can provide exact and more accurate data than can be achieved with graphs and diagrams.

- Tables are widely used and readily understood.

Disadvantages

- Tables can contain too much data so that they become cumbersome and difficult to understand.

- Analysis and relationships often require separate work for the user of the table. For example, new calculations might be needed to compare sales growth rates over time.

Visualising information: Chapter 15

- The most significant data is often difficult to find in tables as all the data is presented – even data that may be less relevant to the user.
- Tables can be disconcerting for those report users who might prefer a more visual style of presentation and are less inclined to understand statistics and numbers.

Test your understanding 3

"Tables can explain why data has changed." Is this statement true or false?

A   True
B   False

3.2 Matrices

Tables can form the basis of a matrix representation of data. A matrix table will often replace raw data with colours, icons, pictures, or even the diagrams and charts that are explained in the next section of this chapter.

Example

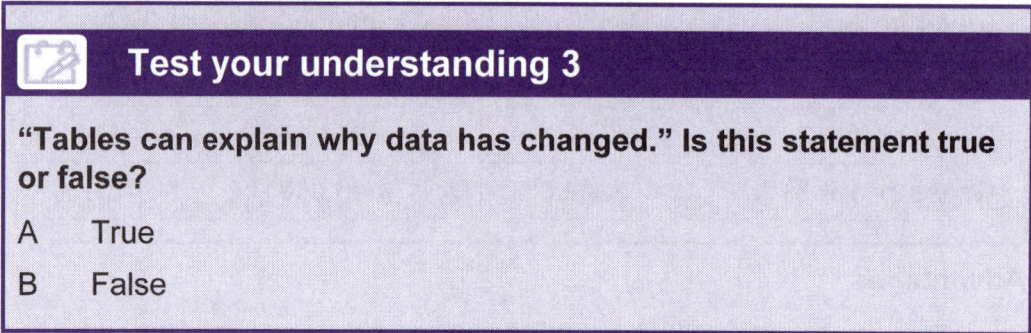

Average cash balance per quarter

	Division A	Division B	Division C
Quarter 1			
Quarter 2			
Quarter 3			
Quarter 4			

In the example above, colours are used to represent the average cash balance held at each division during each quarter of the year. A darker colour indicates that a higher amount of cash is held.

A user of this matrix can quickly see when cash balances are at their highest (quarter 2 has high balances in divisions A and B), when they are at their lowest (in quarter 4 only division C has a high cash balance and the balances at the other divisions are low), as well as examining the balance for each division on its own. This can prove useful in evaluating and adjusting the organisation's cash management strategies. It could, for example, decide that, during quarter 4, some cash should be transferred from division C to division A.

Advantages

- Matrices have the advantage of converting tables to a more visual mode of communication that can quickly highlight key issues for users.
- The most significant data will typically stand out in the matrix (the darkest and lightest colours in our example).

Disadvantages

- The detail is now lost. In the above example there is no way to see the actual cash balance held by each division during each quarter.
- A 'key' will be required before the matrix can be understood. Before anyone can understand the table presented in our example users would need to be told what the dark and light colours represent.

4 Using images to visualise information

Definition

Data visualisation allows large volumes of complex data to be displayed in a visually appealing and accessible way that facilitates the understanding and use of the underlying data.

Charts and graphs are popular ways of displaying data simply using images. Such visual representation of facts plays an important part in everyday life since these images can be seen daily in newspapers, advertisements and on television.

There are various methods of representing data diagrammatically. These include:

- bar charts – simple, component and multiple
- pie charts
- scatter graphs
- single and double line graphs
- area charts.

4.1 Bar and column charts

Bar and column charts are effectively the same idea, with the bars and columns representing data points and the height of the column or length of the bar representing a value. In bar charts, the width of the bar is always the same.

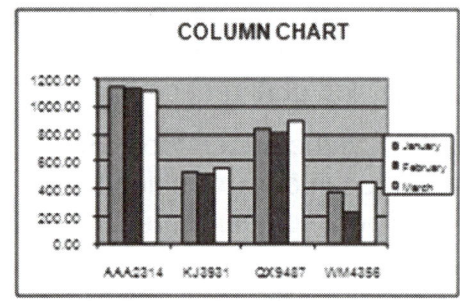 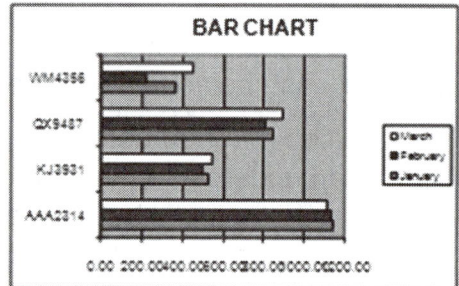

There are many variations of these types of charts such as:

- A single bar (or column) chart which represents one set of information (for example, total sales over the last five years)
- A stacked (or component) bar chart which stacks single data sets on top of each other in order to form an overall single bar.

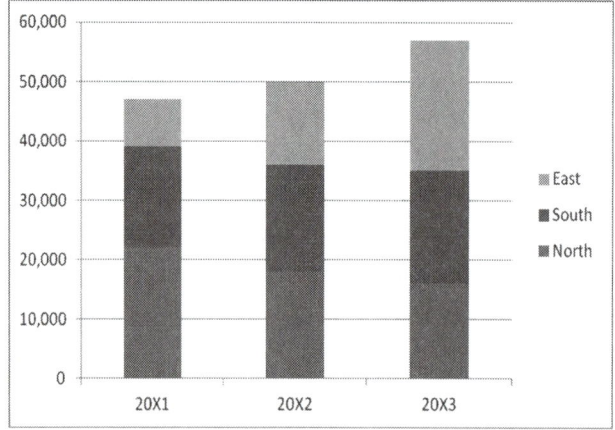

For example, the above column chart illustrates total sales over the last three years. It can be seen from the overall size of the column each year that the overall sales have been increasing. But each column is also shaded for each of the three different sales areas within this company (North, South and East). It can be seen, for example, that in the first year 'North' made up most of the sales column but by the third year 'East' made up most of the sales column. This type of chart has the advantage of the single bar chart in that the total increase in sales can be seen. But it has the added advantage of being able to see the relative proportion of sales made up by each division. However, it is very difficult to determine the absolute change in sales for each component (for example, it is very difficult to tell from the chart whether sales in 'South' have changed each year). If that information is wanted by users, then a compound bar or column chart may be of more use.

Note: the same information could also be presented in the form of a stacked bar chart with the data being represented by component horizontal bars rather than columns.

- A compound bar (or column) chart combines several sets of single bar charts into one overall chart. For example, it may be used to combine the bar charts for sales of individual divisions into one overall bar chart. The stacked column chart used in the previous illustration would be reconstructed as a compound column or bar chart as follows:

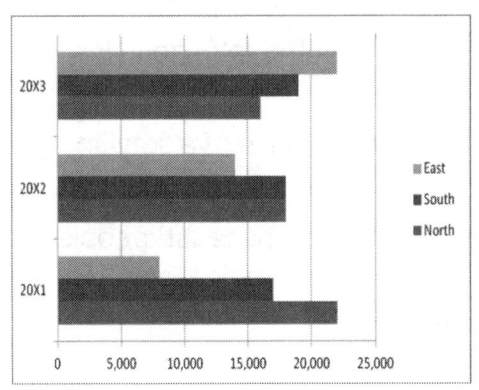
Bar chart

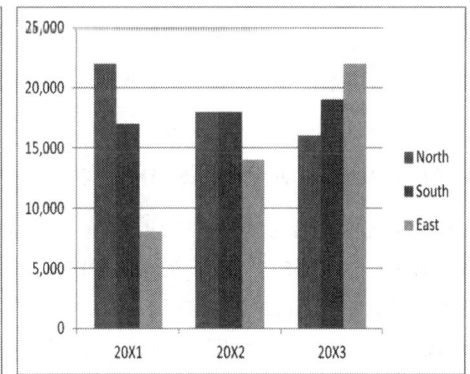
Column chart

In a compound chart we can still see which component makes up the largest share of sales but we can now also get a better illustration of the changes which are happening for each component (for example, we can now see that 'South' has made a gradual increase each year). But we now lose data on total sales. Another problem with compound charts is that they can become clustered and confusing if there are too many components to examine.

Advantages

- Bar and column charts can be used to represent more than two sets of data at once. For example, the axis may be, say total sales and years, whilst each bar or column could represent individual products sold.

- The information can be interpreted very quickly. From a glance at the chart, patterns can be determined and the relative height of each column or length of each bar can be observed.

- It is easy to see the relative importance of each product, say, simply by comparing the height of the column.

- They are widely used tools which are therefore easily understood and communicated.

- Totals can be broken down into components for better analysis. For example, each product's individual sales could be represented by its own individual column or bar.

Disadvantages

- It is difficult to portray accuracy or precision. Bars or columns which are far apart but of a similar height are difficult to compare.

- It can look confusing if too many columns or bars are used. For example, if a company sold 15 different types of products it may be difficult to have 15 columns for each year and to also observe changes for each product over a number of years.

- If totals are broken down into components then the total gets 'lost' and is difficult to determine.

- The chart will need additional information in the form of a 'key' in order to fully convey its message.

- Column charts are more common than bar charts because people are more accustomed to reading numbers on the vertical axis. The use of bar charts places numbers on the horizontal axis and the value of the numbers can become less obvious.

Suitability

Bar and column charts are best used when we want to compare more than one item over time and see their relative importance.

4.2 Pie charts

Pie charts represent proportions of a whole (for example: percentage of AAT students who are over 25) and do not have axes. A pie chart can only have one data series. These types of charts are most effective with a small number of data points – otherwise the chart becomes too busy and crowded.

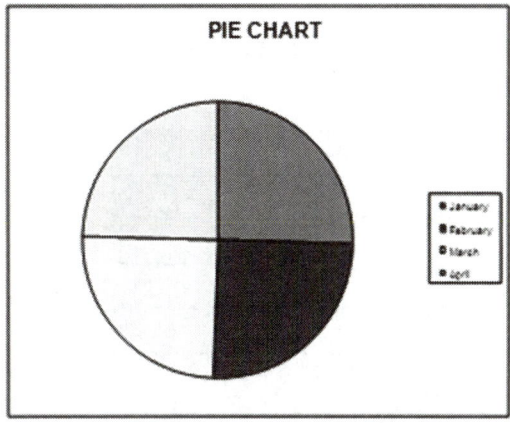

Advantages

- The relative size of each component can quickly be assessed.
- The size of the circle (or pie) can be used to represent the overall total if we are comparing data between a number of periods.
- They can represent lots of complicated data quickly and simply.
- Again, they are widely used and understood.

Disadvantages

- It is difficult to determine exact values.
- It can become complicated if more than one pie is represented with different sizes to represent overall total value.
- They may be too simple for some users who are concerned with the details.
- It can be difficult to make distinctions when values are close together.

Suitability

Pie and doughnut charts are best used when we want to show the relative proportions of multiple classes of data.

4.3 Scatter graph

This type of graph has two value axes and no category axis, and is typically used to show the relationship of two sets of numbers. In the example below the relationship is of sales volume to sales revenue. The data points (represented by diamonds) show the intersection of the two sets of numbers.

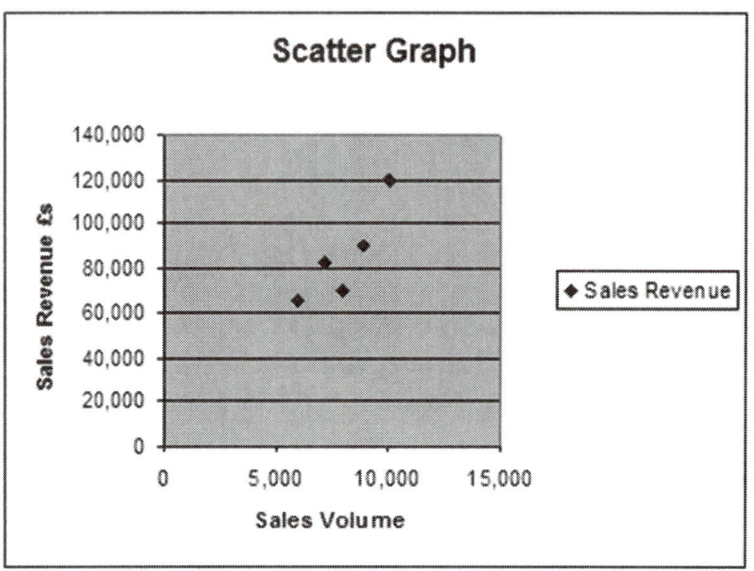

Advantages

- Scatter graphs can be used to quickly identify the 'direction' of the relationship between the two variables. In the example above it can easily be seen that as sales volume increases then sales revenue also, generally, increases.
- Scatter graphs can display a more varied series of data than line graphs. Data doesn't need to be at set intervals and can be both closer and further apart from each other.
- It may be the best way to illustrate a non-linear or random pattern/relationship between the variables.

Disadvantages

- Only two variables can be compared at one time.
- A user might find it difficult to interpret without further information.
- It can be difficult to assess data exactly or accurately.
- If there are only a few data points then the diagram can become misleading and less useful.
- If no relationship exists a flat line may occur which may have little value to a user.

BUSINESS AWARENESS

Suitability

Scatter graphs are a good way of illustrating the lack of a relationship between variables. If data is scattered around the graph it can illustrate that the variables are not related.

4.4 Single and double line graphs

Line graphs are used to plot continuous data and are very useful for showing trends. The more data series there are the more lines you can have on your graph.

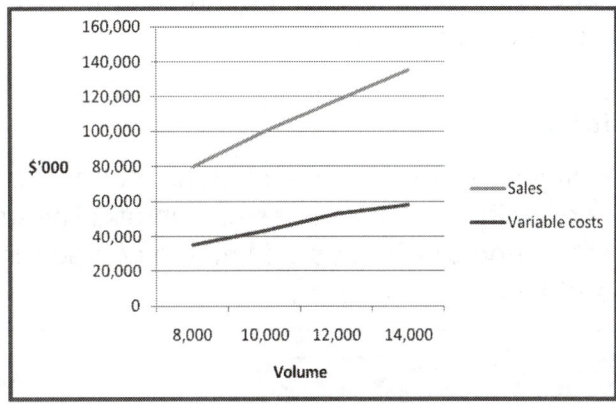

Advantages

- This helps to identify the 'correlation' between the data. The straighter the points are on a line then the stronger the relationship between the data. In the example above the sales line seems fairly straight, which therefore tells us that there is a strong, linear relationship between total sales and volume – as volume increases then total sales will also increase. With the variable cost line it appears to 'tail off' a little, and therefore the correlation between volume and variable costs is less linear.

- More than one set of data can be shown at a time, which can make comparisons easier.

- Line graphs can be used to identify trends. If, for example, there is some seasonality in sales over time, then when this is plotted on a line graph the peaks and troughs should become obvious.

Disadvantages

- It is difficult to use line graphs over very large ranges or where the 'gaps' between data observations are inconsistent. For example, in the above diagram the volume increased by a consistent 2,000 units at a time. The graph becomes less useful if this is not the case.

- When lines intersect or cross and lots of lines have been used the graph can become over-complicated and more difficult to interpret.

Suitability

Line graphs are best used for identifying trends and when there is a strong correlation between the data.

4.5 Area chart

An area chart displays a series as a set of points connected by a line, with the area filled in below the line. It is an extension of a line graph. It is used to show overall totals (the top line) as well as the components from different sources (the different shades).

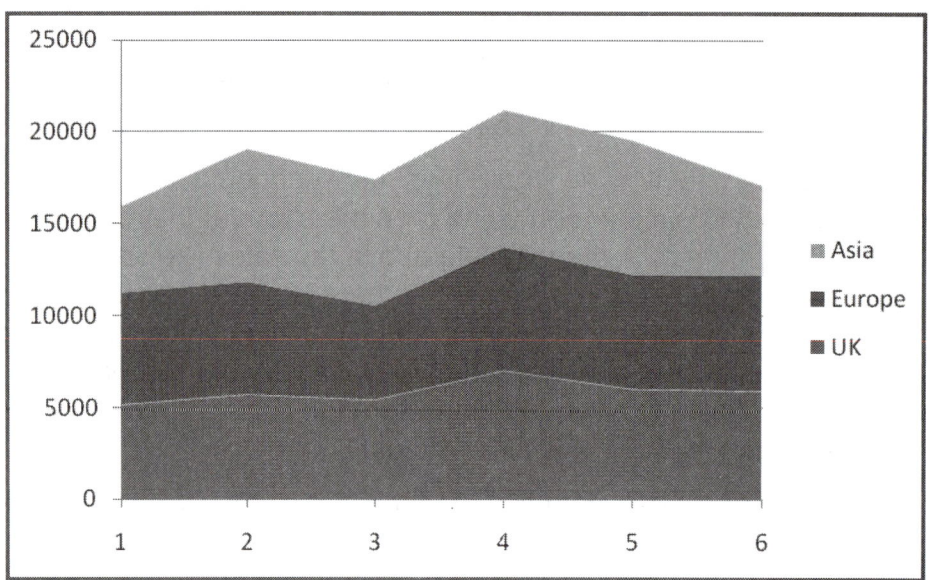

Advantages

- Both the overall total and the component elements can be illustrated.

- Trends in components and in the total can be easily identified.

- The graph illustrated uses an absolute scale to prepare the chart (i.e. the absolute total is used). A percentage scale can be used instead where the total must always come to 100% and this can be more useful in identifying the relative size of each component against another.

Disadvantages

- Only one overall total can be displayed.
- It can be difficult to assess the relative size of each component as the absolute data is difficult to determine. For example, would a user be able to judge the amount of European sales in quarter 3 just from looking at the graph? They would be able to identify that the sales have fallen but it would be very difficult to put a definite value on the size of the fall.
- It can become confusing if there are too many components.
- Small components can be difficult to assess and add little value to the chart.

Suitability

Area charts are best used to display over time how a set of data adds up to a whole (cumulated totals) and which part of the whole each element represents.

4.6 Multiple graph types in one chart

Also known as combination charts, these charts must consist of at least two data series. These charts combine two types of charts or graphs and represent them together.

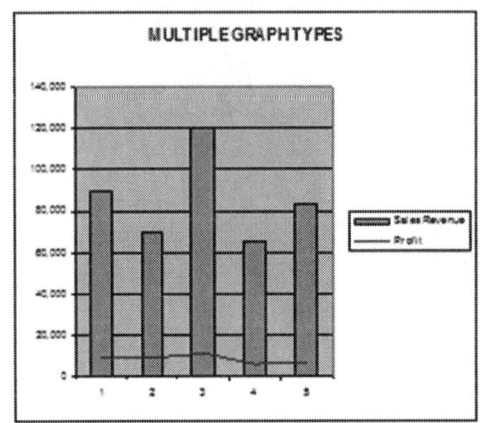 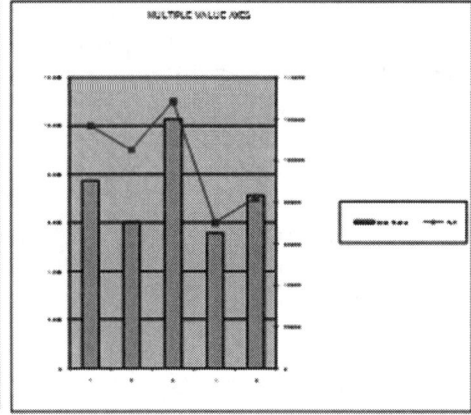

These are examples of a combination of a line graph and a bar chart. These charts combine the advantages of the two graph types used. But they can become more confusing for users and require further explanation.

Test your understanding 4

You have been asked to supply the quarterly sales figures for the last six years using a suitable pictorial representation. What might the appropriate form for such information take?

A Bar chart
B Pie chart
C Area chart
D Table

Test your understanding 5

The following diagram illustrates staff numbers in X Ltd for the period April to June:

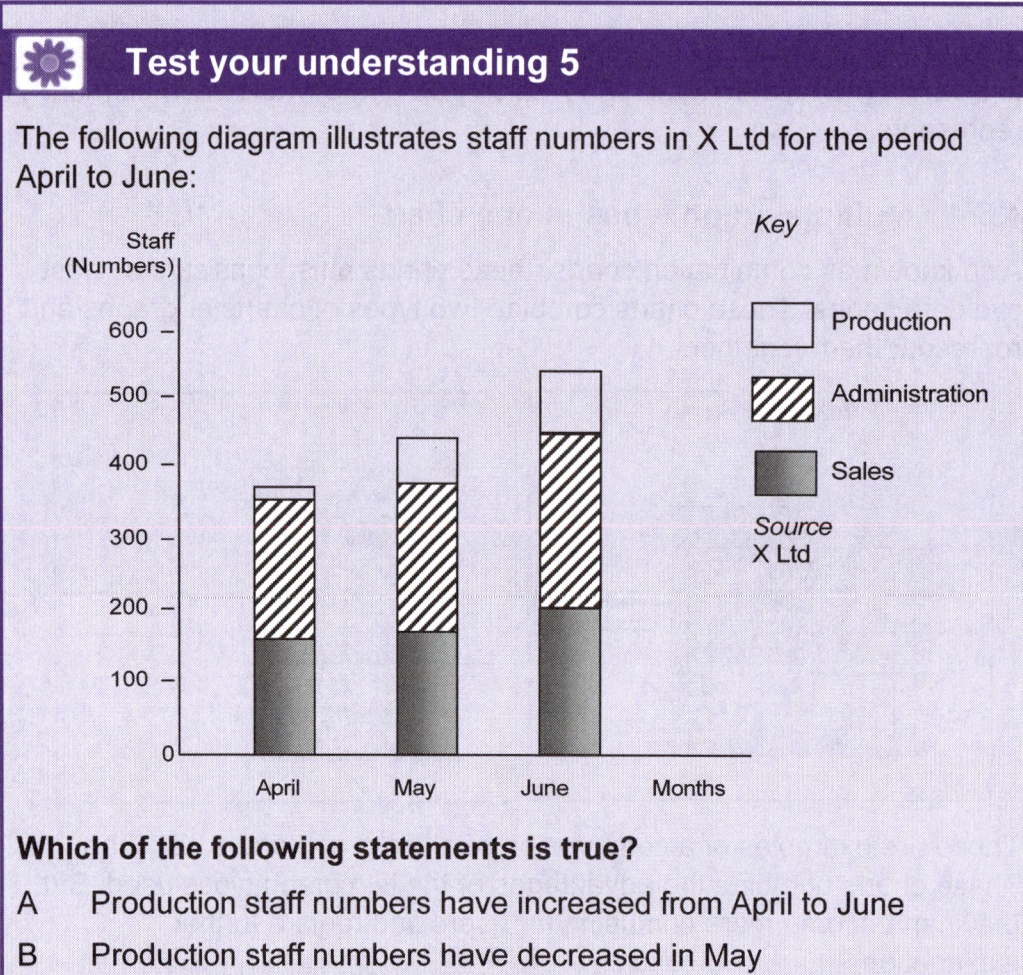

Which of the following statements is true?

A Production staff numbers have increased from April to June
B Production staff numbers have decreased in May
C Sales staff numbers have decreased in June
D Total staff numbers exceeded 500 throughout the period

BUSINESS AWARENESS

5 Using technology in data visualisation

The growing significance of data has seen a rise in the importance of being able to access and understand the data in a clear, concise way. This is where data visualisation fits in. The tools of today's market leaders (Tableau and Qlik,) go far beyond the simple charts and graphs of Microsoft Excel. Data is displayed in customisable, interactive 3D formats that allow uses to manipulate and drill down as required. Central to data visualisation is understanding and ease of use; the leading companies in the field look to make data easier and more accessible for everyone.

Data visualisation aims to remove the need for complex extraction, analysis and presentation of data by finance, IT and data scientists. It puts the ability to find data into the hands of the end user, through intuitive, user-friendly interfaces.

5.1 Dashboards

The most common use of data visualisation is in creating a dashboard to display the key performance indicators of a business in a live format, thus allowing immediate understanding of current performance and potentially prompting action to correct or amend performance accordingly.

> **Example**
>
> This is an example of a dashboard from Edited, a retail data analytics technology company. It demonstrates a summary of the stock movements, replenishment rates and price discounting across a range of retailers in the same sector of the market. The visualised data summarises a vast amount of data into a visually appealing and useful infographic that highlights the key information needed by users.

	Sellout	Replenished	Currently discounted	Avg. Discount
Debenhams	22.4%	19.1%	63.4%	46.3%
House of Fraser	8.7%	17.8%	44.2%	41.5%
John Lewis	42.1%	22.6%	28.1%	32.1%
Marks & Spencer	18.2%	9.0%	52.2%	50.1%

KAPLAN PUBLISHING

Visualising information: **Chapter 15**

The ability to receive real-time information about critical areas and feed this back to staff allowing them to understand current performance and respond accordingly can be the difference between success and failure.

The collection and analysis of the data is underpinned by the ideas of Big Data. However, bringing this data to life in an easy-to-understand and intuitive fashion is the purpose of **data visualisation**.

Organisations are increasingly using dashboards (a collection of key infographics displayed together) to display key performance indicators to staff in real time and to flag areas requiring improvement in order to hit predetermined targets and drive success. This instant feedback allows for action to be taken quickly to highlight and fix potential problems.

 Example

For instance, an IT service desk within a business will use key performance indicator dashboards to monitor and display performance for all staff and the department as a whole.

Metrics such as the number of support tickets logged, time taken to open support tickets, time taken to resolve support tickets and customer satisfaction would all be displayed clearly using graphics. If performance in any of the areas is falling below target levels the graphics will clearly display this, prompting action to resolve the poor performance.

5.2 Features and key benefits

An effective IT data visualisation tool should display these five **features**:

- Decision-making ability – Results focused, it should aid decision-making

- Effective infrastructure – The output is reliant upon sufficient quantity and quality of data

- Integration capability – With existing systems and the business overall

- Prompt discovery of rules and insights – Live data is vital and delay can render any insight useless

- Real-time collaboration – Users must interact with each other and the data

This area of technology is of particular significance to the finance function of an organisation. The provision of information to help support the efficient and effective running of all functions within a business and the business overall is the fundamental purpose of the finance function.

BUSINESS AWARENESS

Big data and data analytics are now mainstream in business. This growth in data and the need to communicate the information and insights to be found within the data makes data visualisation critically important to the finance function. The ability to make data relevant, accessible and easy for all end users is vital.

Key benefits of IT data visualisation tools

- Accessible – traditional spreadsheets and financial reports can be both difficult to understand and unappealing to look at. Modern data visualisation graphics and dashboards are designed to be user friendly and intuitive

- Real time – synchronising real-time data with data visualisation tools gives live up-to-date numbers in a clear, informative style. This allows quicker response to business changes rather than waiting for weekly or monthly reports

- Performance optimisation – the immediacy and clarity of the information being displayed supports better decision making and proactive, efficient utilisation of resources as problems are identified promptly

- Insight and understanding – combining data and visualising it in a new way can lead to improved understanding and fresh insights about the cause and effect relationships that underpin the data.

Test your understanding 6

Which TWO of the following are characteristics of effective data visualisation?

A   Use of jargon
B   Intuitive visuals
C   Audience specific
D   Extensive training used at the same time
E   High level only
F   Paper format only

5.3 Layering data

Another advantage of using IT in data visualisation is that it allows for data to be layered. Dashboards are increasingly being used as a way of allowing users to determine the volume and detail of data that they require.

Layering of data allows users to obtain more detail if they require it simply by selecting an existing piece of data and moving to a layer above or below that (which may even be presented in a different way). Layers above typically have less data, whilst layers below contain more data.

> **Example: Data layering**
>
> The visualisation below is an extract from an accounts receivable report; this simple pie chart gives the user an indication of the ageing of the receivables balances in a clear and concise way. The heavy detail of multiple pages of individual credit customers along with the breakdown of their balances is not needed by most users and this infographic directs users to the key headline information.
>
> Here the figures of AR turnover and the AR turnover ratio are displayed clearly at the top and can be easily compared against budget to get an indication of performance.
>
> A visualisation like this would typically allow users to drilldown into the detail behind the numbers; for instance, by selecting the 90+ days segment of the pie chart, the user would access the customers and balances that make up this figure and further questions could then be asked about these. This is the purpose of layering data and making visualisations intuitive and simple to navigate.
>
>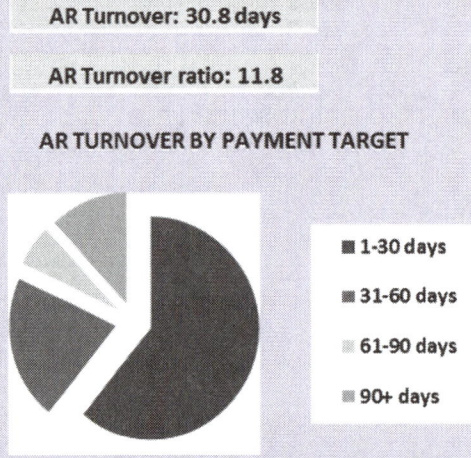

BUSINESS AWARENESS

Matrices are commonly used in IT dashboards as a layer of data (often the top layer). In the earlier example of a table matrix that showed the average cash balance for divisions, this might be the top layer of data in an IT dashboard. A user might then be able to select a particular quarter for an individual division and it would open up a new layer of data. This new layer could convert the table into a more traditional table with the numbers for average cash balances per quarter. There could be further layers underneath this. For example, users could select a number (for example, the average cash balance in quarter 3 for division B) and this would open up a further layer where the highest and lowest cash balances could then be presented.

The more data that is available and required by users, the more layers that the IT dashboard can provide.

5.4 Data outliers

As with any data analysis, care must be taken when interpreting data provided by IT dashboards. One area which needs particular attention is the impact of data outliers on the information provided by a dashboard.

Definition

An **outlier** is an observation that lies an abnormal distance from other values in the data.

This definition leaves it up to the analyst to decide what will be considered abnormal. Therefore in an IT system it may be necessary to determine what are the normal values for data so that outliers can be determined and accounted for.

Example: Data outliers

Data outliers are pieces of data that do not appear to fit into the pattern of normal results.

For example, consider the following data for website visitors over the six months (in thousands):

	Apr	May	Jun	July	Aug	Sep
Visitors	150	140	65	145	150	140

It can be seen that most months are within five thousand visitors of 145,000. But June does not appear to follow this pattern. It is well below the normal results. June's result is an outlier.

Note: outliers are often more easily spotted through the use of data graphs. For example, if the data above was represented as a scatter graph then the June results would very quickly stand out.

If data outliers are included in data the results are skewed towards the outlier. In our example, if June's result is ignored completely and we calculate the average number of monthly visitors to the website we get an average of 145, which would give a very fair representation of the data.

But when June's result is included in the average the average falls to 131.7 giving a very different impression of the overall data. Analysis and interpretation of the data would likewise be very different.

This is not to say that outliers should be ignored completely. The outliers themselves could contain valuable data. In our example, June's result could indicate some seasonality, the impact of negative press reports in the month of June, a website failure in June etc. For that reason data outliers are often investigated separately from data that more readily fits into overall patterns.

Data outliers are more common in Big Data – due to its obvious size and variability. One way of coping with data outliers in Big Data is to use a trimming approach. For example, if we wanted to examine the average time taken per page on visits to a particular page on our website we might 'trim' the data by ignoring the longest and shortest 5% of visitors. This would exclude people who have clicked on the page but left it open long after they have finished reading it as well as excluding people who clicked on the page by accident. The remaining 90% of data would be used in the website analytics to give a more useful piece of information.

BUSINESS AWARENESS

6 Communicating information

6.1 Introduction

There are a number of factors that should be considered when communicating information and data, including

- the house style required,
- the need for confidentiality,
- and the format of the communication to be used.

6.2 House style

Although the basic requirements of each method of reporting will be covered in this chapter it is important to realise that each organisation will have its own style and methods of reporting. These will normally be contained in the organisation's policy manual and house styles should always be followed.

6.3 Confidentiality

It is extremely important that the information that has been requested is sent to the appropriate person and only that person and any others that you are specifically asked to send it to. Often the information is confidential and therefore should be treated with the highest respect and care.

You should ensure that confidential information is viewed by the recipient only, bearing in mind the fact that a manager's secretary or assistant might deal with their incoming mail. If information is extremely confidential it should be marked as such or delivered in person, and each copy of the information should be uniquely numbered. If in doubt, do not pass on confidential information until you have been told specifically to do so by your manager.

6.4 The appropriate format

A number of factors need to be taken into account when deciding on the appropriate format for communicating management information. Some of the factors conflict with each other and it is up to the person who prepared the information to weigh up the various considerations to select the most appropriate communication medium.

The factors to be considered include the following:

Speed and timing

A short memorandum can be prepared and read more quickly than a lengthy written report. Information to be discussed at a meeting must be communicated to the relevant people in time for them to read and understand it. Urgent information can be sent almost instantaneously by email.

The need for a written record

Written information is less open to misinterpretation and a hard copy is available for filing in case queries should arise at a later date.

Confidentiality

The choice of communication medium is extremely important when you are dealing with confidential information. For example with a fax there is the possibility that an unauthorised person may see the message and a telephone conversation could be overheard. Email can also cause problems with confidentiality, for example if the recipient has left their computer unattended.

Cost

Email is a very cheap and rapid communication medium but it may not be suitable for sending confidential information. Fax or post might be cheaper but could cause delays. Sending information by courier is more appropriate for confidential information but it can be expensive. Obviously the cost aspect must be weighed up in the light of all the other factors.

Distance

Email systems, for example, communicate information rapidly and cheaply over large distances whereas post and couriers are slower but provide a more secure service for confidential information.

Complexity

More complex information may be communicated more effectively through a written medium rather than, for example, through a telephone conversation. On the other hand, in a face to face or telephone conversation it is possible for the recipient to ask questions and thus for some interaction to take place.

BUSINESS AWARENESS

 Test your understanding 7

Which of the following methods of communication is likely to be most appropriate for complaining to the organisation's cleaning contractor about the standard of cleanliness in the sales offices?

A Memo
B Telephone
C Letter
D Courier

 Test your understanding 8

Which of the following would not be considered when considering how to distribute a report?

A The cost of preparing the report
B The preparer of the report
C The distance between the preparer and the recipient
D The need for confidentiality

7 Summary

Management require good information to enable them to make decisions, to plan and to control the organisation. Information may be easier to use and more relevant if it is presented in a suitable format, such as a **table or a graph**.

When making a decision on the most appropriate method to use we should consider the nature of data to be presented, the nature of our audience and the method of delivery chosen.

There are many ways in which data can be visualised in order to make it more easy to understand. These include:

- Tables – the systematic arrangement of numerical data to provide a logical account of the results of analysis.

- Simple bar chart – a chart in which each bar represents the variable under consideration.

- Component bar chart – a chart in which each bar is made up of several component parts, which form a logical whole.
- Multiple bar chart – a chart in which two or more related items are to be compared. The bars are placed next to each other and each represents a different item.
- Pie chart – this is useful for easily illustrating data proportions (which are represented as a share of a pie).
- Scatter graph – these are useful for illustrating non-linear relationships.
- Line graphs – these are useful for illustrating linear relationships between two sets of data.
- Area chart – overall and component elements of data are represented by both lines and areas on a chart.
- Matrices – these are a combination of a table and a diagram but require careful explanation before they can be used effectively.

Accounting software packages use dashboards to communicate data to non-technical stakeholders. Layers can be added to the data so that users can determine the amount of data they want to consider.

When communicating data we should consider any relevant house styles and the need for confidentiality, and ensure that we choose the most appropriate format for both the data and the user.

Test your understanding answers

Test your understanding 1

The correct answer is C

The use of complex terms in internal reports is acceptable if they are understood by the recipient. The fact that the recipient is inside the organisation means that they are more likely to understand these complex terms.

The other options are all true for internal reports.

Test your understanding 2

The correct answers is A

Attachments are sent alongside reports or other data and typically contain additional data. This additional data will not necessarily be visualised and may remain in text format.

Test your understanding 3

The correct answer is B

This statement is false. It may be possible to identify that there is a trend or a pattern in the data using a table, but the cause of such changes would still require further analysis and investigation.

Test your understanding 4

The correct answer is A

A bar chart shows not only the actual amount of the data but also the relationship between the various items of data, for example the sales in each year. When using bar charts it is easy to compare the amount of sales achieved each year. A table is not a picture.

Test your understanding 5

The correct answer is A

The area covered by production numbers has increased month to month, as has the sales staff numbers. Total staff numbers did not exceed 500 until June.

Test your understanding 6

The correct answers are B and C

The other options are areas that good visualisation should avoid.

Test your understanding 7

The correct answer is C

A letter provides written evidence of the complaint and is less open to misinterpretation or being overlooked than a verbal conversation on the telephone. A memo is not formal enough for a complaint and a courier would probably be unnecessarily expensive.

Test your understanding 8

The correct answer is B

The nature of the person who prepared the report would not normally be considered when deciding how the report should be distributed.

MOCK ASSESSMENT

BUSINESS AWARENESS

1 Mock Assessment Questions

TASK 1 (20 marks)

This task is about organisations and ethics for accountants.

(a) Identify whether the following statements are true or false.

Statement	True	False
A limited liability company operates as a separate legal entity from its owners		
A sole trader business operates as a separate legal entity from its owners		

(2 marks)

(b) (i) Identify which ONE of the following structures is suited to an organisation in which employees are divided by specialisation.

Statement	✓
Functional	
Divisional	
Matrix	

(1 mark)

(ii) Identify which type of control is described by each of the following statements.

Statement	Centralised control	Decentralised control	Wide span control	Narrow span control
The managerial structure has many levels of management				
Decision making and control is delegated to managers at lower levels in the organisation				
The organisation has less flexibility but a higher level of control				

(3 marks)

Mock Assessment Questions

NW is a utilities provider for residential and business properties operating in the North West of country J. The business was nationalised in the past (state owned) but has more recently become a privatised company. NW has recently won the tender for the North West region, meaning they have a regional, government imposed monopoly for the next few years. The government still regulates the industry and makes decisions on who provides the utilities for each area, but doesn't get involved in the day to day running of the business.

NW pays its shareholders a dividend payment based on a well-publicised dividend policy. NW has surplus funds to invest and there are two options available:

1   To expand into new regional areas in country J by winning more government tenders.

2   To provide utilities in a foreign country.

NW's major shareholder has stated that they are keeping a close eye on the organisation, as profits and dividends have not been as high as expected in recent years.

None of NW's customers account for more than 2% of their revenue, and they don't have an option of who to use as their provider due to a regional monopoly.

Some of NW's employees are concerned about possible redundancies at the company due to new technologies providing many efficiencies in NW's processes. However, they are not unionised and it looks unlikely that they will be able to act collectively against NW.

(c) (i)   Identify which ONE of the following stakeholders is most likely to have a high interest but little power/influence on the decision about which option to invest in.

Stakeholder	✓
NW's major shareholder	
One of NW's customers	
Government of country J	
NW's employees	

(1 mark)

BUSINESS AWARENESS

(ii) Identify which ONE of the following stakeholders is most likely to have a high level of interest and high power/influence on the decision about which option to invest in.

Stakeholder	✓
NW's major shareholder	
One of NW's customers	
Government of country J	
NW's employees	

(1 mark)

(iii) Identify which ONE of the following is the system by which companies are directed and controlled:

System	✓
Corporate governance	
Corporate acceptance	
Corporate compliance	
Corporate refinance	

(1 mark)

(iv) Complete the following statement about a company's structure by selecting ONE option.

In a _____ structure, the upper levels of an organisation's hierarchy retain the authority and make decisions.

Options	✓
Centralised	
Decentralised	
Geographically spread out	
Compliant	

(1 mark)

ABC Co is a well-established firm of accountants with a single office in the city of Standley. ABC Co employs fully qualified professional accountants, part-qualified student accountants and administrative staff.

Mock Assessment Questions

You are Chris, one of the three part-qualified student accountants at ABC Co. You report to Ian, one of the fully qualified professional accountants.

Recently Eliza Brown, one of the fully qualified professional accountants in ABC Co, has been off sick for a week. Your line manager Ian asked you to go through the mail folder on Eliza's desk to see if there was anything that needed to be dealt with urgently. You found the following note:

> **Note from:** Mick Gurdy, Straithard Ltd
>
> **Addressed to:** Eliza Brown, ABC Co. Eliza
>
> I'm pretty disappointed that you haven't answered my emails or texts. I thought I had made it clear to you that I'll let you have that £500 you need for your holiday but only if you go ahead and include on the company's tax return the revenue figure that I gave you. I don't care that it's much less than the figure from the accounts. You know that if you don't do as I say by the end of the month I'm going to tell your firm about the other ways in which you have helped me manipulate our figures in the past. This is your last chance.
>
> Mick

(d) (i) **Identify how Chris' principles are threatened, by completing the following statement:**

This is…..	Gap 1	…..threat to…..	Gap 2

Gap 1 options	✓	Gap 2 options	✓
An advocacy		integrity	
A self-review		confidentiality	
An intimidation		Professional competence and due care	

(2 marks)

Jamie, a member in practice, has been asked to assist a client with interviewing potential new recruits for the finance department. Jamie has since discovered that a close personal friend has applied for the role.

BUSINESS AWARENESS

(ii) Identify which ONE of the fundamental principles needs to be safeguarded in this situation.

Fundamental principle	✓
Integrity	
Objectivity	
Professional competence and due care	
Professional behaviour	

(1 mark)

(iii) Identify which TWO of the following are advantages of a principles-based approach to ethics over a rules-based approach to ethics.

Advantage	✓
Applicable to all situations	
Less chance of people finding loopholes	
Reduced misunderstandings or misinterpretation	
Easy enforcement	

(2 marks)

(e) (i) For each statement below, explain why each of the following actions appears to be in conflict with fundamental ethical principles.

Statement	A likely loss of objectivity	This is an issue of integrity	Potential conflict with professional behaviour
An advertisement for a firm of accountants states that their audit services are cheaper and more comprehensive than a rival firm.			
An accountant prepares a set of accounts prior to undertaking the audit of those accounts.			
A financial accountant confirms that a report on their company is correct, even though the report omits to mention some important liabilities.			

(3 marks)

Mock Assessment Questions

(ii) Professional accountants are required to undertake continuing professional development (CPD). Which ONE of the five fundamental principles is safeguarded by CPD?

Fundamental principle	✓
Integrity	
Objectivity	
Professional competence and due care	
Confidentiality	
Professional behaviour	

(2 marks)

TASK 2 (18 marks)

This task is about analysing the external environment.

Andante Rail (AR) is a company that runs train services between a few holiday destinations in the UK and France via the Channel Tunnel. The UK's government has recently announced additional expenditure on motorways and roads, as well as new health and safety regulations for all rail operators in the country. Additional one-off taxes on rail operators are being proposed in the UK to help pay for road upgrades. This is in addition to a marked rise in the cost of repairs to trains due to a shortage of skilled labour in the country.

However, surveys show that residents of the UK are becoming more environmentally conscious and concerned about congestion on the roads.

Although new internet systems are available that simplify the process of booking train tickets, at AR phone bookings are still the norm and new systems are yet to be introduced to help improve the efficiency of train arrivals and departures.

(a) (i) For each of the three specified PESTLE categories (Economic, Political, Technological), identify ONE threat facing AR. (3 marks)

BUSINESS AWARENESS

(ii) Explain ONE action that AR could take to reduce threats under each category. **(6 marks)**

	Threat	Action to reduce threat
Economic	....	....
Political	....	....
Technological	....	....

(iii) Identify ONE of the remaining PESTLE categories.

....

(1 mark)

Mock Assessment Questions

(b) **Identify which FOUR of the statements below are true about blockchain.**

Statement	✓
Blockchain is regarded as a solution to cyber security risk	
Records in the blockchain are publicly available	
Records in the blockchain are distributed across everyone that is part of the network of participants	
Records in the blockchain are always kept private to enhance security	
The verification of transactions is carried out by computers	
The verification of transactions is carried out by individuals	

(4 marks)

(c) (i) **Identify whether each of the following statements about the duties of directors is TRUE or FALSE.**

Statement	True ✓	False ✓
Directors have a legal obligation to act in the best interests of the company by promoting its success for the benefit of its shareholders.		
A director must avoid any situation which places them in direct conflict with the interests of the company or the performance of any other duty.		

(2 marks)

BUSINESS AWARENESS

(ii) Complete each of the following definitions about unlimited liability partnerships by selecting ONE option:

| An unlimited liability partnership can be defined as: | Gap 1 | In an unlimited liability partnership, the partners' liability is referred to as | Gap 2 |

Gap 1 options	✓	Gap 2 options	✓
A separate legal entity, in which each partner has full personal liability for the partnership debts.		'legal and regulatory'	
Not a separate legal entity, in which each partner has full personal liability for the partnership debts.		'common and indivisible'	
A separate legal entity, in which each partner has partial personal liability for the partnership debts.		'joint and indivisible'	
Not a separate legal entity, in which each partner has partial personal liability for the partnership debts.		'joint and several'	

(2 marks)

Mock Assessment Questions

TASK 3 (17 marks)

This task is about technology, cyber risk and data security.

(a) (i) **Identify which TWO of the following are key features of cloud accounting.**

Feature	✓
Software updates delivered faster and more easily by cloud provider	
Users' ability to connect not dependent on internet connection	
Cloud accounting suppliers not required to adhere to data protection regulations	
Access levels can be controlled	

(2 marks)

(ii) **Identify which ONE of the following is a disadvantage of cloud accounting.**

Disadvantage	✓
Software updates delivery by cloud provider takes longer	
It may become difficult to switch providers/systems	
Access to real-time financial performance is more difficult	
Access to large networks takes longer	

(1 mark)

(b) **Complete each of the following statements about the automation of processes by selecting ONE option.**

_____ GAP 1 _____ tasks (for example, associated with the financial close and regulatory reporting and account reconciliation) are most likely to be automated, but developments in technology are allowing more complex tasks to be automated also.

An organisation considering investing in process automation technology within the finance function would benefit from _____ GAP 2 _____.

BUSINESS AWARENESS

Gap 1 options	✓
One-off	
Repetitive	
Common	
Accounting	
Gap 2 options	✓
Improved accuracy	
Fewer training requirements	
Smoother relationship management processes	
Increased job certainty	

(2 marks)

(c) **Identify which TWO of the following are benefits to business operations offered by the electronic filing of documents.**

Statement	✓
Reliable backup assistance and disaster recovery methods	
Increased data security	
Low initial setup costs	
Increased workplace productivity	

(2 marks)

(d) **Identify the ONE risk below that is NOT a risk to computer systems and the data they contain:**

Risk	✓
Physical damage	
Operational problems	
Data theft	
Financing issues	

(1 mark)

Mock Assessment Questions

(e) **Identify which TWO of the following are principles of data protection.**

Principle	✓
Personal data shall be updated on a minimum of an annual basis	
Personal data held for any purpose shall be held for a minimum of 12 weeks and it shall not be held for more than six years	
Data must be used in a way that is adequate, relevant and limited to only what is necessary	
Data must be accurate and, where required, kept up-to-date	

(2 marks)

(f) **Complete the following statement about data breach by selecting ONE option.**

A data breach must be reported to the relevant supervisory authority within _____ of becoming aware of the breach, where feasible.

Options	✓
24 hours	
72 hours	
1 month	
18 weeks	

(1 mark)

BUSINESS AWARENESS

(g) Identify which quality of a service is described in each of the following statements.

Statement	Intangibility	Simultaneity	Heterogeneity	Perishability
The fact that there is no physical product means that it is difficult to define the 'service' and attribute costs. For example, in the NHS, it is challenging to define what a 'procedure' is.				
Customers often must be present during the production of a service, and cannot take the service home. No service exists until it is actually being experienced/consumed by the person who has brought it.				
Quality and consistency may be inconsistent, because of an absence of standards to assess services against. In the NHS for example, there is no indication of what an excellent performance in service delivery would be.				
The unused service capacity from one time period cannot be stored for future use. Service providers' marketers cannot handle supply-demand problems through production scheduling and inventory techniques.				

(4 marks)

Mock Assessment Questions

Farmer Ltd is purchasing a new combine-harvester for £300,000 and is considering how to fund the purchase.

(h) **Identify the funding source that each of the following characteristics relates to.**

Characteristic	Working capital	1-year loan	Equity finance
We can rely on the excess of current assets over current liabilities to repay the funding every month			
Suitable for long-term funding requirements			

(2 marks)

TASK 4 (8 marks)

This task is about ethical and legal compliance.

B works in a small accountancy practice, as a fully qualified professional accountant.

For years, B has dealt with two competing technology companies, Unwin Ltd and Idris Ltd. The two companies have existing premises in Standley Science Park, where a new building has just been completed.

Idris Ltd and Unwin Ltd are both putting in a bid to lease the whole of the new building. They each asked B to act for them in relation to the bid. When the companies realised they were both interested in leasing the same building, Idris Ltd offered B an extra £3,000 to act for it exclusively; Unwin Ltd also offered B an additional £3,000 for exclusive representation.

Neither company is willing for B to act for both parties with respect to the lease.

(a) **Explain which TWO of B's fundamental principles are threatened by the fact that both Idris Ltd and Unwin Ltd are bidding for the lease on the same building in Standley Science Park.** (4 marks)

BUSINESS AWARENESS

(b) Describe the ethical conflict resolution process that B should undertake in deciding how to act in respect of this matter. Assume that they will be able to resolve the conflict of interest without external professional advice. **(4 marks)**

....
....
....
....
....
....
....
....
....

TASK 5 (9 marks)

This task is about the microeconomic environment and sustainability.

(a) (i) Identify which TWO of the following events will cause a shift in the demand curve of a normal good.

Event	✓
A change in the quantity supplied	
A change in the price of substitutes	
A change in consumer tastes and preferences	
A change in raw material costs	

(2 marks)

BVO is a small business, which manufactures and sells a number of products, including product X (a relatively low-value item). BVO has recently been considering its pricing policy for this product.

It has estimated that if it raises the current selling price (per unit) of product X from $1 to $1.50, annual demand will drop from 100,000 units to 90,000 units.

Mock Assessment Questions

(ii) Which ONE of the following options from the above information is NOT correct?

Option	✓
Product X may be a product that customers buy out of habit	
Product X may have few, if any, substitutes	
Product X may see a sharper fall in demand if the price rise lasts for a long period	
Product X would be more profitable if the price was cut rather than raised	

(1 mark)

(iii) A demand curve is drawn assuming all but one of the following remains unchanged. Which ONE item can vary?

Item	✓
Consumer tastes	
The price of the product	
The price of other products	
Disposable income	

(1 mark)

(b) (i) Organisations should use resources in such a way that they do not compromise the needs of future generations.

What is this a definition of?

Definition	✓
Environmentalism	
Sustainability	
Future-focus	
Redesign	

(1 mark)

BUSINESS AWARENESS

(ii) Identify ONE type of sustainability that each of the following organisational policies relates to:

Organisational policy	Social sustainability	Environ-mental sustainability	Financial sustainability
Jossara assembles clothes out of discarded fabrics manufacturers usually leave behind on sewing tables. Jossara only creates limited edition pieces, minimises the usage of fabric and advocates minimalism to support the overall image of their brand.			
Arundhati employs apple pickers and has recently decided to focus on a programme of affordable housing and workforce development for their staff. In collaboration with local engineers and orchard owners, they have drawn up blueprints for three different housing plans, as well as a partnership with the local community college and mentorships with cider professionals.			
El Mansour Ltd have clearly defined strategic plans and all new projects must be capable of achieving a minimum level of profit within two years, to be accepted.			

(3 marks)

Mock Assessment Questions

An organisation includes the following amongst its stakeholders:

(1) Customers

(2) Trade unions

(iii) Identify which of the stakeholders can be classified as 'connected' stakeholders. Select ONE option.

Stakeholders	✓
(1) only	
(2) only	
(1) and (2)	

(1 mark)

TASK 6 (13 marks)

This task is about communication and visualisation.

Today's date is 4 April 20X6. You work for Sharpkit, a business which sells a range of kitchen knives to consumers.

- Sharpkit is a partnership owned by Aya and Olivia Khan. Sharpkit has a year end of 31 March each year.

- Sharpkit produces and sells six products in total. Its newest product, the Fidle, was introduced two years ago and is proving popular with customers.

- Sharpkit produces its products at its purpose-built factory. Production uses a combination of skilled labour and high technology machinery.

- Sharpkit uses a range of suppliers for material in the production of its products.

- Sharpkit sells its products directly to consumers through its website. All sales are paid for immediately.

- Many consumers will purchase more than one product in each order whilst some consumers will return at a later date and purchase additional products from Sharpkit's range.

- Part of Sharpkit's factory is dedicated to storage of inventory of finished goods so that orders can be delivered to customers within 24 hours of a customer placing an order on Sharpkit's website.

BUSINESS AWARENESS

Production and inventory data for the year ended 31 March 20X6

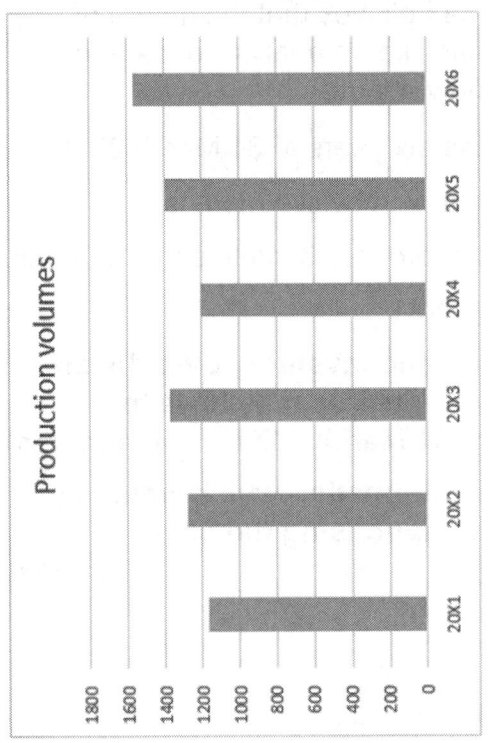

Closing inventory by product (000's of units)

	20X1	20X2	20X3	20X4	20X5	20X6
Radon	10	14	15	14	16	33
Makar	9	10	11	9	11	12
Fidle	0	0	0	0	5	10
Jagal	27	29	31	29	32	36
Farag	20	22	25	23	24	27
Buked	33	37	41	39	42	45
Total	**99**	**112**	**123**	**114**	**130**	**163**

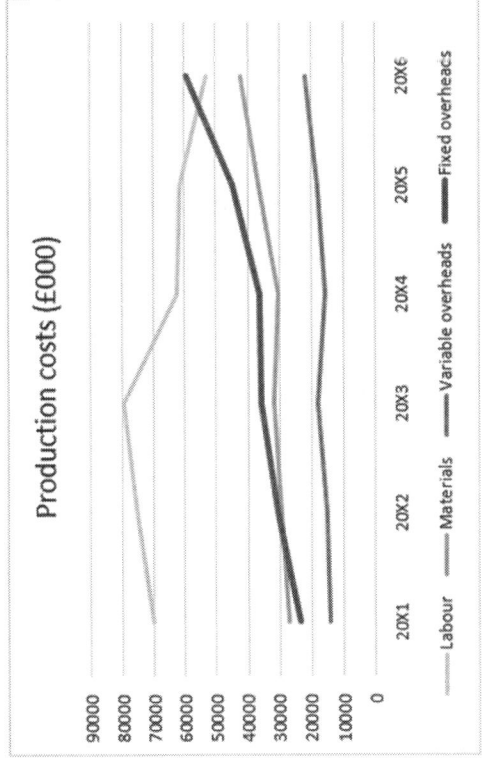

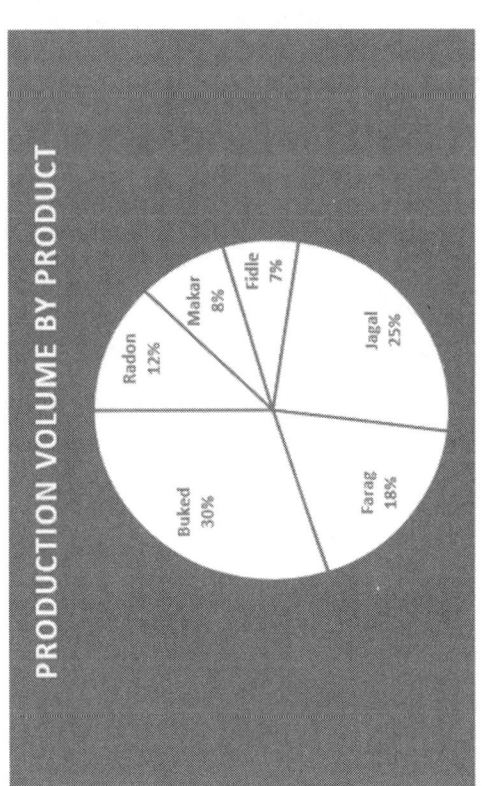

Mock Assessment Questions

Olivia Khan wishes to evaluate the performance of the factory over the last six years and has asked you to help. Olivia believes that the nature of Sharpkit's production is changing but would like an analysis of data to back up this belief. Olivia would like to know about:

- how production has changed over the six years to 31 March 20X6
- whether things might change over the next twelve months
- what further data might be required in order to complete this analysis.

Prepare a response to Olivia in which you:

(a) **Discuss the changes in production and inventory over the six years to 31 March 20X6 and how production may have to change over the twelve months to 31 March 20X7.** (11 marks)

(b) **Identify TWO pieces of additional information which would be useful for the Sales Manager when appraising the Sales Representatives' performance.** (2 marks)

BUSINESS AWARENESS

TASK 7 (15 marks)

This task is risk and Big Data.

(a) Identify ONE appropriate strategy to deal with each of the following risks.

Risk	Transfer	Accept	Reduce	Avoid
Company A has decided to abandon its operations in a politically volatile country where the risks of loss (including loss of life) are considered to be too great, or the costs of security are considered to be too high.				
After a number of incidents in which its 'whatzis' product had failed whilst being used by customers, Company B has been presented with compensation claims from customers inconvenienced by the product failure. The 'whatzis' is highly profitable and it may be that the returns attainable by maintaining and even increasing the 'whatzis' sales are worth the liabilities incurred by compensation claims.				

(2 marks)

Mock Assessment Questions

(b) Which of the four V's of Big Data is illustrated in the following statements? Tick the 'V' that applies to each statement below:

	Variety	Volume	Veracity	Velocity
Six billion people use mobile phones. 50 trillion gigabytes of data will be created by 2025 and around 2.3 trillion gigabytes of data are created each day.				
There are currently 420 million wearable, wireless health monitors; 4 billion hours of video are watched on YouTube every month. 400 million tweets are sent every day, by 200 million users.				
Poor data quality costs the UK economy around $3 trillion a year, and 1 in 3 business leaders do not trust the information they use to make decisions.				
There are currently 20 billion network connections in the world (around 2.5 connections per person) and the New York Stock Exchange captures 1 terabyte of information during each trading session.				

(4 marks)

BUSINESS AWARENESS

(c) (i) Identify whether the following statements about Big Data are true or false.

Statement	True	False
Big Data is structured and stored in consistent formats within databases.		
There is a heightened risk of inaccuracy with Big Data because of the number of different sources used to provide it.		
One advantage of analysing Big Data is that the relationships identified have certain organisational value.		
Big Data refers to the storage of data in excess of one petabyte.		
Big Data is now streaming at such velocity that it is impossible to generate meaningful real-time analysis.		

(5 marks)

(ii) Identify whether the following statements about the difference between risk and uncertainty are TRUE or FALSE.

Statement	True	False
Risk can be quantified by assigning probabilities to the various outcomes		
Uncertainty is when it is hard to predict the probability of a range of future outcomes		

(2 marks)

(d) Identify which ONE of the following is NOT a characteristic of good information.

Not a characteristic of good information	False
Relevance	
Cost effectiveness	
Interchangeability	
Accuracy	
Timeliness	

(2 marks)

Mock Assessment Questions

BUSINESS AWARENESS

2 Mock Assessment Answers

TASK 1

(a) Identify whether the following statements are true or false.

Statement	True	False
A limited liability company operates as a separate legal entity from its owners	✓	
A sole trader business operates as a separate legal entity from its owners		✓

(2 marks)

(b) (i) Identify which ONE of the following structures is suited to an organisation in which employees are divided by specialisation.

Statement	✓
Functional	✓
Divisional	
Matrix	

(1 mark)

(ii) Identify which type of control is described by each of the following statements.

Statement	Centralised control	Decentralised control	Wide span control	Narrow span control
The managerial structure has many levels of management				✓
Decision making and control is delegated to managers at lower levels in the organisation		✓		
The organisation has less flexibility but a higher level of control	✓			

(3 marks)

KAPLAN PUBLISHING

Mock Assessment Answers

(c) (i) Identify which ONE of the following stakeholders is most likely to have a high interest but little power/influence on the decision about which option to invest in.

Stakeholder	✓
NW's major shareholder	
One of NW's customers	
Government of country J	
NW's employees	✓

(1 mark)

(ii) Identify which ONE of the following stakeholders is most likely to have a high level of interest and high power/influence on the decision about which option to invest in.

Stakeholder	✓
NW's major shareholder	✓
One of NW's customers	
Government of country J	
NW's employees	

(1 mark)

(iii) Identify which ONE of the following is the system by which companies are directed and controlled:

System	✓
Corporate governance	✓
Corporate acceptance	
Corporate compliance	
Corporate refinance	

(1 mark)

BUSINESS AWARENESS

(iv) **Complete the following statement about a company's structure by selecting ONE option.**

In a _____ structure, the upper levels of an organisation's hierarchy retain the authority and make decisions.

Options	✓
Centralised	✓
Decentralised	
Geographically spread out	
Compliant	

(1 mark)

(d) (i) **Identify how Chris' principles are threatened, by completing the following statement:**

This is…..	Gap 1	…..threat to…..	Gap 2

Gap 1 options	✓	Gap 2 options	✓
An advocacy		integrity	✓
A self-review		confidentiality	
An intimidation	✓	Professional competence and due care	

(2 marks)

(ii) **Identify which ONE of the fundamental principles needs to be safeguarded in this situation.**

Fundamental principle	✓
Integrity	
Objectivity	✓
Professional competence and due care	
Professional behaviour	

Mock Assessment Answers

Jamie needs to safeguard the fundamental principle of objectivity. Their friendship may colour their judgement in favour of their friend.

(1 mark)

(iii) **Identify which TWO of the following are advantages of a principles-based approach to ethics over a rules-based approach to ethics.**

Advantage	✓
Applicable to all situations	✓
Less chance of people finding loopholes	✓
Reduced misunderstandings or misinterpretation	
Easy enforcement	

(2 marks)

(e) (i) **For each statement below, explain why each of the following actions appears to be in conflict with fundamental ethical principles.**

Statement	A likely loss of objectivity	This is an issue of integrity	Potential conflict with professional behaviour
An advertisement for a firm of accountants states that their audit services are cheaper and more comprehensive than a rival firm.			✓
An accountant prepares a set of accounts prior to undertaking the audit of those accounts.	✓		
A financial accountant confirms that a report on their company is correct, even though the report omits to mention some important liabilities.		✓	

(3 marks)

BUSINESS AWARENESS

(ii) Professional accountants are required to undertake continuing professional development (CPD). Which ONE of the five fundamental principles is safeguarded by CPD?

Fundamental principle	✓
Integrity	
Objectivity	
Professional competence and due care	✓
Confidentiality	
Professional behaviour	

(2 marks)

TASK 2

(a) (i) For each of the three specified PESTLE categories (Economic, Political, Technological), identify ONE threat facing AR.

(ii) Explain ONE action that AR could take to reduce threats under each category.

	Threat	Action to reduce threat
Economic	Changes in interest rates or tax rates could lower demand for rail travel **(1 mark)**	Offer a range of discount holidays **(1 mark)** and payment options to enable customers to spread the cost **(1 mark)**
	Reduced disposable income and therefore lower demand for holidays and rail travel **(1 mark)**	Increase range of locations **(1 mark)** for example in other UK destinations **(1 mark)**
	Exchange rate could impact on the location holiday makers choose to travel to **(1 mark)**	
	Exchange rates could increase the cost of the French hotels and stays for their customers **(1 mark)**	

Mock Assessment Answers

Political	New government expenditure on roads and motorways may affect demand for train travel **(1 mark)**	Increase communication on environmental impact and green credentials of train travel vs. road/motorway travel **(1 mark)**
	Proposed additional one-off taxes on rail operators to help pay for road upgrades will increase costs **(1 mark)**	Campaign for 'clean' travel and against taxes on rail operators **(1 mark)**
Technological	Competition have online booking facilities, which may reduce AR's market share **(1 mark)**	Invest in booking system **(1 mark)** to enable online booking **(1 mark)**
	AR's costs are high, as staff are required to take all bookings details **(1 mark)**	Improve AR's website to enable online booking **(1 mark)** which will mean staff can deal with a higher volume of bookings **(1 mark)**

(iii) Identify ONE of the remaining PESTLE categories.

Social

Environmental

Legal **(1 mark)**

(b) Identify which FOUR of the statements below are true about blockchain.

Statement	✓
Blockchain is regarded as a solution to cyber security risk	✓
Records in the blockchain are publicly available	✓
Records in the blockchain are distributed across everyone that is part of the network of participants	✓
Records in the blockchain are always kept private to enhance security	
The verification of transactions is carried out by computers	✓
The verification of transactions is carried out by individuals	

(4 marks)

BUSINESS AWARENESS

(c) (i) Identify whether each of the following statements about the duties of directors is TRUE or FALSE.

Statement	True ✓	False ✓
Directors have a legal obligation to act in the best interests of the company by promoting its success for the benefit of its shareholders.	✓	
A director must avoid any situation which places them in direct conflict with the interests of the company or the performance of any other duty.	✓	

(2 marks)

(ii) Complete each of the following definitions about unlimited liability partnerships by selecting ONE option:

An unlimited liability partnership can be defined as:	Gap 1	In an unlimited liability partnership, the partners' liability is referred to as	Gap 2

Gap 1 options	✓	Gap 2 options	✓
A separate legal entity, in which each partner has full personal liability for the partnership debts.		'legal and regulatory'	
Not a separate legal entity, in which each partner has full personal liability for the partnership debts.	✓	'common and indivisible'	
A separate legal entity, in which each partner has partial personal liability for the partnership debts.		'joint and indivisible'	
Not a separate legal entity, in which each partner has partial personal liability for the partnership debts.		'joint and several'	✓

(2 marks)

Mock Assessment Answers

TASK 3

(a) (i) Identify which TWO of the following are key features of cloud accounting.

Feature	✓
Software updates delivered faster and more easily by cloud provider	✓
Users' ability to connect not dependent on internet connection	
Cloud accounting suppliers not required to adhere to data protection regulations	
Access levels can be controlled	✓

(2 marks)

(ii) Identify which ONE of the following is a disadvantage of cloud accounting.

Disadvantage	✓
Software updates delivery by cloud provider takes longer	
It may become difficult to switch providers/systems	✓
Access to real-time financial performance is more difficult	
Access to large networks takes longer	

(1 mark)

BUSINESS AWARENESS

(b) **Complete each of the following statements about the automation of processes by selecting ONE option.**

_____ GAP 1 _____ tasks (for example, associated with the financial close and regulatory reporting and account reconciliation) are most likely to be automated, but developments in technology are allowing more complex tasks to be automated also.

An organisation considering investing in process automation technology within the finance function would benefit from _____ GAP 2 _____.

Gap 1 options	✓
One-off	
Repetitive	✓
Common	
Accounting	
Gap 2 options	✓
Improved accuracy	✓
Fewer training requirements	
Smoother relationship management processes	
Increased job certainty	

(2 marks)

(c) **Identify which TWO of the following are benefits to business operations offered by the electronic filing of documents.**

Statement	✓
Reliable backup assistance and disaster recovery methods	✓
Increased data security	
Low initial setup costs	
Increased workplace productivity	✓

(2 marks)

Mock Assessment Answers

(d) Identify the ONE risk below that is NOT a risk to computer systems and the data they contain:

Risk	✓
Physical damage	
Operational problems	
Data theft	
Financing issues	✓

(1 mark)

(e) Identify which TWO of the following are principles of data protection.

Principle	✓
Personal data shall be updated on a minimum of an annual basis	
Personal data held for any purpose shall be held for a minimum of 12 weeks and it shall not be held for more than six years	
Data must be used in a way that is adequate, relevant and limited to only what is necessary	✓
Data must be accurate and, where required, kept up-to-date	✓

(2 marks)

(f) Complete the following statement about data breach by selecting ONE option.

A data breach must be reported to the relevant supervisory authority within _____ of becoming aware of the breach, where feasible.

Options	✓
24 hours	
72 hours	✓
1 month	
18 weeks	

(1 mark)

BUSINESS AWARENESS

(g) Identify which quality of a service is described in each of the following statements.

Statement	Intangibility	Simultaneity	Heterogeneity	Perishability
The fact that there is no physical product means that it is difficult to define the 'service' and attribute costs. For example, in the NHS, it is challenging to define what a 'procedure' is.	✓			
Customers often must be present during the production of a service, and cannot take the service home. No service exists until it is actually being experienced/consumed by the person who has brought it.		✓		
Quality and consistency may be inconsistent, because of an absence of standards to assess services against. In the NHS for example, there is no indication of what an excellent performance in service delivery would be.			✓	
The unused service capacity from one time period cannot be stored for future use. Service providers' marketers cannot handle supply-demand problems through production scheduling and inventory techniques.				✓

(4 marks)

Mock Assessment Answers

(h) Identify the funding source that each of the following characteristics relates to.

Characteristic	Working capital	1-year loan	Equity finance
We can rely on the excess of current assets over current liabilities to repay the funding every month	✓		
Suitable for long-term funding requirements			✓

(2 marks)

TASK 4

(a) **Explain which TWO of B's fundamental principles are threatened by the fact that both Idris Ltd and Unwin Ltd are bidding for the lease on the same building in Standley Science Park.**

Objectivity – because it is difficult to act without a perception of bias when the two clients' interests are in such conflict because they both want the lease.

Confidentiality – because they have confidential information in respect of each client. **(4 marks)**

(b) **Describe the ethical conflict resolution process that B should undertake in deciding how to act in respect of this matter. Assume that they will be able to resolve the conflict of interest without external professional advice.**

B should:

- consider relevant facts/ethical issues involved/their fundamental principles/any established procedures in their firm

- establish alternative courses of action, establish which is most consistent with the fundamental principles and establish the consequences of each

- seek advice about the matter within their firm, and document the substance of the issue and discussions. **(4 marks)**

BUSINESS AWARENESS

TASK 5

(a) (i) Identify which TWO of the following events will cause a shift in the demand curve of a normal good.

Event	✓
A change in the quantity supplied	
A change in the price of substitutes	✓
A change in consumer tastes and preferences	✓
A change in raw material costs	

(2 marks)

(ii) Which ONE of the following options from the above information is NOT correct?

Option	✓
Product X may be a product that customers buy out of habit	
Product X may have few, if any, substitutes	
Product X may see a sharper fall in demand if the price rise lasts for a long period	
Product X would be more profitable if the price was cut rather than raised	✓

(1 mark)

(iii) A demand curve is drawn assuming all but one of the following remains unchanged. Which ONE item can vary?

Item	✓
Consumer tastes	
The price of the product	✓
The price of other products	
Disposable income	

(1 mark)

Mock Assessment Answers

(b) (i) Organisations should use resources in such a way that they do not compromise the needs of future generations.

What is this a definition of?

Definition	✓
Environmentalism	
Sustainability	✓
Future-focus	
Redesign	

(1 mark)

(ii) Identify ONE type of sustainability that each of the following organisational policies relates to:

Organisational policy	Social sustainability	Environ-mental sustainability	Financial sustainability
Jossara assembles clothes out of discarded fabrics manufacturers usually leave behind on sewing tables. Jossara only creates limited edition pieces, minimises the usage of fabric and advocates minimalism to support the overall image of their brand.		✓	

BUSINESS AWARENESS

Arundhati employs apple pickers and has recently decided to focus on a programme of affordable housing and workforce development for their staff. In collaboration with local engineers and orchard owners, they have drawn up blueprints for three different housing plans, as well as a partnership with the local community college and mentorships with cider professionals.	✓		
El Mansour Ltd have clearly defined strategic plans and all new projects must be capable of achieving a minimum level of profit within two years, to be accepted.			✓

(3 marks)

An organisation includes the following amongst its stakeholders:

(1) Customers

(2) Trade unions

(iii) **Identify which of the stakeholders can be classified as 'connected' stakeholders. Select ONE option.**

Stakeholders	✓
(1) only	✓
(2) only	
(1) and (2)	

(1 mark)

Mock Assessment Answers

TASK 6

(a) Discuss the changes in production and inventory over the six years to 31 March 20X6 and how production may have to change over the twelve months to 31 March 20X7.

Question	Answer (Indicative content)
(a)	Conclusions: • Labour costs have fallen consistently since 20X3 • Fixed overheads have risen consistently every year • This may indicate a switch away from hand-made to more machine-made products • Production in 20X1 was below 1,200 units and then grew for two years • There was a fall in production in 20X4 which was also followed by two years of growth • The fall in production in 20X4 caused a reduction in all variable costs for that year • Production in 20X3 and 20X5 were very similar but material and variable overhead costs were higher in 20X5 in total indicating that material and variable overhead costs per unit have been increasing • The Buked product is the company's biggest product in terms of production. The Fidle product now makes up 7% of total production • Inventory levels have generally been linked to changes in production • Inventory levels have usually been in line with the percentage of production of each product • But the Radon product has shown a significant increase in inventory in 20X6 Changes over the next twelve months • Production could follow the pattern of a drop following two years of growth • The Radon product may becoming less popular (given its rise in inventory) and production of this product could be reduced

BUSINESS AWARENESS

	• Labour costs are likely to continue to fall • Fixed overheads are likely to continue to rise (fixed overheads will not fall if production falls) • The Fidle product will make a larger percentage of production

Marks	Descriptor
0	No response worthy of credit.
1–3	The answer is not explained, or only states production has been increasing or sales of the Buked are highest (or basic points similar to this which do not recognise there is a trend/pattern).
4–8	An answer which demonstrates a good understanding of the patterns in the data provided, where there have been upward trends in the data and where there have been steady decreases in costs over the six years with an attempt made to link the data from the different sources.
9–11	An answer which demonstrates a clear understanding of the patterns in the data provided, where there have been upward trends in the data and where there have been steady decreases in performance. A strong answer will link the data between the different sources, for example the rise in production to the rise in inventory, or the fall in production to the fall in material and variable overhead costs.

(11 marks)

(b) Identify TWO pieces of additional information which would be useful for the Sales Manager when appraising the Sales Representatives' performance.

Question	Answer (Indicative content)	Marks
(b)	• Sales volumes/sales by product **(1 mark)** • Production by product over the last six years **(1 mark)** • Production cost by product **(1 mark)** • Sales forecasts for 20X7 **(1 mark)** • Material costs per supplier **(1 mark)** Other relevant points may be awarded marks	Max 2 marks

Mock Assessment Answers

TASK 7

(a) Identify ONE appropriate strategy to deal with each of the following risks.

Risk	Transfer	Accept	Reduce	Avoid
Company A has decided to abandon its operations in a politically volatile country where the risks of loss (including loss of life) are considered to be too great, or the costs of security are considered to be too high.				✓
After a number of incidents in which its 'whatzis' product had failed whilst being used by customers, Company B has been presented with compensation claims from customers inconvenienced by the product failure. The 'whatzis' is highly profitable and it may be that the returns attainable by maintaining and even increasing the 'whatzis' sales are worth the liabilities incurred by compensation claims.		✓		

(2 marks)

BUSINESS AWARENESS

(b) Which of the V's of Big Data is illustrated in the following statements? Tick the 'V' that applies to each statement below:

	Variety	Volume	Veracity	Velocity
Six billion people use mobile phones. 50 trillion gigabytes of data will be created by 2025 and around 2.3 trillion gigabytes of data are created each day.		✓		
There are currently 420 million wearable, wireless health monitors; 4 billion hours of video are watched on YouTube every month. 400 million tweets are sent every day, by 200 million users.	✓			
Poor data quality costs the UK economy around $3 trillion a year, and 1 in 3 business leaders do not trust the information they use to make decisions.			✓	
There are currently 20 billion network connections in the world (around 2.5 connections per person) and the New York Stock Exchange captures 1 terabyte of information during each trading session.				✓

(4 marks)

Mock Assessment Answers

(c) (i) Identify whether the following statements about Big Data are true or false.

Statement	True	False
Big Data is structured and stored in consistent formats within databases.		✓
There is a heightened risk of inaccuracy with Big Data because of the number of different sources used to provide it.	✓	
One advantage of analysing Big Data is that the relationships identified have certain organisational value.		✓
Big Data refers to the storage of data in excess of one petabyte.	✓	
Big Data is now streaming at such velocity that it is impossible to generate meaningful real-time analysis.		✓

(5 marks)

(ii) Identify whether the following statements about the difference between risk and uncertainty are TRUE or FALSE.

Statement	True	False
Risk can be quantified by assigning probabilities to the various outcomes	✓	
Uncertainty is when it is hard to predict the probability of a range of future outcomes	✓	

(2 marks)

(d) Identify which ONE of the following is NOT a characteristic of good information.

Not a characteristic of good information	False
Relevance	
Cost effectiveness	
Interchangeability	✓
Accuracy	
Timeliness	

(2 marks)

Index

4th Industrial Revolution, 243

A

AAT ethics guidelines, 234
Ability to undertake Big Data analytics, 294
Absorption costing, 100, 106
Advocacy, 214
Area chart, 316
Artificial intelligence, 243, 247
Attributes of good quality information, 282
Authorised disclosure, 230
Authority of directors, 25
Availability of information, 171

B

Bar and column charts, 310
Barriers to entry, 169
Big Data, 243, 288
    analytics, 293
    benefits, 291
    characteristics, 289
    definitions, 288
    pyramid, 294
    risks, 292
Blockchain, 97, 243, 249, 250, 251, 252
    key features of a blockchain, 250
    typical stages in a blockchain transaction, 252
Bruntland report, 178
Business
    cycles, 140
    environment, 132
    ethics, 198
    partnering, 104
    risk, 112

C

Centralisation and decentralisation, 74
Championing sustainability, 189
Changes in
    disposable income, 140
    technology, 145
Characteristics of
    good information, 283
    professional communication, 300
Charity commission, 20
Chief financial officer, 104
Cloud computing, 97, 243, 262, 263
    features of cloud computing, 263
    private cloud, 262
    public cloud, 262
Collective goals, 2
Commercial
    governance, 72
    organisations, 5
Communicating information, 325
Companies Act 2006, 21, 23, 27
Competition, 167
Conceptual framework, 204
Conditions of
    demand, 158
    supply, 162
Confidence, 212
Confidentiality, 203, 208, 220, 221
Connected stakeholders, 44
Controlled performance, 2
Core competencies, 258, 259
Corporate
    culture, 201
    governance, 73
    Social Responsibility (CSR), 183
Credibility, 212

Index

Criminal property, 224
Culture, 188
Customer due diligence, 234
Cyber risk, 115

D

Dashboards, 319
Data, 283
   analytics, 97, 102, 243, 257, 293
   controllers, 270
   outliers, 323
   security, 274, 277
   tables, 306
   versus information, 282
   visualisation, 243
De minimis, 226
Dealing with ethical conflicts, 216
Debt, 14
Demand, 157
Demographic changes, 143
Difference between risk and uncertainty, 110
Diligence, 208
Directors, 22
Directors' duties, 23
   duty to act, 24
   duty to promote, 24
   general duties, 23
   powers, 24
Dissolution of the partnership, 32
Distribution of assets, 33
Divisional: geographic structure, 67
Due care, 203

E

Economic environment, 139
Effect of a change in partner, 33
Employment Act 2015, 27
Employment/Unemployment, 142
Entrepreneurial structure, 62
Environmental factors, 149
Equilibrium, 164

Equity, 13
Ethical
   codes, 200
   influences, 199
Ethics of technology usage GDPR, 270
Exchange rates, 139
Expertise, 212
External stakeholders, 45

F

Failure to report, 229
Familiarity, 214
Features and key benefits, 320
Finance function, 88
   interface with operations, 92
   key roles – enables, 88
           – narates how, 89
           – shapes how, 89
   outsourcing functions, 261
   roles of the finance function, 88
Finance professional process automation, 246
Financial
   conduct authority, 20
   governance, 73
   risk, 120
Functional/departmental structure, 63
Functions of an organisation, 88
Fundamental principles, 203
Funding, 12

G

General Data Protection Regulation (GDPR), 270
Goodwill, 34
Governance, 72
   in a business context, 72

H

Hierarchy of management, 79
Human Resource Management (HRM), 99
Human resources, 88, 99

BUSINESS AWARENESS

I

Impact on structure, 146

Imports/exports, 137

Independence, 206

Individual demand, 157

Inflation, 141

Information, 285, 287
  requirements, 282
  systems, 286

Integration, 224

Integrity, 203, 205, 220, 221

Interest rates, 139

Internal stakeholders, 42

Intimidation, 214

IT, 88
  modern organisation, 101

K

Key Performance Indicators (KPIS)
  IT, 103
  sales and marketing, 98

L

Layering, 224
  data, 322

Legal factors, 148

Legislation governing financial statements, 21

Limited liability, 26
  companies, 5

Location, 171

M

Management
  control, 285
  hierarchy, 77

Managing director, 23

Market demand, 158

Matrices, 308

Matrix structure, 68

Mendelow's
  matrix, 51
  power-interest matrix, 51

Method of delivery, 306

Methods of communicating, 300

Methods of communication, 301

Microeconomics, 156

Minority and majority shareholders, 29

Money Laundering, 224
  Regulations 2007 (2007 regulations), 226
  reporting officer, 227

Motivation, 100

Multiple graph types in one chart, 317

N

Nature of the
  audience, 305
  data, 305

Non-governmental organisations, 8

Non-profit, 5

Number of sellers and buyers, 168

O

Objectivity, 203, 206, 221

Operational
  control, 285
  planning, 77
  risk, 114

Operations, 88
  management interface with finance, 92
  production, 94
  purchasing, 92

Organisational structure, 62

Other types of governance, 73

Outsourcing, 258, 260, 261
  disadvantages of outsourcing, 260

P

Partners'
  authority, 31
  salaries, 31

Index

Partnership(s), 5
   agreement, 31

Personal advantage, 208

PESTLE
   acronym, 132
   analysis, 133

Pie charts, 313

Placement, 224

Political influences, 136

Prejudicing an investigation, 233

Presentation of data, 305

Price mechanism, 164

Primary and secondary stakeholders, 45

Private
   limited companies, 6
   sector, 7

Proceeds of Crime Act 2002 (POCA), 226

Process automation, 243, 244

Product features, 167

Production, 90, 94, 95

Professional
   and technical competence, 207
   behaviour, 203, 211
   competence, 203
   courtesy, 212

Professionalism, 212

Protected disclosure, 230

Prudent, 209

Public Interest Disclosure Act (PIDA) 1998, 237

Public
   limited companies, 6
   spending, 138

Purchasing, 92, 93

R

Regulatory
   and legal governance, 73
   bodies, 20

Reputational risk, 117

Rights of shareholders, 28

Risk(s), 190
   and return, 111
   and uncertainty, 111
   attitude of stakeholders, 55
   identification and evaluation, 122
   management, 122
   of not acting sustainably, 179, 180

S

Safeguards, 214, 215

Sales and marketing, 88, 97, 98

Scatter graph, 314

Self
   -interest, 213
   -review, 213

Separation of ownership and control, 10

Share of residual profit, 31

Shareholders, 26

Shifts in supply or demand, 165

Single and double line graphs, 315

Social
   arrangements, 2
   factors, 143
   pressure, 200

Sole traders, 5

Sources of big data, 289

Span of control, 70

Stakeholder
   conflict, 50
   needs analysis, 48

Strategic planning, 77, 285

Structure and governance, 79

Supply, 161
   chain, 103, 104
   curve of a firm, 161

Suspicious activity reports, 227

Sustainability, 178, 184

T

Tactical
   information, 286
   planning, 77

Tall and flat organisations, 70, 71

TARA framework, 123

Taxation, 137

Terrorism Act 2000 (TA 2000), 226

Terrorism Act 2006 (TA 2006), 226

Terrorist financing, 225

The Code of Ethics for Professional Accountants, 203

The Institute of Business Ethics, 203

Threats, 213
    and safeguards, 213

Tipping off, 232

Trading partnerships, 32

Transaction costs, 260

Trends, 144

Trust, 214

Types of
    director, 23
    information systems, 286
    risk, 112

U

Unlimited liability partnerships, 30, 35

Upside risks and downside risks, 110

Using technology in data visualisation, 319

V

Visualise information, 309

W

What is risk?, 110

Whistleblowing, 236

Who are stakeholders, 42

Working capital, 14

Index